Patricia S. E. Darlington, PhD
Becky Michele Mulvaney, PhD

Women, Power, and Ethnicity
Working Toward Reciprocal Empowerment

Pre-publication
REVIEWS,
COMMENTARIES,
EVALUATIONS . . .

"*Women, Power, and Ethnicity* is a groundbreaking work, an admirably thorough and sensitive investigation into how women view and use power in every arena of their daily lives. Darlington and Mulvaney offer a nuanced understanding of how power has been used and understood previously and, in an original model of what they call reciprocal empowerment, how it can and should be used in the future. In this thoughtfully designed study, they provide readers with a broad survey of women from seven different cultural and ethnic backgrounds living in the United States.

Readers from a variety of fields will find this book a very valuable contribution to their understandings of the complicated relationships of women and power. With sharp perception, the authors situate each group in historical context and then proceed to privilege these women's voices, modeling reciprocal empowerment in their practice even as they research it. The authors are flexible and responsive to what they find. Darlington and Mulvaney respect and honor their respondents' voices by ultimately revising their own understanding of reciprocal empowerment, in order to better reflect real women's understandings of power. The wise and practical suggestions in the conclusion should stimulate and inspire thought, discussion, further research, and, yes, political action. This book is an excellent resource that lays the groundwork for generations of future scholars, activists, and citizens."

Suzanne M. Daughton, PhD
Associate Professor,
Southern Illinois University—
Carbondale; Editor,
Women's Studies in Communication

More pre-publication
REVIEWS, COMMENTARIES, EVALUATIONS . . .

"By highlighting the issue of ethnicity, this book breaks new ground in research on women and power. While it provides, for the first time, a look at some of the differences among women in their attitudes toward power, this book also provides a window into some strong similarities across groups. It reveals the attraction many women apparently feel toward a model of power that involves reciprocation, equality, and mutual respect. It shows how wary many women are of the traditional forms of power they see being practiced in political life, and thus suggests one reason why many women report they are uncomfortable with politics. The authors' findings may provide the basis for changing the language we use to speak about power, and thus our willingness to embrace power in the quest for social change."

Hilary M. Lips, PhD
Professor of Psychology,
Radford University

"Darlington and Mulvaney present a model of power that avoids the pitfalls of earlier masculinist and feminist approaches that focused solely on taking or giving. Reciprocal empowerment is a 'degendered form of interaction' that nevertheless fully acknowledges the ways in which women of many backgrounds have found their way to empowerment and change without sacrificing self or others. The authors survey women of seven different backgrounds to see how women with different experiences relate to power and to the authors' model of reciprocal empowerment. The result is an empirically based, very informative assessment of female attitudes about power that is multiethnic and multiracial and that challenges simplistic notions of power. This book is a major achievement that should inform future discussions and research about women and power."

Susan Love Brown, PhD
Associate Professor,
Department of Anthropology,
Florida Atlantic University

The Haworth Press®
New York • London • Oxford

NOTES FOR PROFESSIONAL LIBRARIANS AND LIBRARY USERS

This is an original book title published by The Haworth Press, Inc. Unless otherwise noted in specific chapters with attribution, materials in this book have not been previously published elsewhere in any format or language.

CONSERVATION AND PRESERVATION NOTES

All books published by The Haworth Press, Inc. and its imprints are printed on certified pH neutral, acid free book grade paper. This paper meets the minimum requirements of American National Standard for Information Sciences-Permanence of Paper for Printed Material, ANSI Z39.48-1984.

Women, Power, and Ethnicity

Working Toward Reciprocal Empowerment

HAWORTH Innovations in Feminist Studies
J. Dianne Garner
Senior Editor

Reproductive Hazards in the Workplace: Mending Jobs, Managing Pregnancies by Regina Kenen

Our Choices: Women's Personal Decisions About Abortion by Sumi Hoshiko

Tending Inner Gardens: The Healing Art of Feminist Psychotherapy by Lesley Irene Shore

Racism in the Lives of Women: Testimony, Theory, and Guides to Anti-Racist Practice by Jeanne Adleman and Gloria Enguídanos

Advocating for Self: Women's Decisions Concerning Contraception by Peggy Matteson

Feminist Visions of Gender Similarities and Differences by Meredith M. Kimball

Experiencing Abortion: A Weaving of Women's Words by Eve Kushner

Menopause, Me and You: The Sound of Women Pausing by Ann M. Voda

Fat—A Fate Worse Than Death?: Women, Weight, and Appearance by Ruth Raymond Thone

Feminist Theories and Feminist Psychotherapies: Origins, Themes, and Variations by Carolyn Zerbe Enns

Celebrating the Lives of Jewish Women: Patterns in a Feminist Sampler edited by Rachel Josefowitz Siegel and Ellen Cole

Women and AIDS: Negotiating Safer Practices, Care, and Representation edited by Nancy L. Roth and Linda K. Fuller

A Menopausal Memoir: Letters from Another Climate by Anne Herrmann

Women in the Antarctic edited by Esther D. Rothblum, Jacqueline S. Weinstock, and Jessica F. Morris

Breasts: The Women's Perspective on an American Obsession by Carolyn Latteier

Lesbian Stepfamilies: An Ethnography of Love by Janet M. Wright

Women, Families, and Feminist Politics: A Global Exploration by Kate Conway-Turner and Suzanne Cherrin

Women's Work: A Survey of Scholarship By and About Women edited by Donna Musialowski Ashcraft

Love Matters: A Book of Lesbian Romance and Relationships by Linda Sutton

Birth As a Healing Experience: The Emotional Journey of Pregnancy Through Postpartum by Lois Halzel Freedman

Unbroken Homes: Single-Parent Mothers Tell Their Stories by Wendy Anne Paterson

Transforming the Disciplines: A Women's Studies Primer edited by Elizabeth L. MacNabb, Mary Jane Cherry, Susan L. Popham, and René Perry Prys

Women at the Margins: Neglect, Punishment, and Resistance edited by Josephina Figueira-McDonough and Rosemary C. Sarri

Women's Best Friendships: Beyond Betty, Veronica, Thelma, and Louise by Patricia Rind

Women, Power, and Ethnicity: Working Toward Reciprocal Empowerment by Patricia S. E. Darlington and Becky Michele Mulvaney

The Way of the Woman Writer, Second Edition by Janet Lynn Roseman

Women, Power, and Ethnicity
Working Toward Reciprocal Empowerment

Patricia S. E. Darlington, PhD
Becky Michele Mulvaney, PhD

with assistance from
Deana Awadallah, Melody Leite, and Kelly Brill

The Haworth Press®
New York • London • Oxford

The Haworth Press, Inc., 10 Alice Street, Binghamton, NY 13904-1580.

Cover design by Marylouise E. Doyle.

Library of Congress Cataloging-in-Publication Data

Women, power, and ethnicity : working toward reciprocal empowerment / Patricia S. E. Darlington, Becky Michele Mulvaney.

p. cm.

Includes bibliographical references and index.

ISBN 0-7890-1058-5 (alk. paper)—ISBN 0-7890-1059-3

1. Women—United States—Attitudes. 2. Minority women—United States—Attitudes. 3. Women immigrants—United States—Attitudes. 4. Power (Social sciences)—United States—Public opinion. 5. Ethnicity—United States. I. Darlington, Patricia S. E. II. Mulvaney, Becky Michele.

HQ1421 .W656 2003
305.4'0973—dc21

2002068605

We dedicate this book to our families

ABOUT THE AUTHORS

Patricia S.E. Darlington, PhD, is an associate professor of communication at Florida Atlantic University, in Boca Raton, where she is director of the undergraduate intercultural communication sequence and has developed and teaches both graduate and undergraduate courses in that area. Dr. Darlington researches and writes extensively in the areas of culture, primarily in the areas of women and culture. She is also president and CEO of the Center for Personnel Resources, Inc., a Florida-based management resources and consulting firm that specializes in diversity training in the workplace.

Becky Michele Mulvaney, PhD, teaches in the department of communication at Florida Atlantic University, in Boca Raton. Her research and teaching interests include rhetorical history, theory, and criticism, rhetoric and social movements, women's studies, and ethnic studies. Dr. Mulvaney is the author of *Rastafari and Reggae: A Dictionary and Sourcebook.* She has published several essays on the rhetorical dimensions of reggae music, including one with co-author Patricia Darlington that appeared in the international journal of art and culture, *Czas Kultury.*

CONTENTS

Foreword

Questions of women and, most commonly, of powerlessness remain at the heart of gender definitions and practices. For many, the equation of women with power is simply an oxymoron. As no less a luminary than Aristotle put it: "Woman is as it were an impotent male." Potency or power, in both its abstract and concrete connotations, continues to be associated almost exclusively with men and defined as domination and control.

Thus, power in some ways is a veritable dirty word for women. Power is regularly used against women, and in relation to the self it remains variously unimaginable, unmentionable, and hence unnameable. This was driven home to me recently in a class I teach, "Women, Violence, and Resistance." One of our readings spoke of "self-power" as a woman's most intrinsic birthright, and I asked students to address this concept. Several of them told me privately that they were at a loss to define power and asked me to suggest additional readings on the topic. Along with my usual sources, I now have an additional one to recommend most highly: Patricia Darlington and Becky Mulvaney's *Women, Power, and Ethnicity.*

This important, closely argued, and carefully researched book demonstrates an understanding that women, historically positioned as subordinate to men and in power-marked class and race relations to one another, approach questions of power differently from men as well as differently from one another. Darlington and Mulvaney provide histories of women's experiences in seven different ethnic groups and survey and interview individual members of these groups about their experiences and beliefs concerning power in a number of spheres. They find that women generally identify with the traditional model of power as domination and control, but immediately appreciate other models when they are presented with an articulated alternative during the interview process. This alternative often is implicit in their statements linking power with respect, equality, and mutuality—forms of influence that they exercised mainly in the family and in the community. Of significance, this was most marked with Native American women who have a tradition of gender equality and complementarity. Yet women from all ethnic groups gravitated toward respectful and mutual modes of power. As Darlington and Mulvaney comment: "They may not have had a name for this alternative, but they recognized it and appreciated it when they saw it."

Clearly, for women to attain, define, and exercise power in ways that do not recapitulate the traditional model of force, domination, and control, naming and education are essential. Naming is crucial to the social construction of reality, to the validation of experience, to the acceptance of the existence of a phenomenon, and, indeed, to further bring that phenomenon into being. Darlington and Mulvaney name a concept that I would very much like to see brought into wider use, in both the private and public spheres: *reciprocal empowerment* as an optimal understanding of power. It differs even from prior feminist notions of empowerment in that it explicitly embraces *active* mutuality and refuses any sacrifice of a woman's self. They explain: "Reciprocal empowerment is a discursive and behavioral style of interaction grounded in respectful reciprocity initiated by people who interact on an equal footing and have a sense of personal authority." Its attributes include "self-determination, independence, knowledge, choice, action, and decision making with competence, compassion, companionship, and consensus to enhance oneself and others, thereby creating an environment that fosters equality, mutual respect, mutual attention, mutual engagement, mutual empathy, and mutual responsiveness."

Darlington and Mulvaney's careful research reveals that despite recent advances, many women remain uneducated about the ways that alternative models of power exist and can be brought to bear in both the private and public spheres. To address this, they recommend education, both formal and informal, through schools as well as community forums and workplaces. That multitiered education is itself furthered through Darlington and Mulvaney's efforts here in giving voice to women in a male-dominant culture that sometimes overtly and sometimes covertly conspires to silence women. Feminist educational efforts will be enriched by their elucidation of a viable and transformative type of power, one that has grown out of women's historical experiences in both resisting dominance and in creating private spheres for growth in the family as well as in a community. A new term—*reciprocal empowerment*—has entered the vocabulary, and that is a gift to us all.

Jane Caputi
Professor of Women's Studies
Florida Atlantic University

Preface

Are powerful women just men walking around in dresses? This question arose as a result of an experience one of us had while attending a conference on women and power. The keynote speaker at that conference, a well-known business executive, was emphatic in her statements urging women that "to be powerful you must learn to act like a man. Be willing to forgo friendships, especially with other women. Don't expect to have a family if you want to get to the top, and you better learn how to sacrifice." Halfway through her presentation, the room that had earlier been filled to capacity with women began to empty rapidly. At the end of her talk, four women remained in the room. All four women—who totally disagreed with the speaker's ideas—stayed not to offer congratulations on a job well done, but to offer a challenge to the presenter. All four had stories of powerful women they knew who did not epitomize any of the attributes of control and domination to which the speaker alluded.

After the conference, the two of us discussed this incident and realized that we were both concerned that some women may have adopted traditionally male patterns of behavior in an effort to gain and maintain power in the public sphere (in business, industry, politics, academics, and the like). Popular self-help and how-to manuals are replete with evidence to suggest that some women may indeed be assuming or are being advised to mimic traditional power behaviors in order to succeed (Josefowitz, 1980).

Our personal observations and informal conversations with other women, however, led us to believe that not all women are subscribing to the traditional concept of power. We were convinced that women are indeed practicing some form of power and in many cases they consider themselves powerful. We found ourselves faced with several related questions. If women are not subscribing to the traditional concept of power, what kind of power are they practicing? Can women describe this power? If not, can they recognize it if presented with descriptions of it? Do women from different ethnicities living in the

United States use the same forms of power? In what contexts do they perceive power being practiced?

To answer these questions, we first immersed ourselves in the relevant literature on power and, more specifically, on women and power. Thus, we researched social science literature that describes a traditional male-oriented patriarchal form of power that we refer to in this book as *traditional power.* We then looked at some of the feminist literature on power that focused primarily on the *empowerment* concept made popular in the 1970s and 1980s. This led us to later feminist literature, particularly from the discipline of social work, that introduced us to the concept of *personal authority.* The research, coupled with further informal discussions with women, led us to believe that women have definite feelings about identifying with some of these forms of power when they are presented with descriptions of them. They were quickly able to identify what they do not like, but found it more difficult to state coherently what they prefer in terms of practicing power. Based on our readings and initial observations, we constructed an alternative model of power. We then decided to undertake a preliminary investigation into whether the description of this new model would resonate with a small group of women. This book centers on that investigation.

Following a discussion of the methodology used to conduct this investigation, we present in Chapter 1 our review of the literature on women and power. Chapter 1 concludes with a presentation of the model we created to introduce the concept that we call *reciprocal empowerment.* In subsequent chapters, we present the results of our ethnographic investigation.

Using a qualitative methodology, we began the process of examining how women feel about various forms of power. The purpose of our study was to determine what women from different racial/ethnic backgrounds living in the United States think about the attributes that we associated with four different forms of power: traditional power, empowerment, personal authority, and reciprocal empowerment. Pearson and Cooks (1995) suggest that rules governing research have been based in the male perspective; thus, gender research should challenge the traditional research paradigm. That is, generally these rules sustain sexist and androcentric values, do not make research available to those who need it most, create exploitative and elitist relationships between researchers and participants, and fail to acknowledge the political nature of the research being conducted. We agree with Pearson and Cooks's criticisms, and we designed our study in an effort to develop a qualitative methodology which, at the very least, avoids some of the pitfalls of the male perspective. We also followed Pearson and Cooks's advice for a feminist construction of research methods.

Pearson and Cooks suggest that in doing feminist research, women and their experiences should be valued. To do this, we surveyed and interviewed women in their own cultural environments whenever possible, and we asked them to use their own language in talking about their experiences as women in their particular racial/ethnic communities as well as in American society. Furthermore, our use of open-ended interview questions allowed for the kind of transaction between researcher and participant that Pearson and Cooks advocate. Their proposal that feminist research should recognize the constructed nature of gender undergirds the theoretical framework of our entire research project as discussed in Chapter 1. Finally, Pearson and Cooks urge feminist scholars to do research that has value for women. They suggest research should "deal with practical situations that characterize the ordinary lives of women" (1995, p. 343). We have followed this guideline by asking women about their perceptions of power in relation to their positions in American society, in their own racial/ethnic communities, and as women in both contexts. We also asked them about their perceptions of power in terms of their experience at work, in the family, and in relation to their involvement with religion and politics. Our goal in this research project was to begin to determine the type of power women practice or would prefer to see practiced in various contexts. Furthermore, we hoped to determine some of the possible constraints certain forms of power may place on women in these various contexts. We may then be able to use this process to help women recognize the value of an alternative concept of power that, with its emphasis on reciprocity, "frees people from those conditions that are oppressive to them" (Pearson and Cooks, 1995, p. 343).

In conducting our study, we identified women of several ethnicities based on the demographics of our South Florida community. For this study, ethnicity pertains to a racial, national, cultural, or religious group. Specifically, we identified African-American women, Asian-American women, Caribbean-American women, European-American women, Latin American women, Middle Eastern-American women, and Native American women. We contacted between fifteen to twenty-five women from each of these specific groups, resulting in a total of 136 women. We conceived of this as an introductory study using a small sample size, and we acknowledge that these racial/ethnic groups, or ethnicities, are gross categories that do not represent the uniqueness and distinctiveness of the various cultural groups subsumed under these broad categories. For example, although we recognize the significant cultural distinctions between Cuban-American and Puerto Rican-American women, we chose, for ease of identification, to represent them both using the umbrella term Latin American women. Similarly, the umbrella term Caribbean-American women was used to describe women from island nations such as Jamaica, Haiti, and the Dominican Republic.

We conducted our research using two methods of data collection. First, we created a survey consisting of fifty-two statements comprising attributes of the four models of power. We tailored the survey statements to elicit responses about the participants' personal feelings concerning attributes of the four power models. The survey contained fourteen statements representing traditional power, fourteen representing reciprocal empowerment, and five each on empowerment and personal authority. We then randomized the survey statements so that no two statements describing the same power paradigm appeared consecutively. We asked participants to select their responses from a five-point scale in which 1 = strongly agree, 2 = somewhat agree, 3 = neither agree nor disagree, 4 = somewhat disagree, and 5 = strongly disagree.

Our second method of data collection consisted of an interview composed of thirty open-ended questions designed to determine participants' perceptions about power. We chose to adopt the open-ended format to avoid participants giving responses influenced by our wording. Although in the survey we wanted to see how our participants would respond to our descriptions of specific power attributes associated with the four paradigms, in the interview we wanted to see what attributes would emerge when the women were free to create their own descriptions of power. We designed the first five questions to elicit responses regarding (1) participants' individual perceptions of power, (2) their perceptions of what power means in American society, (3) in general, their perceptions of what power means in their own culture, (4) their perceptions of what kind of power they—as women—have in U.S. society, and (5) their perceptions of what kind of power they—as women—have in their culture. We designed the remaining twenty-five questions to elicit responses regarding power in four different areas: work, family, religion, and politics. Specifically, we asked the respondents about their perceptions of how power *is used* and *should be used* in these areas. In order to evaluate ease of comprehension, we administered both the survey and the interview to several groups of undergraduate students in the Department of Communication at Florida Atlantic University. Based on the results, we reworded several survey statements and interview questions before conducting our study. To each survey and interview packet we attached a consent statement that also provided the research participant with a guarantee of confidentiality.

To analyze the survey data, we collapsed points one and two to create an "agree" category, and did the same with points three and four to create a "disagree" category. We then sorted results based on the particular power model to which the women were responding. We documented all interview responses in writing, and generally we transcribed responses verbatim except when editing was necessary for clarity. We interpreted responses in two ways: first, we noted the frequency in the use of particular terms, and then we associated these terms with the four power paradigms under examination. In determining which statements to associate with a particular paradigm, we first looked for a specific mention of an attribute from that model in the participant's statement; we then did a contextual reading of each statement to determine how the attribute was being used. For example, a statement that read "I think power should be used to assert control over other people," was interpreted as a traditional power statement; whereas, a statement that read "I like to have control over my own life" was not associated with traditional power. In certain responses, statements that did not technically use an attribute associated with one of the models we identified with a particular model based on our original definition of that model. For example, the statement "I like to have control over my own life" was interpreted as a personal authority statement, again, based on our definition of personal authority. Finally, we made note of words or terms used repeatedly by specific groups of women and which were not part of the original descriptive attributes of the models. We did this because we began to recognize that significant power descriptors were being used by women of particular ethnicities, but which we had not included in the original list of attributes associated with each model.

Chapters 2 to 8 each begin with a historical context introducing the particular ethnic group of which the women are a part. This is followed by a description of the demographics as well as a discussion of both the survey and the interview results. In Chapter 9, we compare the results of the survey and interview for all ethnicities, and we discuss what these findings say, overall, about reciprocal empowerment and women from various ethnicities.

Acknowledgments

We are indebted to the many people who assisted us in bringing this project to completion. We thank Dorothy Leland for naming our concept of power and for her substantive comments in the first stages of our project. We thank our department chair, Susan Reilly, for her exuberant support for our work. We also thank Susan and our colleagues Christine Scodari, Noemi Marin, and Enid Sefcovic for their substantial and perceptive comments and suggestions on an earlier draft of Chapter 1. We thank Kate Hawkins, our respondent at the Seventieth Annual Meeting of The Southern States Communication Association, whose comments and encouragement are greatly appreciated. We also want to thank Helen Ross for her patience and careful eye in proofreading the final manuscript. Of course we are indebted to Elaine Stern, our administrative assistant, for putting up with us, providing us needed supplies, and giving us motherly advice. We also thank Elcin Babacan, Jon Wyman, and Jorden Covert for seemingly endless photocopying and much-needed levity. We are ever thankful to our "Ethnicity and Communication" class members, spring semester 2000, whose research and assistance with the design and implementation of our survey and interview were instrumental to the completion of our project. In addition, Blake Reznik refined the first drafts of the survey and interview tables and Lisa Walkowich graphically reproduced the first drafts of the power diagrams. Kelly Brill patiently refined all the final tables and figures for the book. We are indebted to the significant contributions of Deana Awadallah and Melody Leite, who tallied the survey results and transcribed responses from all 136 interviews in a clear format for our analysis. In our meetings with them, they also provided us with their own insights concerning the results they were recording. In addition, Deana did all the background research on the introduction to Chapter 6 on Latin American culture and proofread the Middle Eastern introduction in Chapter 7 for cultural accuracy. We also wish to thank Dan McDonald, communications director of the Big Cypress Seminole Reservation in Hollywood, Florida, for granting us access and making arrangements to allow interviewers to talk with women at the reservation headquarters. Last, and most important, we thank all the women who participated in our study. Their generosity in giving us their time and in sharing with us their thoughts, feelings, and insights make up the substance of this work.

Chapter 1

Power: Past, Present, and Future

As the twenty-first century opens with women assuming positions of social leadership, the dynamics of the social construction of power need to be examined. Connell (1987) notes that many social scientists viewed power as a socially mediated construct in which particular transactions involving power are easy enough to observe. However, he suggests that it is often difficult to see beyond individual acts of force or oppression to a structure of power, a set of social relations with some scope and permanence. Social science theorists, though, usually present power in ways that can be characterized as patriarchal, a situation typically problematic for women. Feminist writers have tackled the complex problems inherent in configuring a feminist framework for power that does not replicate the problems of a masculinist approach, and two alternatives to traditional power have been presented: an early conception of empowerment constructed as a culturally feminine paradigm, and more recently a perspective variously called personal authority (Rampage, 1991; Miller and Cummins, 1992), self-definition (Collins, 1990), or personal agency (Yoder, 1999). Our review of the literature reveals that scholars such as Collins (1990), Ferree and Martin (1995), Josefowitz (1980), and Reid-Merritt (1996) noted the limitations of the traditional power and empowerment models; however, little has been done in a systematic way to offer alternatives.

We believe that none of these perspectives of power, taken alone, is adequate to address the changing roles of women or the social and political challenges we face in the twenty-first century. We argue that a new model of power is needed, one that in part combines aspects of the existing models, but one that also transcends these previous notions, comprising a whole greater than its component parts.

In this book we propose and describe a new model of power that we call reciprocal empowerment. We also offer an initial investigation of how reciprocal empowerment and other socially constructed concepts of power are viewed by women of various ethnicities. This chapter introduces and discusses this model and its relationship to discursive and behavioral practices. First, we define reciprocal empowerment and note its attributes. Second, from a feminist perspective, we examine the traditional power construct as a socially mediated, patriarchal model that focuses on the ideas of self versus other. We also examine the early conceptions of empowerment and more recent discussions of personal authority. Third, we propose our reciprocal empowerment model, arguing that, for some feminists, this model may present an alternative preferable to existing constructs of power. In the subsequent chapters, we present results of a qualitative study that illustrate how reciprocal empowerment, as well as other concepts of power, are perceived and experienced by women of various ethnicities.

We define reciprocal empowerment as a discursive and behavioral style of interaction grounded in reciprocity initiated by people who feel a sense of personal authority. The personal authority aspect of reciprocal empowerment provides an individual with a level of knowledge necessary to develop a heightened self-confidence that can then lead to action. This action can, in turn, facilitate movement from the private to the public sphere. Reciprocal empowerment enables people with mutual self-interests to rise above obstacles based on social and political structures and to use personal authority to discuss and act on issues openly and honestly in order to effect change. The process of engaging in reciprocal empowerment requires that the participants have enough self-confidence and respect for others to assist them without sacrificing self. The process also requires that participants be skilled in active listening to be sufficiently knowledgeable to mediate reasoned discussions that can create mutually beneficial outcomes. Although the process facilitates reasoned discussion, it does not entail abandoning one's own stance to avoid antagonism. The fact that reciprocal empowerment focuses on mutuality works to provide a process that eliminates the potential for interactions to degenerate into traditional power-over exchanges.

This process transcends existing notions of power that contain tensions embodied in gendered discourse. Typically, power has been masculinized by the public discourse of patriarchy. Reciprocal empowerment offers a degendered form of interaction that transcends both the masculinized models of power as well as the feminized empowerment model popular during the first wave of feminism.

Reciprocal empowerment combines the attributes of *self-determination, independence, knowledge, choice,* and *action* embodied in the personal authority model with the early empowerment model's attributes of *compassion, companionship, collectivity, consensus,* and *competence* to enhance *oneself* and *others,* thereby creating an egalitarian environment that fosters *mutual attention, mutual empathy, mutual engagement,* and *mutual responsiveness.* Reciprocal empowerment, therefore, combines the personal authority construct with the early empowerment conception to form a nongendered, nonhierarchical model. The paradigm includes the internal and external, involving both the process of gaining power and the results that are produced by having power, albeit a power that differs from the traditional perspective.

Before beginning our discussion, we feel it necessary to respond to a charge put forth by Dow (1995), who suggests that because feminist approaches and women's experiences cannot be viewed as monolithic, feminist scholars should "discuss the feminist assumptions that fuel their scholarship" and "engage with the implications of those assumptions" (p. 112). Various scholars (Alcoff, 1988; Jaggar, 1983; Jaggar and Rothenberg, 1984; Weedon, 1987) describe different feminist perspectives and discuss their theoretical implications at length. Among these perspectives are liberal, radical, socialist, cultural, and Marxist feminism, as well as feminist poststructuralism, and women-of-color feminism. Jaggar and Rothenberg (1984) note that women-of-color feminist theorists do not utilize any single theoretical framework, and we, too, do not adhere to a particular perspective. We do, however, share assumptions associated with some of these feminist approaches. These assumptions direct the character of our reciprocal empowerment model. For example, we embrace the values of individual dignity, equality, and autonomy postulated by the liberal theory of human nature (Jaggar, 1983). This view accepts the potential for personal agency which we realize has been questioned extensively by poststructuralist feminists and which we discuss later. However, we do not subscribe to the separation of the public and private spheres historically fostered by liberal theory. In addition, we agree with black feminists (among others) who note the ethnocentricity of liberal feminism, a perspective that historically ignored the interrelations between racism and sexism.

We also share the concern of women-of-color feminists whose writings "reflect a concern that the complexities of race and gender (and often class as well) be explored simultaneously. They caution us against hasty over-generalizations about women's situation, generalizations that have often reflected only the experience of white, middle-class women" (Jaggar and Rothenberg, 1984, p. 89). We acknowledge that the different experiences of women are significant. For example, Humm (1992) states that "a black woman's family and labor market experience might shape her economic inequality but also, and often, the family might be a source of succor and collective support. Therefore, the strident feminist calls in the 1970s for abortion on demand could not adequately address these black understandings of the family and of sexuality" (p. 122); furthermore, it must be recognized that race, class, and gender are "*interlocking* systems of oppression not additive systems . . . [and that] most [black and Asian feminists] take feminism to involve a recognition of 'multiple identities'" (p. 122).

Although women-of-color feminists highlight the influence of culture and ethnicity, they should not be confused with cultural feminists, some of whom, Alcoff (1988) suggests, advocate essentialism. We, too, wish to avoid the essentialist perspective, which, according to Foss, Foss, and Griffin (1999) is "the view that women and men are biologically determined" (p. 171), and instead suggest that previous models of power, early empowerment, and personal authority arose out of or developed in response to patriarchy, a set of structural relations existing in "the institutions and social practices of our society . . . in which women's interests are subordinated to the interests of men" (Weedon, 1987, pp. 2-3). Weedon defines patriarchy as a structure embedded in social institutions and practices, and suggests that it should not be confused with any so-called inherent qualities of individual men and women.

We also wish to avoid charges of relativism that may be raised about the concept of reciprocal empowerment by stating that its practice does not necessarily or always involve questions of moral or epistemological relativism. The attributes or characteristics inherent to the process of reciprocal empowerment do reflect certain values, such as equality and respect; hence, reciprocal empowerment can be used fully only by participants willing to abide by such values. As such, we take a stance in developing our model that lies between absolutism and unbridled relativism. Alcoff (1996) describes this position in her discussion of Putnam:

> We have reason to doubt specific claims and to take issue with other cultures' beliefs on specific issues, but because these doubts are based on specific reasons (such as lack of evidence, failure to cohere with our other beliefs on the subject, and so on), they do not lead to the all-encompassing suspension of belief that a total relativism implies. (p. 180)

Similarly, we agree with the rational relativistic view articulated by LaFollette (1991):

> Thus, we should instruct each other in the basic principles inherited from the past (respect for persons, reverence for human life, etc.) and act upon those as circumstances warrant. Then, we must listen and talk. We must non-defensively hear other's evaluations of our actions and non-condemnatorily offer reactions to theirs—all the while acknowledging our and their fallibility. (pp. 152-153)

This discussion, then, defines our position as feminists who embrace the potential for personal agency, are sensitive to the differences in women's experiences, do not subscribe to the separation of the public and private spheres, are mindful of patriarchy as a set of structural relationships enacted via discourse, and are unconvinced by arguments espousing essential differences between women and men.

POWER: ITS VARIOUS FORMS

To address issues related to power, empowerment, and personal authority, it is important to discuss the historical and social use of the terms as they relate to men and women.

Traditional Power

Power as a construct has been around since the emergence of humans in society. Numerous writers and researchers have examined the term and detailed its various uses, meanings, and implications. *Merriam-Webster's Collegiate Dictionary* (1993) offers as some of its definitions of the term *power* the following: (1) possession of control, authority, or influence over others, (2) physical might, (3) political control or influence, and (4) the ability or capacity to exercise control. The dictionary gives the following words as synonyms: authority, control, sway, command, and dominion. These synonyms indicate that the concept of power has historically not been intended to connote a female's position in many aspects of society except, perhaps, within the family structure.

Social Science Perspectives of Power

Merriam-Webster's popular definition of power as "the ability or capacity to exercise control" differs little from social science definitions and conceptions. A review of the social science literature shows that, until recently, very little usage of the term related to women, with most discussions using men as referents and emphasizing influence and control. Furthermore, definitions of power are based on wealth, resources, influence, control, and physical strength. They characterize power as the ability to get someone to do what you want despite initial resistance, and they discuss power as a form of control over resources. Lips (1991) suggests that these definitions view power as a commodity, but she argues that "Power is the process of bargaining and compromise in which priorities are set and decisions made in relationships" (p. 4). Similarly, Janeway (1980) sees power not as a commodity, but as something we *do*. Power, then, is not a thing available only to the elite, but rather a process we all engage in.

Connell (1987) posits that power may be a balance of advantage or inequality of resources in a workplace, a household, or a larger institution. According to Goodrich (1991), "those who dominate have much more power-to than do their subordinates, and thereby they have the means to increase their domination. Key for that purpose is the power to name and define things" (p. 8). This ability to impose a definition of the situation, to set the terms in which events are understood and issues discussed, to formulate ideas and define morality—

in short, to assert hegemony—is an essential part of traditional concepts of social power.

According to Miller and Cummins (1992), in the past, power has been theorized in terms of men's experiences. For example, in psychology, power is discussed as a picture of struggle, and power is measured by the ability to dominate another, to win a conflict, and to exert power over another person. Similarly, in social exchange theory, human interaction is said to involve "exertion of influence mediated through control of both tangible and intangible resources" (Miller and Cummins, 1992, p. 416). In sociology, Max Weber (1969) describes power as the "chance of man or a number of men to realize their will in a communal action even against the resistance of others who are not participating in the action" (p. 24). In fact, Duffy (1986) notes that in patriarchal conceptions of power, recurrent themes include resistance, conflict, force, domination, and control. The conceptual basis of these definitions rests in a win-lose or power-over paradigm. In short, these definitions of power focus on structural hierarchies and interpersonal terms.

Foucault also focused on structures of power. He offered a theory of power in relation to the body that has helped feminists explain the oppression of women. McNay (1992) writes that Foucault believed "systems of power bring forth different types of knowledge which, in turn, produce effects in the bodies of social agents that serve to reinforce the original power formation" (p. 148). Foucault's conception of power as it relates to the body and to sexuality has been used by feminists to combat essentialist perspectives. However, the post-structuralist denial of individual intentions and Foucault's early dialogue regarding personal agency creates significant problems for feminism. So, although Foucault's theory of power neatly allows feminists to argue the social construction of gender, we stand—with theorists such as Alcoff (1988), Giddens (1979), and McNay (1992)—in opposition to his denial of personal agency.

McNay (1992) notes that "Foucault's lack of a rounded theory of subjectivity or agency conflicts with a fundamental aim of the feminist project: to rediscover and re-evaluate the experiences of women" (p. 3). Numerous theorists have grappled with this problem in postmodern theories in ways that redeem individual intention and action. For example, Alcoff (1988) rejects the total denial of personal agency by post-structuralists and postmodernists. She combines ideas from Teresa de

Lauretis and Denise Riley to develop a concept of positionality that also recognizes the importance of identity politics. Alcoff (1988) argues that, "If we combine the concept of identity politics with a conception of the subject as positionality, we can conceive of the subject as nonessentialized and emergent from a historical experience and yet retain our political ability" (p. 433). She further explains that this alternative conception would not view a woman merely as a passive recipient of an identity, but that "she herself is part of the historicized, fluid movement, and she therefore actively contributes to the context within which her position can be delineated" (p. 433). In developing her stance, Alcoff draws from de Lauretis's concept of gendered subjectivity in "relation to concrete habits, practices, and discourses while at the same time recognizing the fluidity of these" (p. 431).

In addition, McNay (1992) points out that even Foucault in his later work attributed "a certain degree of autonomy and independence to the way in which individuals act, especially in the ordering of their day to day existence" (p. 61). Similarly, Giddens (1979) advances the concept of the duality of structure, "which relates to the *fundamentally recursive character of social life, and expresses the mutual dependence of structure and agency*" (p. 69). As McNay (1992) explains, "The relationship between structure and agency must be grasped as dynamic, not static; existing structures are reproduced by human agents who modify and change these structures to differing degrees as they are shaped by them" (p. 60).

We affirm the feminist commitment to recognizing women's experiences, and we agree with the complementary stances of Alcoff, Giddens, and McNay. We argue, then, that although people are certainly influenced by social structures, human agents also have the ability to effect change. We suggest that this can be done through both behavioral and discursive strategies and that these strategies are filtered through the prism of power.

Lips (1991) supports a gendered theory of power, noting the Western stereotype that women and men use different methods to get what they want. She suggests that this stereotype holds true when women use hidden influence strategies because they lack legitimate power and have less control over resources. Lips argues that indirect, helpless strategies stereotypically attributed to women take the largest toll on self-esteem. This calls attention to issues that center on the notions of the public and the private spheres.

Historically, and in many cultures, the home has been the domain of the woman, primarily where duties of child rearing and the general management of the home are concerned. Even this arena, however, has its limitations for women in terms of power. Habermas (1989), in his development of the concept of the public sphere, recognized that the public sphere did not fully achieve its goals of equality and participation by all. Property ownership, in practice, was necessary for membership in the public sphere, and Landes (1995) adds that the bourgeois public sphere "was for the most part a restricted male preserve" (p. 96). Furthermore, although women have some power over child rearing and a few other aspects of home life, historically men have had ultimate authority in the home. Goodrich (1991) points out that a woman's "much-touted reign" in the private sphere is an illusion: "The gifts and labors she provides there are discounted by very reason of their being expected and considered natural. Further, they have no collectable value in the marketplace and grant her no usable credentials in the 'public' sphere" (p. 7).

As a result of structural differences among the public sphere, the market, and the family, Landes (1995) notes that a number of concerns were considered private and "treated as improper subjects for public debate" (p. 98). Landes also argues that:

> The virtues of universality and reason are offset by the role they play within a system of Western cultural representation that has eclipsed women's interests in the private domain and aligned femininity with particularity, interest, and partiality. In this context, the goals of generalizability and appeals to the common good may conceal rather than expose forms of domination, suppress rather than release concrete differences among persons or groups. (p. 99)

Landes' discussion illuminates the assumptions inherent in Western rationality that have worked to exclude women from the public sphere.

Feminist Responses to Power

Along with Landes, other feminist researchers tackled the issues of power as a function of the public/private sphere dichotomy. They spent a great deal of time debating power; they argued that power differences exist between women and men; and they pondered whether women should strive for power-over or work to define new, nonhierarchical approaches to power. As Lips (1991) asks, "If women simply work their way into existing power hierarchies instead of challenging the notion that power must come from the top down, will any basic changes in human relationships really result?" (p. 7).

Some feminist theorists argue that patriarchal institutions have manufactured differences among social groups, privileging the public over the private. As Yeatman (1987) explains, "the ruling paradigms or theoretical frameworks in social science are flawed by a masculinist bias which is indicated in an arbitrary privileging of the public aspect of social existence" (p. 159). This masculine bias extends to preferred speech styles and forms of association (Fraser, 1990-1991; Campbell, 1989). Ironically, as Fox-Genovese (1991) states, "the dominant male culture nonetheless itself depended, in the lives of individual men, upon a repressed domestic sphere that was represented as custodian of all the qualities the public sphere could not tolerate" (pp. 16-17). Certain topics, styles of speech, and issues are considered legitimate only in one or the other of the spheres. The consequences of this structured dichotomy are that certain groups (especially women and minorities) are denied access to the dominant "means of interpretation and communication." This obviously has tremendous impact on anything political, and traditionally domestic or private sphere concerns are typically considered nonpolitical.

As with feminists of the early contemporary women's movement in the United States who argued that the personal is political, we agree it is important to dissolve the arbitrary barriers between the public and the private spheres. For example, Reid-Merritt (1996), in her book *Sister Power: How Phenomenal Black Women Are Rising to the Top,* writes that, "phenomenal women are in the process of creating a new leadership model that has several distinguishing characteristics, including an unusual perception of power, decision making through consensus building, hard work, tenacious drive, and a willingness to break the rules" (p. 189). She notes many feminists have observed that women seem to have a different perception of the world and a different way of wielding power. This is in contrast to the traditional power paradigm which values control-over, dominance, and authority, and assumes that human society is inherently and necessarily hierarchical. This notion, in turn, is justified by major public social structures including religion, politics, and economics, through which these attributes form the standard of what is considered worthwhile or desirable. As Tong (1989) puts it:

> With man's desire to control the monolith "woman/nature" was born patriarchy, a hierarchical system that values power-over. Originally developed to ensure the human community's survival, power-over rapidly became, under patriarchy, a value cultivated simply for the experience of being the person in charge, the law giver, the "boss," number one in the "pecking order" . . . the masculine world can accommodate only those values that serve it. It has room for "true grit," "doing what you have to do," and "the end justifying the means." (pp. 99-100)

Similarly, Starhawk (1987) identifies power-over as the type of power that is oppressive, exploitative, and divisive, reinforcing obedience in patriarchy. She links power-over to domination and control and argues that:

> Power-over shapes every institution of our society. This power is wielded in the workplace, in the schools, in the courts, in the doctor's office. It may rule with weapons that are physical or by controlling the resources we need to live: money, food, medical care; or by controlling more subtle resources: information, approval, love. We are so accustomed to power-over, so steeped in its language and its implicit threats, that we often become aware of its functioning only when we see its extreme manifestations. (p. 9)

It is obvious, then, some feminists have challenged the value orientation inherent in the traditional power paradigm. These challenges were evidenced in the formulation of the early empowerment paradigm in which some feminists attempted to wield power through the attributes associated with giving to others rather than with domination and control.

Power As Empowerment

As the attributes *control* and *control-over* seem inexorably tied to any definition of the term *power,* so are several attributes associated with or tied to any definition or discussion of the traditionally feminine concept of empowerment. These include consensus, collectivity, compassion, companionship, and competence (Wheeler and Chinn, 1991; Schaef, 1995; Andrews, 1996).

Jean Baker Miller (1977) is one of the first theorists to have argued that feeling powerful does not have to imply following the traditional masculine model of competition and control. Goodrich (1991) describes empowerment as "a benevolent but unilateral transaction in which one person enhances another's ability to feel competent and take action, that is, enhances another's power-to" (p. 20). Similarly, Miller (1991) states that:

> we women have been most comfortable using our powers if we believe we are using them in the service of others. . . . One instance is in women's traditional role, where they have used their powers to foster the growth of others—certainly children, but also many other people. This might be called using one's power to empower another—increasing the other's resources, capabilities, effectiveness, and ability to act. (p. 38)

Andrews (1996) further describes empowerment as follows:

> In historical times as well as today the toil and work of women is not recognized as valued work. The value of women has for the most part been measured by men. Now in all parts of the world we can find women who are taking into their own hands how they will be valued. . . . Women know that they are valued less than men in all sectors of national life: economic, political, social and cultural. They know that the brokers of power will never give up their power, so women around the world must learn how to empower themselves. Their empowerment will take on a very different face from that of the dominating, exploiting, oppressive, authoritative power of the present day brokers of power. . . . Women are finding their power—becoming empowered—through cooperating, compassion, consensus, community, and competence. (pp. 2-3)

This form of power, which is the constant giving to others, however, appears insufficient for women working toward social and political change, and Avis (1991) takes it a step further by suggesting that more is needed:

> Empowerment is a holistic process which involves our comprehensive integration of (1) a political understanding of the oppression of women, including its embeddedness in the culture, its maintenance in family relationships, and its internalization with individual women; with (2) a high degree of respect for women, their strengths, and their self wisdom; and (3) an understanding of change at individual, family, and larger system levels. (p. 199)

It is evident that the value orientation associated with early empowerment focuses on nurturance, caring, and community, but primarily as it benefits others. Little inherent value or worth is given to individuals except in terms of what they do for others, and even then perhaps only in the private sphere. It appears that with the early empowerment paradigm, feminists attempted unsuccessfully to gain recognition for the value of these attributes within the larger social structure.

The original concept of empowerment, "giving power to other women" (Steinem, 1983, p. 228), then, has been found lacking. Goodrich (1991), however, points out that the concept of empowerment has been broadened by authors such as Surrey (1987) to indicate a mutual process. "Both participants in a relationship can interact in ways that increase connection and enhance personal power for each. These interactions involve *mutual attention, mutual empathy, mutual engagement,* and *mutual responsiveness*" (italics added, Goodrich, 1991, p. 20). Mutual empowerment entails "the psychological reality of the other as part of an ongoing, continuous awareness beyond the momentary experience, and to 'take the other into account' in all one's activities" (Surrey, 1987, p. 6). Goodrich (1991) goes on to say that "Power—energy to act—is thus grounded in emotional and equitable relationship rather than in imposition or intimidation or privilege" (p. 21).

Similarly, Lips (1991), although supporting the concept of empowerment, emphasizes the need for mutuality and warns against the binary thinking that emphasizes differences between men and women by suggesting that "cautious women might do well simply to revel in the empowerment that comes with the realization that there is no magical correctness at all about the masculine way of doing things, that feminine approaches to getting things done are not in any way second-rate, and that men can learn as much or more that is useful from the feminine style as women can from the masculine one" (p. 90).

These broadened conceptions of empowerment suggest that individuals have the need to support themselves while supporting others and that women in particular are no longer content with simply giving or taking. Instead, they are intent on developing mutually enhancing interactions.

Power As Personal Authority

A third conception of power focuses on the intrapersonal realm and is concerned with personal authority which Rampage (1991) states is "the most fundamental form of power" (p. 110). She argues that:

> Personal authority is . . . the power to be *self*-determining, to act rather than react, to choose the terms on which to live one's own life. It is thus distinguished from the more common understanding of power as the ability to exercise control over others. Personal authority must also be distinguished from authority which comes by virtue of an association with another in authority (e.g., a powerful person), or with an institution which is vested with authority by some common or formal agreement among members of a society (e.g., the Supreme Court). (p. 110)

It is apparent that the attributes associated with personal authority include *self-determination, knowledge, action, choice,* and *independence*. Rampage suggests, however, that typically personal authority has been demonstrated mostly by men because it is associated with male gender expectations.

Rampage (1991) reviews feminist theorists who have tried to explain why women have trouble with personal authority. She concludes that "*social* norms and expectations regarding appropriate female behavior, rather than biology, discourage women from seeing themselves as capable, independent knowers, able to make choices about their lives regardless of the approval or disapproval of others" (p. 111).

It is evident that this form of power remains within the current patriarchal system of values, returning to a concern with self and self-improvement, and to a large degree leaving behind the early feminist concept of supporting others. It is also evident that none of the three conceptions of power—traditional power, empowerment, or personal authority—taken individually have fully served the needs of women.

Miller (1991), however, offers an insightful explanation that may well account for why reciprocal empowerment, which combines empowerment and personal authority, may be the perspective preferred by many women. In terms of some women's views of power, Miller states that:

> I think most women would be most comfortable in a world in which we feel we are not limiting, but are enhancing the power of other people while simultaneously increasing our own power. . . . The part about enhancing one's own powers is extremely difficult for women. When women even contemplate acting powerful, they fear the possibility of limiting or putting down another person. They also fear recognizing or admitting the need, especially the desire, to increase their own powers. (p. 39)

Although early conceptions of empowerment were concerned primarily with the "other," and personal authority is concerned primarily with "self," the reciprocal empowerment model we propose, emphasizes a great concern for the other, and also takes into consideration the self. Social changes now occurring suggest that some women are indeed taking steps to strengthen their individual positions while still giving of themselves to care for and nurture others. It is for this reason that we offer reciprocal empowerment as an alternative perspective of power.

RECIPROCAL EMPOWERMENT: A NEW APPROACH

The results of Miller and Cummins's (1992) work, along with those of myriad other researchers, support the notion that women would actively seek to isolate themselves from traditional power identifications, and evidence also exists to support Miller and Cummins in their effort to further investigate the notion of women's acceptance of power as personal authority, with its attendant attributes of knowledge, action, self-determination, choice, and independence. However, recent literature supports the idea of women's rejection of the power construct and the early conceptions of the empowerment construct for the acceptance of personal authority, *but* only as a necessary component of a new nonhierarchical paradigm. As noted earlier, Rampage (1991) posits that personal authority is associated with self-determination, action, and choice. That is, personal authority is a required first step to gain/possess any form of power.

The traditional power model is driven by the individual's need to conquer or have dominion, authority, and sway over another primarily to the benefit of the individual wielding the power, as does the personal authority model, which appears to be hinged on the notion of satisfying one's own needs. On the other hand, the reciprocal empowerment paradigm we describe carries with it the idea of sharing, a combining of the good of the individual or group with a structure or system in which individuals or groups work toward the common good—a combining of the self and other. Reciprocal empowerment combines both aspects to create a more universal give-and-take perspective of influence. It also combines the aspects of the internal and external considerations discussed previously.

Graphic Illustrations of Power, Empowerment, Personal Authority, and Reciprocal Empowerment

The illustrations (Figures 1.1 through 1.4) offer graphic representations of the various concepts of power we have discussed: power, empowerment, personal authority, and reciprocal empowerment.

Model A (Figure 1.1) represents traditional power and is associated with the attributes of domination, conflict, force, winning, resistance, competition, physical strength, control, sway, wealth, authority, resources, coercion, and struggle. The literature reviewed suggests that these attributes are tools used to gain power for the self generally by taking from others. We have chosen the triangle because it illustrates the hierarchical character of the traditional power construct.

Model B (Figure 1.2) represents the early empowerment paradigm and is associated with the attributes of compassion, collectivity, consensus, companionship, and competence. This model and its attributes are generally associated with giving to others without necessarily considering the self. The inverted triangle illustrates that early empowerment is really traditional power stood on its end. It simply emphasizes the view of those who give rather than those who take.

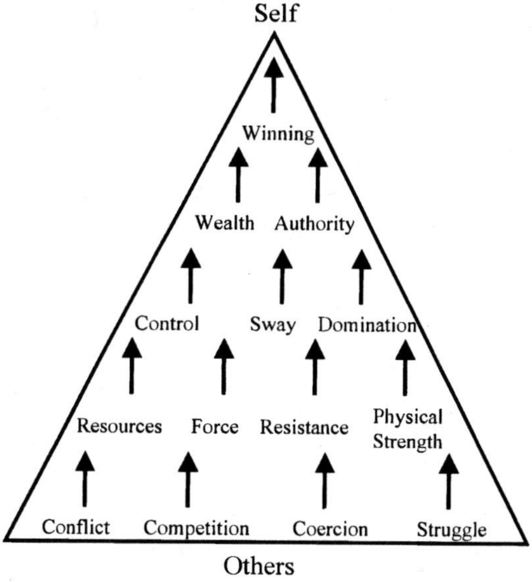

FIGURE 1.1. Model A: Traditional power (others supporting self) and its attributes

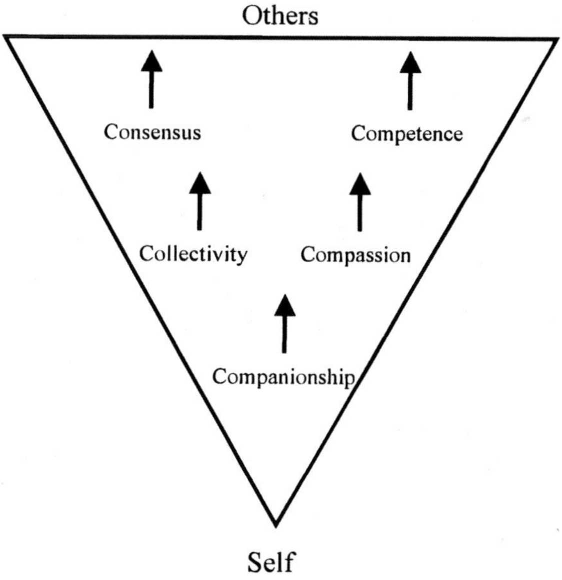

FIGURE 1.2. Model B: Empowerment (self supporting others) and its attributes

Model C (Figure 1.3) represents the personal authority paradigm and is associated with the attributes of knowledge, choice, self-determination, action, and independence. The literature suggests that this model, like the traditional power model, has been associated with gaining power for the self, but without necessarily taking from or giving to others. We depict personal authority as a circle in which self—in gaining knowledge, independence, self-determination, and the ability to act and make choices—supports self, but does not necessarily break from the self-oriented cycle to share power. Keep in mind that personal authority—a historically masculine paradigm which some feminists have only recently begun to embrace—has been perceived as a necessary foundation of power. We too consider it a fundamental part of power and a necessary component of Model D, reciprocal empowerment.

We choose the spiral to illustrate Model D (Figure 1.4) because the shape connotes growth and evolution (Cirlot, 1962). In addition, Andrews (1996) suggests that empowerment from within is horizontal and circular, moving up and in a spiral. We suggest that it is this combination of personal authority and early empowerment that allows women access to areas traditionally controlled by men, since men

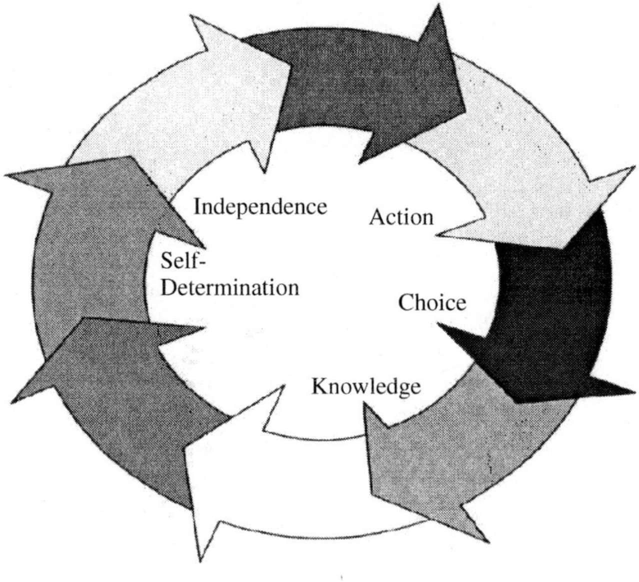

FIGURE 1.3. Model C: Personal authority (self supporting self) and its attributes

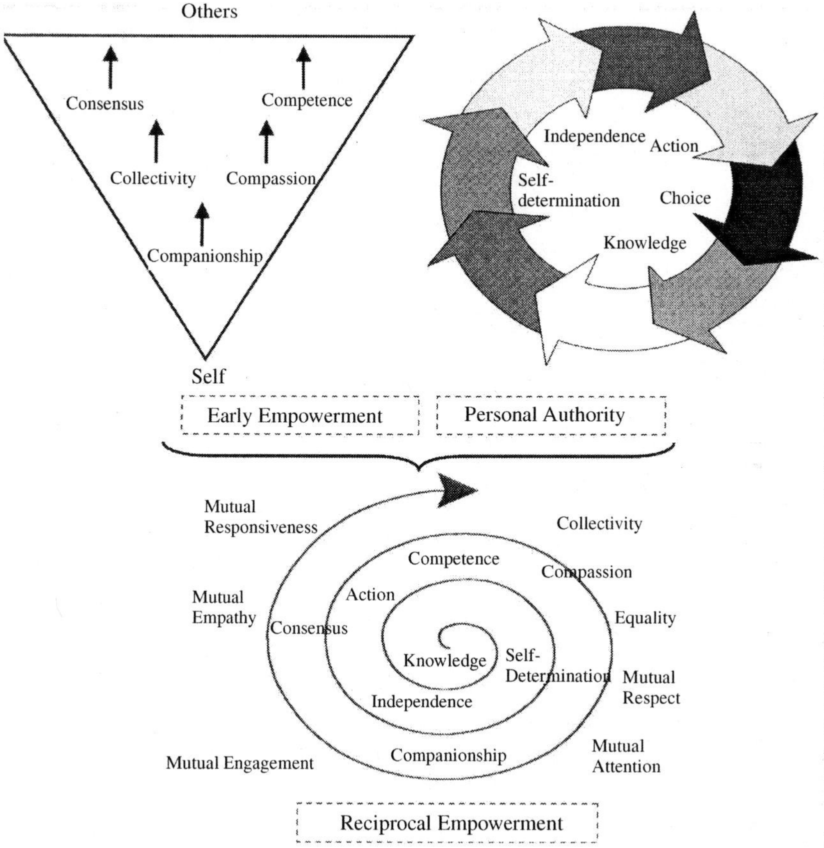

FIGURE 1.4. Model D: Reciprocal empowerment (self supporting self and others) and its attributes

have always employed the personal authority attributes as the foundation of their traditional power. Having personal authority, therefore, allows women to practice the attributes they have always used (early empowerment) to provide a unified process and a product that works toward the common good.

Other researchers who recognized the need to combine personal strength with sharing include Starhawk (1987), whose discussion of "power-with" resembles the merging of empowerment and personal authority in our model. She defines power-with as

> the power of a strong individual in a group of equals, the power not to command, but to suggest and be listened to, to begin something and see it happen. The source of power-with is the willingness of others to listen to our ideas. . . . Power-with is more subtle, more fluid and fragile than authority. It is dependent on personal responsibility, on our own creativity and daring, and on the willingness of others to respond. (pp. 10-11)

Our graphic representation of reciprocal empowerment accurately depicts the fluidity that Starhawk attributes to power-with.

Reciprocal Empowerment in Action

In addition to the graphic illustrations, we offer one example of reciprocal empowerment in action: civil rights advocate Fannie Lou Townsend Hamer, who lived from 1917 to 1977. A Mississippi Delta sharecropper's wife with little education, Hamer went on to become a national civil rights leader after her initiation into political activism when she was denied the right to vote in 1963. Hamer was a field secretary for the Student Nonviolent Coordinating Committee, a cofounder of the Mississippi Freedom Democratic Party, a teacher for the Freedom Riders, an organizer for the Poor People's Campaign, and founder of the Freedom Farm Cooperative in the Mississippi Delta. She worked to get black women and men to unite to preserve the black family and was one of the first to argue against blacks fighting in U.S. wars. Her simple, common sense rhetoric was characterized by religious imagery, reference to biblical scripture, earthy humor, and the use of song. According to Price and Markham (1994), she "set forth the issues in words people from all walks of life could understand, told them forcefully what each of them could do, provided a model of the power of each person through her own example, and then sent her audiences out singing to try to do it" (p. 428). An example of this comes from a 1972 speech in which Hamer targeted middle-class black women who had failed to respect her work in the human rights movement:

> Whether you have a Ph.D., or no D, we're in this bag together. And whether you're from Morehouse or Nohouse, we're still in this bag together. Not to fight to try to liberate ourselves from

> the men—this is another trick to get us fighting among ourselves—but to work together with the Black man, then we will have a better chance to just act as human beings, and to be treated as human beings in our sick society. (Price and Markham, 1994, p. 431)

Reciprocal empowerment, as a combination of personal authority and empowerment, is evident in this speech as Hamer used her words to conjure feelings of mutuality between herself and the audience. Although reciprocal empowerment is typically exhibited in discursive interactions, its characteristics can be found within a single speech. For example, Hamer's speech is peppered with the pronoun "we," and she repeats the phrase "we're in this bag together." She also states that "we" need to "work together with the Black man," which is evidence of her willingness to work cooperatively in a community to achieve mutual benefit. Hamer gives herself and others the choice of taking action "not to fight to liberate themselves from the men . . . but to work together with the Black man." This is a clear demonstration of individual choice and action, two attributes of personal authority, combined with the attributes of empowerment—cooperation, collectivity, community, and so on.

Our choice of Fannie Lou Townsend Hamer as an illustration of reciprocal empowerment is not accidental. Despite being doubly oppressed on the basis of both race and gender, historically many black women have combined personal authority with the early empowerment attributes to demonstrate reciprocal empowerment in their words and actions. We recognize that on the surface this may appear contradictory based on the historical practices of institutional and organizing silence as experienced by marginalized groups such as black women. However, according to Clair (1998), "numerous scholars have advanced Gramsci's notions of hegemony and coercion, allowing us to see that multiple voices are positioned in a variety of places within an ever shifting and changing set of social relations" (p. 67). For example, Braxton and Zuber (1994) discuss an 1861 account of slave life written by Harriet Jacobs. Originally published using the pseudonym Linda Brent, the autobiographical nature of this account was not revealed until after its publication. In their analysis of Jacobs' writing, Braxton and Zuber note that breaking silence in this way may come at great cost, but through such expression one can tell not only a story of oppression, but also a story of resistance.

It is these shifting and changing social relations, identified by Clair and illustrated by Braxton and Zuber, that we feel have historically allowed black women such as Hamer and Jacobs to come to voice within their own cultural milieu and have more recently allowed them a voice in the larger social environment. That is, until recently, they practiced reciprocal empowerment only within their own communities where black women were situated to better resist patriarchal power. Black women represent an example of Engel's notion that proletarian women, because they work outside of the home, have a greater measure of equality with their mates (Tong, 1989). Typically, black women have worked outside of the home, first because they were forced to as slaves, and later because of economic necessity. This economic situation allowed black women a certain social positioning that afforded them the tools to engage in what Collins calls "breaking the silence," or "coming to voice" (Collins, 1998). Collins has suggested that black women have used these tools which include the privileged knowledge (a vital attribute of the prevailing power paradigm) gained by working as domestics within white households to increase their positions within their communities, thereby increasing their ability to help others. According to Collins (1998), "Ironically, in fulfilling the emotional labor of caring for whites, males, and/or the affluent, these same mammy workers gain access to their private, usually hidden knowledge" (p. 49). Furthermore, Collins posits that:

> By invoking the authority of lived experience, African-American women confronted seemingly universal scientific truths by citing examples from their own experiences. The purpose was not simply to insert the missing experiences into prevailing wisdom. Instead, when effectively done, claiming the authority of concrete experiences used wisdom to challenge legitimated knowledge. Thus, breaking silence by claiming the authority of individual lived Black female experience offered an effective challenge to elite discourses claiming the authority of science. (pp. 48-49)

It is possible that breaking the silence, or coming to voice could be functions of the attributes of personal authority, thereby giving women such as Sojourner Truth, Harriet Tubman, Mary Bethune, Shirley Chisholm, and Barbara Jordan the strength and wherewithal to make their way into the political system, a realm traditionally reserved only for white males and generally inaccessible to women of *any* color. Furthermore, Reid-Merritt (1996) suggests that for phenomenal black women, "power seems to be a combination of understanding history, being moved by the power of the spirit, and hearing the cries of an oppressed people. They are motivated by their social consciousness and epic memories. They view power in the collective sense" (p. 202). She describes "sister power" as "the collective spirit of culturally conscious Black women committed to principled leadership . . . as women who never lose sight of the need for social change, and who carry their commitment into local neighborhoods, small towns, and big cities, and into the citadel of business and government" (p. 202).

We suggest it is the historically situated position of black women that allowed them to access secret knowledge of elite society and helped them to develop attributes of personal authority. Using this information to challenge society's legitimated knowledge positioned them as activists within communities. It is in this way that black women have a history of speaking from within the reciprocal empowerment paradigm. As Collins (1998) argues, "access to both public and hidden knowledge on both sides of power positions African American women and other similarly situated groups to develop distinctive standpoints on hierarchical power relations" (p. 49). Undoubtedly, this phenomenon bears further exploration, for although black women may use reciprocal empowerment, it is important to determine whether and how women from other ethnicities perceive and practice power.

We began this exploration by reviewing the historical and social use of the concepts of power, empowerment, and personal authority that illustrated the following: (1) many women define/conceptualize traditional power as a culturally masculine construct that supports values they may find undesirable; (2) feminists struggle to develop/conceptualize power in new ways that embody values they find acceptable, and (3) certain groups of women, due to their economic, social, and cultural situations, already practice a combined personal authority/empowerment model in the form of reciprocal empowerment.

We recognize that the components of what we call reciprocal empowerment are not new. Our contribution has been to identify the components of the various concepts of power, examine their individual uses, strengths, and weaknesses, and then begin the process of investigating the dynamics that result from combining them. In doing so, we chose to give this perspective of power an identifiable name: reciprocal empowerment.

Finally, we want to make clear that first and foremost our model of reciprocal empowerment is descriptive. It describes a process influenced by a particular concept of power. It is this process that we chose to examine by talking to seven culturally diverse groups of women about their perceptions and use of power.

Chapter 2

African-American Women and Power

THE STRENGTH OF A NATION: A BRIEF HISTORY OF AFRICAN-AMERICAN WOMEN

Although some members of this group may be recent immigrants to the United States, most African Americans trace their personal history to slavery. Today, according to Reid (1984), black women live with multiple jeopardies as they battle issues of gender, race, and class. They encounter gender discrimination both inside and outside their communities and experience racism from both of these arenas as well. Reid also suggests that although it has been given little consideration, the combined influence of gender and race broadly impacts the personal development of black women. Gutiérrez (1990) notes that oftentimes African-American women are hindered by fewer years of education, higher rates of unemployment, overrepresentation in low-status, low-paying jobs, and significantly higher rates of poverty than that of whites and even black men. Furthermore, within the professional realm, African-American women are commonly underrepresented in positions of power and are generally denied sufficient access to necessary social and material resources. To combat these problems, Gutiérrez advocates an empowerment perspective. She argues that issues of power and powerlessness are central to the experiences of women of color.

To understand the position of an African-American woman, then, it is essential to describe historical factors that contributed to the social, political, economic, and legal aspects of her culture. However, the daunting task of describing the transatlantic slave trade, antebellum slavery, and the residual effects of this brutal system is beyond the scope of this book and has been discussed and analyzed by many scholars from a variety of academic disciplines. Here we provide a brief overview of slavery, summarize the role of African women in

American slave and postemancipation society, and then focus on the effects of this historical experience on contemporary African-American women's lives in the United States.

African-American Women, Slavery, and Postemancipation

According to Burnside and Robotham (1997), the Spanish first imported African slaves to the North American mainland in 1565. By 1725, the American colonies had a population of at least 75,000 slaves. Just two years later, the Quakers—who would play a prominent role in the abolition movement—began arguing for the end to the institution of slavery in America. Although the transatlantic slave trade was officially outlawed in 1824, slaves in the United States were not freed until Abraham Lincoln issued the Emancipation Proclamation in 1863. Estimates of the number of Africans who traveled to the Americas on the ships of the Middle Passage range anywhere from eight to fifteen million. The human suffering and death caused by the institution of slavery as well as its far-reaching effects can hardly be overstated. Burnside and Robotham explain that

> Africa would suffer an enormous depletion of its population, while the Americas would be bolstered by the forced immigration of a significant new race of people who would contribute their energies to the building of the New World alongside European settlers and native inhabitants. . . . Slavery would finally be brought to an end in European countries and their colonies as a direct result of the struggles of Africans against their enslavement in the Americas, and the support and activism of those who empathized with their plight. (p. 28)

Watkins and David (1970) recognize that the American black woman has occupied a unique if unenviable position in the United States. Historically, she has carried the weight of inferior status and prejudice derived from both her sex and race. According to Watkins and David, the most accurate account of the African-American woman's place in America begins in the antebellum period, when black women were brought to America to labor and breed more slaves, and continues to today's complex society of culturally specific advances and ever-changing roles. In our study, we focus on the roles of the African-

American woman and her life as an American. We do not attempt to compare women of African cultures to the culture of African-American women. Although residual links to Mother Africa exist, most cultural connections to Africa were forcefully severed during the slave trade. African-American women's slow yet distinct assimilation into American society can be characterized as a change from marginalization to significant cultural icon. Gilmore (1996) writes that from the debris of disenfranchisement, black women discovered fresh approaches to serving their communities and crafted new tactics designed to forge their way into the social spotlight.

Many have attempted to explain the marginality of African-American women by examining social dislocations such as poverty, unemployment, school dropout rates, and the like. However, Watkins and David posit that the most indelible experiences of black women in the United States grew out of the treatment they received as slaves. Hard labor, poor food, little shelter, and the inhumane breeding of more slaves were all part of the African-American woman's historical experience. Emancipation brought few significant improvements to the lives of black women and their families, and the absolute power of whites versus the powerlessness of black women often made compliance necessary for these women's survival. Therefore, although their status changed from slaves to freewomen, the conditions of their lives and their social environment for decades to follow were still governed by exploitation. Their roles as wives and mothers were significantly influenced by social, political, and economic structures. Even as a married woman, the black woman was not immune to the sexual advances of white men. As a mother, she was forced to watch her daughters relive the same injustices she endured. Experiences such as these chiseled the mold for much of the culture of contemporary African-American women.

The history of the image of black women in the United States begins with the antebellum period in which race and gender played a large role in the social hierarchy. The African-American woman carried the dual stigma of being female and black in a society that devalued both. Jewell (1993) contends that American society is replete with cultural images based on race, ethnicity, gender, and class. When race, ethnic background, gender, and class are combined, a plethora of diverse cultural images emerges. Jewell observes that although cultural images of most ethnicities have changed over time, the cultural images of African-American women have undergone only minimal change. Research on cultural images of African-American women has revealed that, until the 1980s, essentially four categories were used to portray African-American women. According to Jewell, these categories were "mammy," "Aunt Jemima," "Sapphire," and "Jezebel" (the "bad black girl"). The introduction of new portrayals of African-American women during the 1980s was accompanied by two practices. On one hand, more positive images were presented ("Claire Huxtable" of *The Cosby Show*). On the other hand, African-American women were still being presented using the negative stereotype of the bad black girl ("Shug Avery" of Alice Walker's *Color Purple*). Images that symbolize African-American womanhood have, with few exceptions, been defined as negative by the majority of African-American scholars. These images, believed to have evolved during slavery, portray black women as the antithesis of the American image of beauty and femininity. These portrayals perpetuated the social disenfranchisement of the African-American woman and perhaps contributed, to a large degree, to the stunted growth of the black woman in the United States. With mass media snipping at the heels of an otherwise largely underrepresented and misrepresented culture, the African-American woman was forced to represent herself in the home and in the workplace in order to salvage the dignity and respect popular culture denied her.

Historically, employment for black men was sporadic and difficult to maintain; inadequate wages forced black women into the workforce oftentimes as the sole providers for their families. Neverdon-Morton (1989) states that between 1895 and 1925, most black females were not college or vocational school graduates. Although successful black women entrepreneurs existed in all the regions of the United States, the majority of African-American women in the workforce held menial, unskilled, low-paying jobs geared toward women. Neverdon-Morton also reports that in 1900, there were 1,316,872 black women in the United States, constituting 11.4 percent of the total female population. In addition, of those black women, 34.8 percent were wage earners. The struggle to balance equally important roles in the household and the workforce has perpetuated the disintegration of the already fragile world of African-American women in the United States. For example, absence from the home for long periods in order to earn money for the family often resulted in problems within the African-American woman's home. Lack of day care, inadequate health care, and poor living conditions were some of the concerns that plagued the lives of many black working women. These problems negatively impacted the individual African American as well as the race as a whole, so that African-American women—both the literate and the uneducated, the professional and the unskilled—found it within their best interest to work together to make their lives easier and more enriching. They found their outlet in the dynamic world of politics, and although African-American women did not achieve direct representation in a timely manner, indirect representation served as their magic carpet into the life they hoped to pass on to future generations.

Roles of African-American Women

From as early as the behind-the-scenes activism during the Civil War and again during the civil rights movement, the African-American woman has been involved in politics in this country in one way or another throughout her history. Gilmore (1996) believes that the result of this involvement was a greater role for black women in the interracial public sphere. Prior to the Voting Rights Act of 1965, black women were not voters, but they made themselves clients—citizens who needed government grants for civic improvement in their neighborhoods—and in that role they became spokespeople for and motivators of black citizens. Gilmore believes that black women also claimed a distinctly female moral authority, and the deep camouflage of their leadership style—their womanhood—helped them remain invisible as they worked toward political ends.

The relationship between black and white women in the early 1900s is important to an understanding of the role African-American women played in past politics. To compare black women's progressivism to white women's progressivism, Gilmore believes we must be cautious at every turn because black and white women had vastly different relationships to power. For example, white middle-class women lobbied to obtain services *from* their husbands, brothers, and sons. On the other hand, black women lobbied to obtain services *for* their husbands, brothers, and sons. When white women received the right to vote and black men were prevented from exercising their newly won right to vote, African-American women felt left out of the public sphere altogether. Gilmore further suggests that it was this split in legal justice and fair representation that led black women to persuade white female philanthropists to transcend race and recognize class and gender similarities. Black women had two political goals: to gain a foothold for African-American opinion in regard to public and state services, and to begin to clear a path for the return of African Americans to the ballot box. Through political means, the black woman worked to improve her status in a society that barely recognized her existence, and she forced those with political power to recognize the plight of her husbands, brothers, and sons. Politics, however, was not the only tool used by African-American women. Black women also became involved in religious work that focused on social issues important to their communities.

Gilmore places significant emphasis on the role of the church and organized religion in the lives of African-American women and their attempts to gain power and respect. In the wake of disenfranchisement, African Americans turned to their churches for consolation and political advice. Black men, however, began to fear the potentially disastrous mix of politics and religion. African-American women used their church organizations to push for community improvement. This alternative involved less risk than preaching inflammatory sermons of protest and civil rights. The church became a center for organized protest that functioned as a moral arena from which to effect change. In addition, the work that black women did in Sunday schools was designed to help build better homes for their children, to better educate them, and to build stronger communities. These women needed little urging. They embraced their roles and basked in their unique ability to execute them. As a result, home became a centerpiece of African-American life that resonated throughout the changing culture of African Americans. The African-American woman's involvement with religion was closely tied to both her political and her home life; this masterfully woven tapestry served as a stepping-stone for the life that the African-American woman envisioned for herself, her family, and the generations to come.

African-American women and their roles in the workforce, the political sphere, and religion helped clear the path for increased affluence and social standing in a society that historically held her and her family in low regard. Today, the constant struggle for power still shapes the day-to-day life of African-American women.

ANALYSIS OF ETHNOGRAPHIC FINDINGS

Demographics

Seventeen African-American women completed the survey and interview. The women ranged in age from eighteen to fifty-five, with ten women falling between the age of eighteen and twenty-five. Fourteen of the women identified themselves as single and three as married. Five of the women's household incomes ranged between $15,000 and $25,000, five women had household incomes over $76,000, and the rest were spread out between $26,000 and $65,000. One respondent did not report her household income. All were high school graduates, some were seeking an undergraduate degree, and some had already earned graduate or professional degrees. Sixteen of the women identified their race as black and one as African-American black. All seventeen women identified their ethnicity as African American.

Analysis of Survey

Fourteen survey statements were designed to evaluate participants' level of agreement versus disagreement with society's use of traditional power attributes. These were compared with fourteen statements designed to measure participants' level of agreement versus disagreement with their personal use of these same attributes (see Table 2.1). For the survey statements that question the women's personal feelings toward traditional power attributes, a majority supported only three of the fourteen attributes: resources, struggle, and competition. For example, fourteen women agreed with the statement "I feel that if I have access to resources I can exercise power." Ten women agreed with both of the following statements: "I feel that struggle is acceptable in order to exercise power," and "I feel that it is acceptable to compete with others in order to exercise power." The highest level of disagreement was with the terms force, physical strength, and control-over. For example, thirteen women disagreed with the statement "I feel that it is acceptable to use force in order to exercise power." An even split between agreement and disagreement existed in response to the statement "I feel that wealth is necessary in order for me to be powerful."

TABLE 2.1. African-American Women: Personal Feelings Regarding Power and Society versus Power and Self

Traditional Power and Society				Traditional Power and Self			
Attribute	**Agree**	**Disagree**	**N A/D**	**Attribute**	**Agree**	**Disagree**	**N A/D**
Domination	14	2	1	Domination	8	9	0
Conflict	4	6	7	Conflict	4	8	5
Force	7	6	4	Force	2	13	2
Win	6	8	3	Win	4	10	3
Struggle	11	1	5	Struggle	10	3	4
Resistance	12	3	2	Resistance	6	9	2
Competition	13	1	3	Competition	10	3	4
Physical strength	8	7	2	Physical strength	4	11	2
Control-over	15	0	2	Control-over	3	11	3
Sway others	14	0	3	Sway others	6	8	3
Wealth	17	0	0	Wealth	8	8	1
Authority	15	1	1	Authority	8	6	3
Resources	14	2	1	Resources	14	1	2
Coercion	11	0	6	Coercion	6	8	3

n = 17
N A/D = Neither agree nor disagree

When asked to respond to statements questioning their perception of society's use of traditional power attributes, a majority agreed that society uses ten of the fourteen attributes. All the women agreed with the statement "Society teaches that, in order for one to be powerful, one needs wealth." This was followed by the statements about society's use of control-over, authority, domination, sway, and resources. A high number of "neither agree nor disagree" responses were given to the statements mentioning the attributes conflict and coercion.

The women agreed that both they and society consider resources, struggle, and competition necessary components of power. The women also felt that neither they nor society use conflict or require winning in order to gain power. Control-over was the sole attribute that yielded a distinct divergence between participants' use and their perception of society's use. In this case, eleven of the women personally disagreed with control-over, whereas fifteen of them felt that society uses this attribute.

Of the five statements highlighting empowerment attributes, three received majority agreement by the women (see Table 2.2). These were the statements that read "I feel that it is important to be compassionate regardless of whether or not it benefits me as long as I empower others," "I feel that it is important that I be willing to reach consensus whether or not it benefits me as long as I empower others," and "I feel that my competence should be used to empower others regardless of whether or not it benefits me."

Five statements were designed to measure the women's attitudes regarding personal authority attributes (see Table 2.3). All these at-

TABLE 2.2. African-American Women: Personal Feelings Regarding Empowerment

Attribute	**Agree**	**Disagree**	**N A/D**
Collectivity	5	6	6
Companionship	5	9	3
Compassion	12	4	1
Consensus	11	1	5
Competence	10	4	3

n = 17
N A/D = Neither agree nor disagree

TABLE 2.3. African-American Women: Personal Feelings Regarding Personal Authority

Attribute	Agree	Disagree	N A/D
Ability to take action	17	0	0
Ability to choose	16	0	1
Self-determination	16	0	1
Knowledge	16	0	1
Independence	16	0	1

n = 17
N A/D = Neither agree nor disagree

tributes received overwhelming majority agreement among the African-American women. The statement "I feel that it is important to take action in order to gain and use personal power" received unanimous agreement, and sixteen of the women agreed with all the remaining personal authority attributes.

Fourteen survey statements were associated with reciprocal empowerment (see Table 2.4). The African-American women surveyed agreed with all fourteen attributes, with five attributes receiving fifteen or more agreements. The statements "I feel that by having the ability to choose I empower myself and others," "I feel that by having the ability to act I empower myself and others," and "I feel that by having knowledge I empower myself and others" received sixteen agreements each. The statements "I feel that by being independent I empower myself and others" and "I feel that by having self-determination I empower myself and others" both received fifteen agreements. The reciprocal empowerment statements that received the highest levels of agreement from the women were all drawn from the personal authority component of the reciprocal empowerment model. The statements "I feel that empowering myself and others creates an atmosphere of mutual attention" and "I feel that empowering myself and others creates an atmosphere of mutual empathy" received the lowest levels of agreement, ten and nine respectively. Although nine of the women agreed with the statement related to mutual empathy, a similar number (seven) chose to neither agree nor disagree.

TABLE 2.4. African-American Women: Personal Feelings Regarding Reciprocal Empowerment

Attribute	Agree	Disagree	N A/D
Mutual responsiveness	12	2	1
Competence	14	0	3
Compassion	12	2	3
Independence	15	0	2
Ability to choose	16	0	1
Collectivity	10	2	5
Companionship	10	3	4
Ability to take action	16	0	1
Self-determination	15	0	2
Mutual engagement	12	2	3
Knowledge	16	0	1
Consensus	11	1	5
Mutual attention	10	4	3
Mutual empathy	9	1	7

$n = 17$
N A/D = Neither agree nor disagree
Note: Where totals equal less than *n,* there were instances of no response.

Analysis of the Interview

To analyze the interview results we categorized and described the responses in terms of their relation to the four power models under examination. We did this by first looking at the five introductory questions concerning (1) what power means to the women as individuals, (2) what they think power generally means in American society, (3) what power means in their ethnic community, (4) whether, as women, they have power in American society, and (5) whether, as women, they have power in African-American culture (see Table 2.5). We then evaluated responses regarding their perceptions of how power *is* and *should be used* in the areas of work, family, religion, and politics (see Table 2.6).

TABLE 2.5. African-American Women: Responses to Introductory Interview Questions and the Relationship of These Responses to the Power Models

Introductory Interview Questions	Traditional Power	Empowerment	Personal Authority	Reciprocal Empowerment
What does the word *power* mean to you as an individual?	7	0	5	1
What do you think the word *power* means in American society today?	15	0	0	0
What do you think the word *power* means in your culture?	6	0	4	1
As a woman, what kind of power do you think you have in U.S. society?	0	0	5	0
As an African-American woman, what do you think the word *power* means in your culture?	6	0	6	1

n = 17
Note: Total numbers may not match *n* since in some cases responses could not be associated with a power model. Zero equals no responses or responses could not be associated with a model.

Introductory Questions

In responding to the first question that asked the women what power means to them as individuals, seven of the women described traditional power. Control and authority were mentioned most frequently. For example, one woman said, "I think power is a form of control and authority," and another said, "Power is a position of authority, to have some kind of control." In their responses, five women used words associated with personal authority. One woman said, "To have the ability to choose and make decisions, to be completely independent." One response, although not specifically using a reciprocal empowerment attribute, we interpreted as reciprocal empowerment. To this woman, power meant "The ability to inspire others and yourself to achieve our potential and work beyond it." Terms that ap-

TABLE 2.6. African-American Women: Interview Responses to Questions About Work, Family, Religion, and Politics

How Power *Is Used*				
	Traditional Power	**Empowerment**	**Personal Authority**	**Reciprocal Empowerment**
Work	15	0	1	0
Family	8	0	2	0
Religion	0	0	0	0
Politics	1	0	0	0

How Power *Should Be Used*				
	Traditional Power	**Empowerment**	**Personal Authority**	**Reciprocal Empowerment**
Work	0	1	0	0
Family	0	1	0	0
Religion	0	1	0	0
Politics	0	0	0	0

n = 17

Note: Total numbers may not match *n* since in some cases responses could not be associated with a power model. Zero equals no responses or responses could not be associated with a model.

peared frequently, but that we could not associate with any of the power models included "decision making" and "free."

In response to the question about the meaning of power in American society today, fifteen of the respondents named traditional power attributes. Control, money, and domination were the attributes most frequently identified. Two responses included domination: "I think power is generally associated with control or domination over someone or something" and "Control and influence over others. Domination and oppression are themes that rule supreme." Politics and oppression were also mentioned a number of times in the responses to this question.

When asked what they think the word *power* means in their particular culture, six respondents used traditional power attributes in their statements, four used personal authority attributes, and one made a statement that matches reciprocal empowerment. The traditional power attributes were the same as those found in earlier responses, and the personal authority responses included choice, the ability to act, and knowledge. For example, one woman responded, "Having the ability to choose and make decisions, take control, and use resources such as knowledge to gain personal power, which would allow one to survive in today's society." One response that we could not associate with any of the power paradigms, but which spoke very strongly of a personal feeling from a member of the African-American community, follows: "Power is not so much a concept in the African-American community as it is a void. I think it is generally accepted that power is something black Americans don't have." Another response, the first one to introduce the concept of skin color, was "Justice for all—freedom to have control in one's home, community, and society at large—not being judged by one's color, but by the content of one's heart."

As women in U.S. society, the respondents indicated no identification with traditional power. Instead, five of them associated their power in U.S. society with personal authority. One woman said, "Personally, I have power here because I choose to work and pay my own bills and be independent," and another said, "I think I have equal power to men to be able to do what I choose."

The final introductory question asked what they as African-American women think power means in their culture. This elicited six traditional power responses. Influence, authority, and control were terms used most frequently, followed by money and domination. Six personal authority references were made, mostly concerning independence and knowledge. Finally, we believe that reciprocal empowerment surfaced again here in this response: "To rise above what society expects and to have a positive influence on your community."

Work

Sixteen of the African-American women said they were employed outside the household. All sixteen of these women felt that people have different kinds of power where they work. Several of the responses described a hierarchical structure, but did not specify the impact of this sort of structure. Of the sixteen women, ten indicated they have a lot or some power, only six associated their power with traditional power, and one woman associated her power with personal authority. For the six who associated traditional power with their jobs, power to them meant responsibility for money, having sway over others, and having authority. Three of the women indicated they had little or no power. One woman's statement follows: "It's all an illusion. None of us have real power. Power comes from within. If one believes she or he has power from outsiders, eventually that power will be *stripped* away from her/him."

Specific examples of how power *is used* on the job included nine traditional power references, primarily having to do with money and control (see Table 2.6). None of the other power models were described in the women's responses. In responding to the question about how they think power *should be used* on the job, only one woman gave a response that could be vaguely associated with any of the power models. We were able to relate that response to empowerment: "Assisting others to achieve their optimal potential in their role in the workplace and as people."

Family

When asked to describe their immediate families, nine of the women indicated a nuclear family structure and eight indicated an extended family structure. In eight instances, a female functioned as head of the household, a male in six instances, and three respondents indicated they shared the position.

In seven instances, the women felt that, in their families, power is demonstrated through traditional power attributes. As with so many of the previous responses given by these African-American women, traditional power in the family also meant control and money. For several respondents, power in the family meant personal authority, and in three instances power meant reciprocal empowerment. Examples of personal authority responses included the attributes independence and knowledge, and one response, although not specifically referring to any of the personal authority attributes, was nonetheless indicative of this perspective: "In my family, power is the ability to take charge of your life and to live it on your terms." Another spoke of "the ability to have control over one's life and circumstances." An example of a reciprocal empowerment statement may be "to be a giver and receiver of love."

Decisions regarding children were made primarily by a female in the household, followed by a shared responsibility between a male and female. In only one instance did a male make the major decisions regarding children; the same held true for decisions regarding housework and finances. Although thirteen women claimed that people have different kinds of power in their families, only three described their power as traditional power, and two described it as personal authority. The three references to traditional power included control, money, and strength. The personal authority references had to do with independence.

Four of the five traditional power responses to the question "Can you give specific examples of how power *is used* in your immediate family?" had to do with money (see Table 2.6). The fifth response was related to control. One respondent said, "My dad makes all the money so he gets the most respect and has the most power." Another respondent said, "Dad makes the rules; Mom usually doesn't have a say. If you break the rules, you suffer Dad's consequences." A response that indicated traditional power, although not drawing from our prescribed list of attributes, follows: "Power in my home is indicative of a game in which my husband attempts to have the final word. However, when this avenue does not provide the desired means to an end, it is necessary for him to concede a degree of his requirement and therefore take other people's ideas under consideration." Several of the respondents used decision making as an indicator of power. For example, "My mother makes all decisions. My father cuts the grass, fixes the car, and baby-sits."

By using the term *consensus,* only one person gave empowerment as an example of how they think power *should be used* in the family. The other responses did not indicate any association with the other power paradigms; however, several other words were used repeatedly: including respect, understanding, shared, and equally. Several responses indicated that power should not be used in the family.

Religion

Ten of the seventeen women belonged to a religious group, including four Baptists, two Catholics, one Jehovah's Witness, one Christian, and one African Methodist. One woman did not identify her religious affiliation. Seven of the ten women felt that people have different kinds of power in their religion. Yet generally they gave no indication of where this power lies, except one respondent who indicated that power in her religion is based on the fact that it is a hierarchical organization.

Of the seven women who answered the question asking what kind of power they have in their religion, three gave responses that indicated they have little or no power. Several women simply mentioned their relationship with God. In describing specific examples of how power *is used* in their religion, one woman made a statement that we interpreted as empowerment (see Table 2.6). She said, "Power is used to assist people in reaching optimal potential on this planet." Another woman said, "Power is used to enforce the will of God," while another said, "The church has the power to make one a believer."

For the most part, the respondents felt that women have no power in religious organizations, except to make decisions about their own faith and their involvement in the church. One woman indicated that, "Women, for the most part, do not hold leadership roles of any significance in the church." However, another woman indicated that, "Based on my observation, women are the true rulers of the church. Men are the figureheads, and they think they rule."

In terms of how power *should be used* in religion, one woman said, "I don't think religion should be about power; I think it should be about one's relationship with God." Another said, "Power should be used to set standards, but there should always be a boundary where standards can be changed." One simply said, "For the glory of God."

Politics

None of the seventeen African-American women interviewed was affiliated with a political organization or cause. Despite their lack of political affiliation and involvement, these women did respond to the final interview question, "How do you see the power roles of women who are affiliated with politics?" Some of these responses were associated with traditional power and a few were associated with personal authority. For example, "Their roles are very influential in passing, interpreting, and making laws. What some of these women say, like Janet Reno, Ruth Bader Ginsburg, and Sandra Day O'Connor, has to be followed without question." Another participant saw women having power in politics because "they're able to voice their opinions . . . and can choose to do what they want." Although not specifying a particular type of power, two of the women had vastly divergent perspectives on the power roles of women affiliated with politics. One said, "Women have a greater presence in the academic, economic, and political arenas than ever before. I think it is inevitable that such a presence will convert to power that will give rise to a voice that will not be silenced or ignored." A less optimistic respondent stated, "Based on my observation, they [women] appear to be figureheads. The men are the rulers in politics."

CONCLUSION

We conclude by discussing the forms of power preferred by the African-American women based on both the survey and interview results. We then discuss terms or statements that emerged from the interviews that we could not clearly associate with our original descriptions of the four power models, and we attempt to determine the significance of these words based on the context in which the words were used.

Results of the survey indicated that the African-American women who participated prefer reciprocal empowerment and personal authority over the other two models. The personal authority attributes contained within the reciprocal empowerment model received the highest level of agreement, and empowerment attributes, which received fairly low levels of agreement when framed strictly as empowerment, received much higher levels of agreement when they were framed as reciprocal empowerment statements. For example, the empowerment statement that read, "I feel that it is important to be a part of a collective regardless of whether or not it benefits me as long as I empower others" received only five agreements, whereas the same attribute written as part of the reciprocal empowerment paradigm, "I feel that by being a part of a collective I empower myself and others," received ten agreements.

The interview results differed quite dramatically from those of the survey. That is, responses to the introductory questions concerning what power means to them as individuals, what they think power means in American society, what power means in their particular culture, and whether, as women, they have power in African-American culture indicated that these African-American women think primarily in terms of traditional power, followed closely by personal authority. The question having to do with whether, as women, they have power in American society, however, did not follow this pattern, with most of the responses here being associated with personal authority.

The questions asking about how power is used both at work and in the family also followed the pattern established in the introductory questions, wherein traditional power attributes were the ones mainly mentioned. Virtually no responses could be associated with any of the four models in response to how power is or should be used in the areas of religion and politics.

As mentioned throughout our discussion, the women used several words that we could not directly associate with the existing attributes of any of the four power models. Overall, decision making as an indicator of power was a term that showed up most frequently. Decision making was mentioned in response to the introductory questions and also with regard to family, work, and religion. This was followed in frequency by equality/sharing. This indicator of power surfaced in the introductory interview questions, especially in relation to the question asking what kind of power they have as women in American society. More specifically, some women considered themselves equal to men in American society, whereas others wished for gender equality. The other areas of the interview in which the women mentioned equality/sharing were family and religion. In terms of family in particular, the women used equality and sharing to describe how power should be used. Respect was another descriptor of power that emerged in all areas of the interview except religion. This was followed by references to freedom, with most of these instances occurring in answers to the question about the meaning of power in African-American culture.

Overall, the results indicate that when allowed to describe power without the benefit of predetermined statements, African-American women describe power in the traditional sense, along with the idea that they do not hold that power within U.S. society. Generally, when traditional power words were not being used, these women described power in terms of other attributes not associated with our models. When given statements with which they were asked to agree or disagree, the women typically identified their preferred form of power as reciprocal empowerment, with particular emphasis on the personal authority attributes within it. Their association of power with reciprocal empowerment, personal authority, and words such as decision making, equality, sharing, respect, and freedom may reflect their historical position in American culture, and may also indicate their desire to live their own lives as they see fit while maintaining respectful, sharing relationships with others.

Chapter 3

Asian-American Women and Power

DIFFERENT HISTORIES AND CHANGING ROLES: A BRIEF HISTORY OF ASIAN-AMERICAN WOMEN

Asian-American women are those women living in the United States who claim heritage from any part of the Asian continent. One obvious fact that makes this subject unwieldy, however, is the very size of Asia. According to Jackson and Hudman (1986), "*Asia* refers to the great landmass stretching from Turkey eastward through the Soviet Union, Saudi Arabia, India, China, Japan, and Indonesia" (p. 290). Asia, then, includes much of the former Union of Soviet Socialist Republics and is the largest continent, containing 17,139,445 square miles. According to the 2000 Census, Asians and Pacific Islanders are the "largest growing ethnic group by percentage" in South Florida, and 10.2 million Asians and close to 400,000 Pacific Islanders currently live in the United States (Gehrke-White, 2001).

Although few participants were of non-Japanese and non-Chinese descent, for the purposes of our study, we significantly narrowed our discussion and analysis of Asian-American women. In this background section we focus on Chinese- and Japanese-American women for four reasons:

1. As mentioned previously, Asia is a particularly large continent, and we cannot begin to do justice to the millions of women of many ethnicities from various parts of Asia.
2. Asia, for many Westerners typically means the Far East, and Japan and China constitute two major cultures of that region.
3. The Japanese and the Chinese represent the two pioneer immigrant groups in the United States who traveled here from the Asian continent (Daniels, 1988).

4. Although many of the women who participated in our study identified themselves broadly as Asian or Asian American, specific answers in their interviews indicated that many were either of Chinese or Japanese descent.

Women in Chinese and Japanese Cultures

The historical experience of Chinese and Japanese women reflects some striking differences. Although geographically these women are relatively close neighbors, historically their cultures treated women in vastly different ways. Simply put, traditional Chinese culture was acutely patriarchal while premodern Japanese culture was matriarchal. In both contemporary China and Japan, however, women currently experience both discrimination and progress.

Precommunist Chinese culture was based predominately on the teachings of K'ung-Fu-tzu (551-479 B.C.) (Confucius). The main doctrine of Confucius was that inequality (of everything including the sexes) is both natural and necessary (Hall, 1997). According to Hall, "their [Chinese women's] lives were among the most restricted and oppressed on earth" (p. 1). Briefly put, Chinese women were economically dependent on their families, could not own property, had no inheritance rights, had no independent status, and, generally speaking, had no source of income (however, rural peasant women developed some sense of independence as they supplemented family incomes by weaving, sewing, etc.). Furthermore, only a few wealthy, urban women were educated, and many women were subjected to forced, arranged marriages. Perhaps one of the few respites to this was the status a woman could attain by having a married son: the son's wife was required to serve her mother-in-law. In addition, despite patriarchal cultural conventions, in practice some older widows ruled their families.

Although in the late nineteenth century strong reform movements existed to protect women, Hall (1997) argues that the communist revolution was the "single most important event in the history of Chinese women" (p. 10). Virtually overnight, Chinese women gained equal rights under the law. The common program (provisional constitution) of 1949 gave women and men "equal rights in all spheres of life," including politics, culture, economics, and social and family life (p. 11). In 1954, the first constitution of the People's Republic of China confirmed the women's rights originally granted in the provisional document. As might be expected, however, equality under the law does not always mean equality in practice, and although the 85 percent of Chinese women who work generally enjoy equality in the workforce, much of Hall's research suggests that Chinese women in the Republic share with U.S. women a glass ceiling. In addition, although strict population control in China has helped to prevent starvation, it has exposed the particularly ugly misogynist practices of "disappearance" and "death at birth" for newborn females. According to Hall, despite all the changes brought by the revolution, a woman's most important function in China remains her position at the center of the family, and motherhood still functions as a fundamental means by which a woman can raise her status, particularly in rural areas.

In direct opposition to Westerners' stereotype of traditional Japanese women as subservient, fragile, and male dominated, historically Japanese culture viewed women as powerful, particularly in terms of their connections with the divine. Iwao (1993) notes that until 1336, Japan was matriarchal. Furthermore, in premodern times, peasant women in Japan enjoyed a great deal of freedom, functioning as both producers and workers. It was only the elite and stoic Samurai culture that organized itself around the patriarchal structure inherent in the Confucian ethic. Furthermore, it was not until early modernization (1868-1912) that Samurai culture penetrated the whole of Japan, asserting into the culture a hierarchical, patriarchal system resulting in the loss of freedom and power for women. According to Von Hassell (1993), the Confucian-based concept of a "family state" (unquestioned obedience to a higher authority in the family as well as to the state) meant that the "values of filial piety and obedience were transferable to the emperor" (p. 554). A woman's individuality was subsumed by her roles, but this ideological construct in which women were responsible for maintaining harmony in the family was contrasted in late nineteenth- and early twentieth-century Japan by the fact that women constituted 69 percent of the labor force.

Today, contemporary corporate-driven Japanese society is controlled largely by men. This situation has had both negative and positive effects on women. On one hand, women striving for a place in the corporate structure have largely felt the effects of sex discrimination. On the other hand, Japanese cultural values have allowed the phenomenon of male workers and female consumers to work to women's advantage. Included in this gender construct is the fact that Japanese women are not looked down upon by men, but rather are given a great deal of power in that they control family finances (including both the power to budget and to spend) and they claim primary responsibility for the family's personal, community, and business relationships. Contemporary Japanese women, then, escape the constraints of corporate life and enjoy access to both time and money. Thus, as Iwao (1993) notes, women have no desire to emulate men, but instead are free to diversify their roles while men remain severely constrained. Consequently, women are calling for a more humane life in Japan (than that offered by the corporate structure), and they play a dominant role in the arts and adult education.

Chinese and Japanese Immigration to the United States

Daniels (1988) notes that Asians traditionally existed outside the canon of immigrant history in the United States. That is, the study of immigration to the United States typically focused on Europe. Furthermore, as Asian Americans early on were treated as a pariah group with little legal or social status, their history in the United States is primarily a negative history, often focusing on what was done to them rather than on what they did (Daniels, 1988, p. 4). Due to the discrimination they faced, Asian ethnic groups in the United States remained their own cohesive and discrete communities.

In some ways, however, early Asian immigrants to the United States were similar to many other immigrant groups: they came during the industrial and agricultural expansion (1850s to 1930s); they arrived with little capital or education; and what they did when they got here (mining and agricultural work) was determined largely by the regions to which they immigrated.

The initial immigration patterns of the two groups we focus on here were somewhat different. According to Daniels (1988), the Chinese began arriving in California during the gold rush of 1849. Those who left China did so as political refugees, as a result of the rapidly increasing population in China and a failing internal Chinese administration. They came to the United States seeking economic opportunity, and they considered themselves sojourners who would eventually return to China. Although the idea of temporary migration to the United States for economic opportunity is common among immigrant groups, the Chinese—unlike so many other immigrants—actually did make money and return home. The gold rush boom in California created a labor shortage the Chinese could fill. In addition, hostilities toward the Chinese and an unbalanced sex ratio due to the immigration of few Chinese women made America an unlikely permanent home.

During the initial phase of Chinese immigration, many of the women who did arrive in the United States were brought by brothel owners as prostitutes and were kept in a state of semislavery. Daniels (1988) reports that in 1880 Chinese men outnumbered Chinese women in the United States 100,000 to 5,000. This imbalance was exacerbated by the 1882 Congressional Act that prevented further immigration from China. Although these factors led many Chinese to stay in the United States only temporarily, they also led those Chinese who remained to maintain the initial immigration pattern of settling in specific areas much longer than usual. This phenomenon created the Chinatowns that still exist today.

Although the Chinese began arriving in the United States in the late 1840s, according to Daniels no meaningful immigration of Japanese to the United States occurred until the 1880s, with Hawaii—not then a state—as the staging point for later immigration into mainland North America. During this period Japan was undergoing rapid modernization which had the effect of displacing many rural Japanese. So, not unlike the Chinese, Japanese sought economic opportunity in America. Although explicit discrimination against the Japanese had begun by the 1890s, and many Japanese women, similar to their Chinese counterparts, were subject to the brothel lifestyle, significant differences between the experiences of the two groups also existed. The Japanese government was aware of what happened to Chinese immigrants and, in an effort to protect its status, carefully oversaw the treatment of its people immigrating to the United States. The Japanese-American experience was largely an urban one, with many Japanese establishing small businesses. In addition, Japanese women immigrated much sooner than had Chinese women, avoiding an unbalanced sex ratio, allowing for quicker development of a significant native-born Japanese-American population, and diminishing the chance that Japanese-American communities would be controlled primarily by first-generation immigrants, who remained unacculturated into old age. A final difference in the experience of these two groups is the degree of discrimination they faced. Although both anti-Chinese and anti-Japanese sentiments existed, Japanese immigration began more slowly than had Chinese immigration, accounting for a slower growth in anti-Japanese sentiment. In addition, the Japanese were not included in the 1882 Exclusion Act, which thwarted the development of dynamic Chinese-American communities early on. However, the advent of World War II sent this situation into a tailspin.

Daniels (1988) reports that World War II destroyed the young but thriving Japanese-American society. Over 70,000 American citizens of Japanese ancestry were imprisoned during the war, and the extent of discrimination against Japanese Americans during the 1940s is well documented. This situation also had the curious effect of giving Chinese Americans a brief period of preferred status over the Japanese. The postwar status of these two Asian groups then reversed. Good political relations with postwar Japan positively affected Japanese Americans, while Chinese Americans began to be associated negatively with "Red" China. Perhaps the precarious situation of both groups understandably perpetuated their closely knit, discrete immigrant cultures. According to Daniels (1988), since 1960 Asia has surpassed Europe as a source of immigrants to the United States. Since the 1970s the term model minority has been applied to Asian immigrants, especially due to the financial success story of many Japanese Americans.

The Effect of Immigration on Chinese and Japanese Women

Early anti-Chinese bias led to the development of several debilitating stereotypes of Chinese-American women. Yung (1998) describes these stereotypes as the "China Doll," the erotic "Suzy Wong" type, and the diabolical "Dragon Lady." These stereotypes functioned to make Chinese women the "other" in American society. They functioned to dehumanize them, and they were used to justify discriminatory immigration laws (White-Parks, 1993). From the beginning, Americans based images of Chinese-American women on questionable nineteenth-century accounts of their sexual habits. As a result, these women were often pictured as dangerous moral and medical threats to American society (Peffer, 1999). The phenomenon of Chinese prostitutes in the United States further added to this stereotype.

They were portrayed as lustful, willing experts at seduction, capable of endangering white families. Peffer (1999) notes that by 1875 the Page Law prohibited Chinese women from entering the United States on the grounds that they were immoral. This, of course, also affected women who wanted to join their husbands in the United States (unwittingly perpetuating the need for prostitutes in the Chinese-American community). It also inhibited the evolution of Chinese-American society, as men could not easily establish families in the United States, thus perpetuating a transient state for Chinese immigrants that lasted much longer than it did for other immigrant groups in the United States.

Those Chinese-American women who did manage to enter the United States obviously faced many challenges. White-Parks (1993) points out that they withstood a double subordination based on both gender and ethnicity. In direct opposition to the Western stereotypes, however, most early Chinese immigrant women were "working class wage earners and wives" (p. 103). These women cooked, cleaned, made clothes and shoes for the family, and gardened. As might be expected, they faced the shock of transition between two very different cultures. To make matters worse, those who followed their husbands to the United States often found their husbands already acculturated, creating distance between spouses. Alienated in a new foreign culture and to some extent from their husbands, these women were often left in isolation to do the housekeeping while their husbands worked. Hence, children became particularly meaningful to the women as their only link to the past and to their home culture.

By the early 1900s, Chinese immigrant women worked long and hard usually at menial jobs, but they "exercised a greater degree of independence and social consciousness than their predecessors in their efforts to participate more fully in the larger society" (Yung, 1986, p. 40). As one woman told Yung, "It's better to be a woman in America. At least you can work here and rule the family along with your husband. In China it's considered a disgrace for a woman to work and it's the mother-in-law who rules" (p. 44). Second-generation Chinese-American women followed their own cultural traditions at home, but tended to emulate Western ways in public. These women still faced limited educational opportunities, in part due to Western prejudices against the Chinese and in part due to a Chinese cultural emphasis on educating males. However, according to Yung, by 1930 more

Chinese girls than Chinese boys in the United States were attending school. In addition, with the advent of women's suffrage in the United States, Chinese women began working for equal rights and became more actively involved in their communities and in their workplaces.

Yap (1989), in her study of Chinese-American women community workers, discovered that contemporary Chinese-American women derive their strength from their accomplishments and from their role as community workers. She also notes that the women's working and leadership styles focus on collaboration and intimacy, and that effective women workers in the community are characteristically articulate, sensitive, cooperative, and willing to compromise. Yap's (1989) research led her to note that Chinese-American "women's roles are no longer centered within the boundaries of familial and kin relations only. For the past forty years, their ties have widened and their visibility as active participants of the community has grown, as they have assumed important positions alongside the men in shaping the forces in the Chinese community" (p. 129).

As with Chinese immigrants, scholars typically discuss Japanese Americans in terms of the immigrant generation from which they come. By 1911, the first generation of Japanese Americans, the Issei, was nearly 50 percent female. Many of these women came to the United States to join their working husbands and were attracted to the promise of adventure, a higher living standard, and the less-hierarchical sex roles associated with America (Spickard, 1996). Issei women functioned as the transmitters of Japanese culture and typically had three other working roles: child care worker, houseworker, and laborer (Nakano, 1990b). Most Issei women worked outside the family (Spickard, 1996). Issei women enjoyed increased authority in the family due to their contributions to the family income. In addition, they were liberated from the constant presence of their mothers-in-law, and they gained more autonomy due to fewer responsibilities than had been associated with the extended family (Nakano, 1990b; Spickard, 1996). However, these circumstances led to unprecedented isolation for women, who were accustomed to the companionship of a large, extended family. In the early years after immigration a Japanese-American wife in the United States had the opportunity to associate only with her husband and his male friends (Spickard, 1996). Many joined women's clubs associated with Buddhist temples and Christian churches. In fact, many Issei women were attracted to Christianity primarily because it allowed them to learn more about American culture. The American emphasis on the individual also was appealing to them.

An Issei phenomenon discussed by Von Hassell (1993) is the culture of silence constructed by the women of this generation. The typical silences shaped by traditional Japanese culture were magnified by the women's immigrant status and their isolation in America. According to Von Hassell, they tended to withdraw into a "private inner world increasingly closed off to the outside" (p. 551). This silence created a tension and lack of understanding between Issei women and their Nisei (second-generation Japanese immigrants) daughters.

The Nisei generation (born between about 1915 and 1940), some of whom experienced interment as children during World War II, maintained strong Japanese values concerning family obligations, but identified primarily with American culture (Nakano, 1990a). They found themselves struggling between the collectivist culture of Japan and the individualistic culture of the United States, resulting in the creation of their own particular subculture. Nisei women typically were humble, hardworking, resourceful, bilingual, and bicultural. They joined the workforce, primarily to fund their children's education. As new occupations were opened up to them after the civil rights movement, they began to learn to balance their obligations to their families with their own growth and fulfillment. By the 1970s, their children were grown and Nisei women began moving into the public sphere doing volunteer work and becoming active in politics.

The Sansei, or third generation (born between 1940 and 1960), grew up in the middle class, became college educated, and developed as its standard the dual-career family. Sansei women were English speaking and reared to assimilate into American culture, but began to redefine their cultural awareness as they raised their own children. Nakano notes that Sansei women have integrated well into American society, but most have not gained access into high-level executive positions or attained considerable political influence.

The Yonsei, or fourth generation, often biracial, "began to construct their own sense of ethnic identity by transforming cultural concepts learned from family history and through study of contemporary Japan and of the Japanese American experience in the United States" (Adler, 1998, p. 154).

In conclusion, although we recognize that categorizing various ethnicities and nationalities into the catchall "Asian American" tends to ignore unique cultural and historical situations (Yap, 1989), we intend here only to give an overview of what the immigrant experience has been like for some of these groups of Asian women. In summarizing the experiences of Chinese and Japanese women, for example, we have been able to illustrate some of the differences between these groups' cultures and experiences while at the same time demonstrating that some of the cross-cultural conflicts and some of the forms of discrimination experienced are similar.

ANALYSIS OF ETHNOGRAPHIC FINDINGS

Demographics

Fourteen Asian-American women completed the survey and interview. The women ranged in age from eighteen to fifty-five, with nine falling between ages eighteen and twenty-five. Ten of the women were single and four were married. Five of the women identified their race as Asian, two as "yellow," one as Filipino, one as Chinese, one as Japanese, and one as West Indian of Asian descent. Three did not respond to the question of race. In terms of ethnicity, seven women identified themselves as Asian, two as Hindu, one as Chinese, one as Pacific Islander, one as Caribbean Islander, one as Chinese-Hawaiian-German-Italian-Austrian, and one did not respond. Six of the respondents had household incomes between $15,000 and $25,000, while two of the respondents had household incomes above $76,000. Four women had graduate degrees; four had undergraduate degrees; one had completed community college, and five were high school graduates.

Analysis of Survey

On the survey statements that questioned the women's personal feelings toward traditional power attributes, a majority of these Asian-American women agreed that society uses eleven of the fourteen traditional power attributes (see Table 3.1). The attributes achieving highest level of agreement among the women were wealth, followed by domination, competition, sway others, authority, and resources.

TABLE 3.1. Asian-American Women: Personal Feelings Regarding Power and Society versus Power and Self

Traditional Power and Society				Traditional Power and Self			
Attribute	Agree	Disagree	N A/D	Attribute	Agree	Disagree	N A/D
Domination	12	0	2	Domination	6	6	2
Conflict	9	2	3	Conflict	9	3	2
Force	8	3	3	Force	1	8	5
Win	9	3	2	Win	6	6	2
Struggle	9	2	3	Struggle	7	4	3
Resistance	6	3	5	Resistance	3	8	3
Competition	12	1	1	Competition	10	1	3
Physical strength	3	8	3	Physical strength	1	11	2
Control-over	11	1	2	Control-over	5	6	3
Sway others	12	2	0	Sway others	6	3	5
Wealth	13	1	0	Wealth	6	5	3
Authority	12	1	1	Authority	6	4	4
Resources	12	1	1	Resources	12	1	1
Coercion	6	1	5	Coercion	3	5	4

$n = 14$
N A/D = Neither agree nor disagree
Note: Where totals equal less than n, there were instances of no response.

The women disagreed with the idea that society uses physical strength, coercion, and resistance to gain or exercise power. When asked about their personal use of traditional power attributes, the majority of the women agreed with three of the fourteen statements: "I feel that conflict is acceptable in order to exercise power," "I feel that it is acceptable to compete with others in order to exercise power," and "I feel that if I have access to resources I can exercise power." Of these three attributes, resources received the highest level of agreement. The use of physical strength was the attribute with which the largest number of women disagreed. The statements "I feel that I must have physical strength in order to be powerful" and "I feel it is acceptable to use force in order to exercise power" received the lowest level of agreement.

Only two statements highlighting empowerment attributes received majority agreement by the women (see Table 3.2). These were compassion and competence. Virtually all of the women agreed with the personal authority attributes, with knowledge receiving the highest level of agreement, followed by the ability to choose and self-determination (see Table 3.3). For example, one statement about knowledge read, "I feel that having knowledge is important in order to gain and use personal power."

In terms of reciprocal empowerment, a majority agreed with all but one of the statements (see Table 3.4). The statement receiving the lowest level of agreement was, "I feel that by being a part of a collective I empower myself and others." The highest levels of agreement were associated with the statements using the attributes knowledge,

TABLE 3.2. Asian-American Women: Personal Feelings Regarding Empowerment

Attribute	Agree	Disagree	N A/D
Collectivity	6	3	4
Companionship	6	2	6
Compassion	9	2	3
Consensus	4	3	6
Competence	11	2	1

n = 14
N A/D = Neither agree nor disagree
Note: Where totals equal less than *n*, there were instances of no response.

TABLE 3.3. Asian-American Women: Personal Feelings Regarding Personal Authority

Attribute	Agree	Disagree	N A/D
Ability to take action	11	0	2
Ability to choose	12	1	1
Self-determination	12	1	0
Knowledge	13	1	0
Independence	10	3	1

$n = 14$
N A/D = Neither agree nor disagree
Note: Where totals equal less than *n*, there were instances of no response.

TABLE 3.4. Asian-American Women: Personal Feelings Regarding Reciprocal Empowerment

Attribute	Agree	Disagree	N A/D
Mutual responsiveness	12	1	1
Competence	12	0	2
Compassion	10	1	3
Independence	13	0	1
Ability to choose	12	0	2
Collectivity	7	0	6
Companionship	8	1	5
Ability to take action	12	1	1
Self-determination	13	1	0
Mutual engagement	9	2	3
Knowledge	13	1	0
Consensus	10	1	3
Mutual attention	8	1	5
Mutual empathy	9	2	3

$n = 14$
N A/D = Neither agree nor disagree
Note: Where totals equal less than *n*, there were instances of no response.

self-determination, independence, mutual responsiveness, competence, ability to choose, and ability to take action. Except for mutual responsiveness, these terms all derive from the personal authority component of reciprocal empowerment. A large number of respondents neither agreed nor disagreed with the statements using the attributes collectivity, companionship, and mutual attention.

Analysis of Interview

The analysis of the four power models, their relationship to the five introductory questions, and responses regarding perceptions of how power *is used* and *should be used* in the areas of work, family, religion, and politics follows.

Introductory Questions

All fourteen of the Asian-American women interviewed answered the five introductory questions that address power as it is perceived by the individual, by American society, by Asian-American culture, by women in American society, and by women in Asian-American society (see Table 3.5). In response to four of the questions, half or more of the women gave statements utilizing attributes of the traditional power model. Three of the women defined power in terms of control as in, "To me, power directly relates to the word *control.* Power is when you have control over someone or something." Two women also mentioned strength, and one each referred to force, authority, and domination. Only one woman mentioned the personal authority attribute of knowledge. Reciprocal empowerment appeared only once, in response to the question asking the women what power means to them as individuals. The respondent stated:

> To me, power is the will and strength of one's heart and mind—not necessarily being physically strong, but having the ability to transform the strength for the mind and heart into action and words that have an effect on one's self and others. I don't think power should be intended for domination or superiority. When a person stands in their truth and still affects others in great ways without the intention of having followers—they are truly powerful.

TABLE 3.5. Asian-American Women: Responses to Introductory Interview Questions and the Relationship of These Responses to the Power Models

Introductory Interview Questions	Traditional Power	Empowerment	Personal Authority	Reciprocal Empowerment
What does the word *power* mean to you as an individual?	8	0	3	1
What do you think the word *power* means in American society today?	12	1	3	0
What do you think the word *power* means in your culture?	8	0	2	0
As a woman, what kind of *power* do you think you have in U.S. society?	3	0	4	0
As an Asian-American woman, what do you think the word *power* means in your culture?	7	0	2	0

n = 14
Note: Total numbers may not match *n* since in some cases responses could not be associated with a power model. Zero equals no responses or responses could not be associated with a model.

Three of the women mentioned status or class ranking. Examples of responses indicating the relationship among status, class ranking, and power follow: Power is "the position you have in life within a group of people—social status" and "respect, honor, and class ranking." Four of the women responded to the question, "What does the word power mean to you as an individual?" by discussing the importance of influence. Examples of these responses included "[To have power means] to influence society. You have a say of what goes on around you"; "the ability to influence others; the ability to overcome obstacles"; and "when someone uses force or influence to have an impact on the lives of others."

In the case of what they think power means in American society today, twelve of the fourteen women used traditional power attributes in their responses. Eleven of the women focused on money and wealth, and one each mentioned authority, force, domination, control, and physical strength. In addition, seven of the women believed that status, class, or position defines power in American society. These responses often linked status to money. For example, one woman said, "Power in today's society means wealth, class, and status," while another said that power is "wealth, status, and the ability to influence society." Of interest, a young woman who just immigrated from China responded to this question by saying power is "more democratic, more sharing—a desire to get power because one has more freedom and because women in China are obedient." One woman mentioned the empowerment attribute competence, and personal authority attributes also surfaced in three responses.

The next question asked the women to describe what power means in their own Asian-American culture. Traditional power attributes appeared most frequently. Five of the women mentioned money, four mentioned control, and three mentioned authority. Again, answers related to money often discussed class or status, which was mentioned four times. For example, one woman said, "The class you are in. Money means everything to Filipinos," while another woman said, "Class ranking—you are born into a family in regards to money." Those who answered by highlighting control often referred to control-over, as in "The ability to exercise control over others." However, one woman specifically referred to power as "The ability to control your household." Authority was linked to both money and control: "[Power is determined by] who holds the money along with who has authority—the right to control others." Personal authority attributes also surfaced in two responses to this question. The personal authority attribute used most frequently was knowledge. Education was also considered a necessary tool to obtain power, and one woman said that "In Asian culture, power means knowledge. Power is a privilege. Those with power respect power and understand that it is something that is earned. Although those who have power do not always use it for the right things, it is also understood that power can be taken away."

In response to the question, "As a woman, what kind of power do you think you have in U.S. society?", three women indicated traditional power attributes, with all of their statements having to do with control. Four participants named personal authority attributes related to knowledge. Seven of the women responded in ways that indicated they believe they have a lot of power; four indicated they believe they have little or no power; and two indicated they believe they have some power. Seven of the answers highlighted gender differences with regard to power. For example, one woman said, "still not as much as men, but the arena for women to exercise power in business is expanding." Yet many of the women who highlighted gender argued that women in the United States are afforded equal, or at least a lot of, power. Such responses included the following: "Much more than where I come from. Women are given equal rights and opportunities and they experience more freedom in every aspect of life. I feel valued and appreciated for my abilities, experiences, and knowledge"; "I feel that in U.S. society the opportunities for women to possess power are more abundant than in my country due to a more liberal way of thinking in this country. Women can become very powerful here"; and "I think women have gained a lot more respect from others and themselves, giving them a greater ability to voice their opinions and stand strongly for their beliefs. I think that women hold a lot of sexual power though." In addition, two women each mentioned respect and influence in describing women and power in the United States.

When asked what they, as Asian-American women, think the word *power* means in their own culture, the women referred to traditional power and personal authority attributes. Three of the women referred to control, two each mentioned authority and money, two mentioned knowledge, and two mentioned being able to voice opinions or to have a say. Two of the women did not respond to this question, and one woman said she believes she has no power at all. Many of the answers to this question referred to power in general in their culture instead of specifically addressing the question of gender and power. However, those women who did address gender all noted that they have more power in the United States than they do, as women, in their own cultures. For example, a Filipino woman said, "Women hardly have any power unless they are American. Women do not get respect." In addition, a Japanese woman who identified women's relationship to power in Japanese culture as a matter of knowledge, influence, respect, and as a legacy also commented: "I am a Japanese woman. Family are your friends. It is quite uncommon for women unrelated to be friends. I believe it is like that on purpose." A number of responses to the five questions could not be directly associated with any of the power models. However, the words influence, class, status, and respect recurred frequently.

Work

Eight of the fourteen women interviewed said they work outside the home. The type of work they do and their roles at their jobs were quite varied. One woman who initially said she does not work outside the home indicated that she holds a tennis scholarship at a state university and answered some of the subsequent questions about work.

The nine women clearly indicated that they believe people have different kinds of power where they work. Two women indicated that position determines the kind of power one has at work and one mentioned influence. One of the women noted gender stereotypes related to a specific profession: "Yes, guys are taken more seriously because guys should know more about computers." Many of the women who recognized differences in power at work described them in terms of the hierarchical structure of the workplace: "Yes, administration—highest level; upper level staff—nurses; activities department, front desk, receptionist, and maintenance; lower-level staff care managers, kitchen staff," and "Yes, power is outlined so there are no questions: director, assistant director, marketing managers from the various departments, assistants to the manager, then teams under them. There is no question of who tells who to do what."

When asked the more personal question about what kind of power they think they have on the job, six of the women responded in ways that suggested they believed they have some power, one woman believed she has a lot of power ("I feel as if I am in the upper level staff"), and three indicated they thought they have little or no power. One of these women responded by saying, "I have a lot of control, but not much power. I have access to resources and many friends, but my position does not possess much influence." Some of the words the women used in their responses that they tended to associate with power included resources, decision making, influence, position, and leadership.

When asked if they could provide an example of how power *is used* at their job, traditional power attributes were described when several women mentioned either specific or general circumstances which highlighted control (see Table 3.6). One woman said, "The

TABLE 3.6. Asian-American Women: Interview Responses to Questions About Work, Family, Religion, and Politics

How Power *Is Used*

	Traditional Power	Empowerment	Personal Authority	Reciprocal Empowerment
Work	6	0	0	0
Family	6	1	3	0
Religion	0	0	0	0
Politics	0	0	0	0

How Power *Should Be Used*

	Traditional Power	Empowerment	Personal Authority	Reciprocal Empowerment
Work	0	1	0	0
Family	1	0	0	0
Religion	0	0	0	0
Politics	0	0	0	0

n = 14
Note: Total numbers may not match the number of participants responding since in some cases responses could not be associated with a power model. Zero equals no responses or responses could not be associated with a model.

boss tells employees what to do." Another woman said, "The manager can tell you what to do. The department manager can overpower them," and another described her workplace quite negatively: "The director sits in his office all day. That is a way in which he says to others he is unapproachable because he is on top, and the assistant uses her position to often be rude and condescending to those who work in the various departments. Positions give some egos and the ego creates the power."

The final question related to work asked the women, "How do you think power *should be used* on your job?" We could associate only one response with the empowerment model: "It should be used to empower others and to create a better work environment." Other than that, no particular characterization stood out as the favored choice of these women. Their answers ranged from providing motivation and leadership to fostering understanding and confidence, to getting the job done, accommodating workers, and allowing freedom of expression. All these answers suggested that the women believed a more relaxed, comfortable environment in which workers are allowed to speak out would encourage productivity. For example, one woman said, "Power should be used to create a work environment in which all the employees feel free to express their ideas and are motivated enough to ensure their respective jobs are done on time and accurately." However, two of the women indicated that power on the job was fine as it was currently practiced.

Family

When Asian-American women described who they included in their immediate family, nine of them described an extended family and five described a nuclear family. Eight of the women indicated that a male was the head of household, four of the women indicated that a female was the head of household, and two respondents noted that more than one family member shared the role of head of household. One of these women said, "No one; everyone should share in the power," and the other said, "Since we live in this country, it is a partnership. Back in my country it would be my husband."

Six of the women indicated that females made the major decisions regarding children in their families, three said that their fathers made these decisions, four indicated that the decision making concerning children was shared by a mother and father or a husband and wife, and one woman said the children made these decisions (perhaps they are adult children). As for decisions concerning housework, eleven said women took this role, two said decisions about housework were shared, and one indicated that the children made these decisions. In terms of finances, six of the women said these decisions were shared by a mother and father or husband and wife, four stated that a male made these decisions, and four said a female made these decisions.

When asked, "What do you think the word power means in your family?" the women made several references to traditional power attributes. Four of the women discussed attributes of authority and two referred to control. One woman of Chinese descent stated,

> In my immediate family, power is authority to a certain point, but respect throughout. In the older generations of my Chinese

> side of the family it is traditional that power means control. The males have most of the authority. Their choices affect the whole family, but in my immediate family we all have an effect on each other that doesn't come from force or the mind-set that we are going to control others.

Knowledge was the only personal authority attribute named in response to this question. In addition, sex and race were highlighted by one woman as playing a significant role in determining power, even in the family: "Power in my family is not a constant. Sometimes I feel more powerful than my husband, and there are days that no matter what, I am determined to control everything. While most often power is determined by sex and race in our family, you try to create a world that you would like to deal with daily." Several other words used by the women in response to this question could not specifically be associated with any of the power paradigms. They included success, respect, and age, and one woman each mentioned honor, loyalty, legacy, and leadership.

When asked if people in their families have different kinds of power, ten of the women said yes and four said no. Some extended answers to this question suggested decision making, respect, understanding, fairness, and age were all important factors. Several of the responses simply described division of labor within the family: "Not really, my mom and dad are equal. My father takes care of the bills. My mother takes care of the groceries and extra necessities, and, "Yes, I have more power with my children while my husband has more power with the financial decisions."

Responses to the question "What kind of power do you have in your immediate family?" elicited a variety of responses. Five of the women indicated they have some power while three noted they have a lot of power. Their responses varied from the ability to make peace to the ability to give compassion. One woman said, "I have the power to make peace between my families when there are disagreements. For some reason I can help calm/relax the people and help them release their tension, anger, and fears." Another expressed elements of empowerment when she said she felt that the kind of power she has in her family is "the power of love, compassion, and the ability to determine her freedom." One woman perceived her ability to voice an opinion and give suggestions regarding decision making as a form of power in the immediate family.

When asked to give specific examples of how power *is used* in the immediate family, the women felt that power is used in their families to influence decision making and to guarantee a freedom to choose (see Table 3.6). Statements indicating this included: "Parents make decisions for my brothers and me. If Dad says 'no' to something and Mom says 'ok' then Dad's word is final," and "Giving the children freedom to choose which university they want to go to."

A majority of the women seemed to have no qualms voicing their opinion that power *should be used* equally in the family. They indicated this in responses such as, "they should treat each other equally. They should decide on everything together to create an equal family," and "I believe in equality. Everyone's opinions should be respected and accepted." Some women indicated that respect should be a consideration in deciding how power is used in the family, and that decision making is a use of power. One woman also indicated that power should be used to teach, to discipline, and to live.

Religion

Seven of the fourteen Asian-American women belonged to a religious group. Of these, three identified themselves as Hindu, two as Christian, one as Catholic, and one as Baptist. In response to the question "Do people have different kinds of power in your religion?" seven of the women said "yes" and most went on to state that this power was held in the hands of God and the priests. In terms of their own power in their religions, one woman responded that she had "none, I follow Christ," and only four of the rest of the eight women felt they have some kind of power. Their responses included statements such as, "[I have the power to] go pray freely, go into temple, no real restrictions to this," and "I am one of the followers; therefore, I make up and am part of the whole system. It's individuals like myself that enable the system to work." One woman indicated that her power in her religion comes simply from her being a member of the Baptist church, and another stated that she has the "power of compassion."

Examples of how power *is used* in their religion included: "Power is used through social castes and social status and on the beliefs of Hinduism. For example, deeds from the present life affect what one would be reincarnated as in the next life." Other examples of the use of power in their religions came from a Christian who said it is used "to forgive and to heal," and from a Hindi who felt that it allows people to "go pray freely, but big ceremonies, marriage, death, and childbirth require a priest."

Although they, as individuals, may not feel that they have a lot of personal power, their responses to the question "What kind of power do women have in your religious organization?" seemed to indicate women in general had some power roles. For example, one Hindu woman said, "More than men, because light is burnt by the women, [and women are] given holy food and wine first." Another Hindu woman said, "Women and men have important roles in the religion, each have different functions and without one the other would have a hard time functioning."

The question asking the women how they think power *should be used* in their religions yielded few responses and none that could be associated with the power models. Some of the responses included, "to spread the word of God and Christ," "to teach, be the peacemaker (like the Pope), and bring unity to the world," and "I never really thought about it, but it should be used for the good."

Politics

The section of the interview dealing with politics rendered almost no responses. Only one of the fourteen women said she was politically affiliated, and that she was a Republican. However, she said little in response to any of these questions except that power should be used "to encourage people to vote and be aware of the issues."

Despite the fact that Asian-American women on the whole were not personally affiliated with politics, ten of the women did respond to the final interview question, "How do you see the power roles of women who are affiliated with politics?" Six of the women gave responses indicating that they felt women are gaining power in politics. For example, one woman said, "Women are gradually becoming more powerful. I think eventually we will become the 'higher' sex." Another compared the roles of women in the United States to Asian countries: "Recently, women are respected for their roles in politics. Women in politics obviously are role models and powerful sources for women in general to carry their opinions, views, and voices across the nation for different aspects of life, although this is not prevalent in most of the Asian countries." Despite the optimism of some of these women, one woman offered a cynical view of women and politics: "In politics, I see women as either puppets put into strategic places to calm media and society, or as crabs crawling over each other to get ahead. Either way there is no real unity, and women are used to play out a false political scheme which gives them a false sense of power."

Four of the women gave yet another view indicating they believe men still have more political power than women. One of these women said, "I think women involved with politics have to back up everything they say a hundred more times than what a man would have to. Their logic and reasoning and presence is judged so much more than others. I think that women's supporters are mostly women or people who can look past stereotypes and prejudgments."

CONCLUSION

In the survey, both traditional power and personal authority attributes emerged most frequently as the models of power with which these Asian-American women agreed. In terms of traditional power, the women identified with statements naming the attributes conflict, competition, and resources. As for personal authority, the women identified most frequently with the attribute knowledge. The women also agreed with all but one of the reciprocal empowerment attributes, and the reciprocal empowerment attributes that received the highest level of agreement were all associated with personal authority.

Traditional power and personal authority attributes also emerged most frequently in the women's responses to the interview questions. The results of the introductory questions suggest that although Asian-American women, as individuals, may see themselves as powerful, their power comes from a different source than the power they see being used in American society. They continually used phrases such as, power is the "ability to influence society," and "influence within the family . . . is power in my culture" when referring to their power as individuals. However, when referring to power in society the terms most frequently used were wealth, money, control, and authority.

Furthermore, seven women who used some of the traditional power attributes when responding to the question about women and power in their specific culture spoke in general terms instead of addressing the question of how power relates specifically to women in their culture. Of those women who did respond directly to the question "As an Asian-American woman, what do you think the word *power* means in your culture?", several indicated that they think they have no power. Some compared their lack of power in their own cultures to the power of American women in the United States. An East Indian woman said, "To have a say in America, it doesn't matter if you're male or female, you have more of a say than in India if you are a woman." A Filipina responded, "Women hardly have any power unless they are American. Women do not get respect." One of the few women who indicated some traditional power within her culture was a Japanese woman who said, "Power in Japanese culture for women is a traditional power. Power is a legacy, meaning the knowledge of mothers and grandmothers, etc. Influence within her family, how much respect she gains and allows to be passed on to those she raises is power in my culture."

Two clear distinctions emerge from the results of the first part of the interview concerning perceptions of power. First, Asian-American women distinguish between the nature of power in the public sphere generally and their use of power as women in both the private and public spheres. Second, their responses highlighted perceived differences between women's roles in Asia and in the United States.

In response to questions asking how power is used on the job and in the home, Asian-American women again referred primarily to attributes associated with traditional power and to a lesser extent with personal authority. When asked how they thought power should be used in these arenas, we could not associate the responses with any of the four power models. The questions on religion and politics elicited even fewer responses that could be associated with the paradigms. Of the questions that asked how power *is used* and how it *should be used,* only one woman responded using an empowerment attribute. When asked to describe what kind of power she has in her religion, she responded that she has "the power of compassion."

As alluded to earlier, several words recurred in the interview that we could not easily associate with the four power models. These words included freedom, equality, class, status, position, respect, and decision making. In all cases these words were used to characterize power within particular contexts and in response to specific types of questions. For example, in responding to the question of how power should be used in the family, equality occurred eight times, and class, status, or position appeared fifteen times. Although scattered throughout the interviews, these words were used most frequently in response to the introductory questions that asked the women about their individual perceptions of power, their perceptions of power in American society, their perceptions of power in their own personal ethnic communities, and their perceptions of power as women in their own ethnic communities. We find it interesting that equality is an attribute that Asian-American women desire, while status—as can be gleaned from both the interview results and historical information—is strongly associated with their home cultures. These answers suggest to us that as Asian Americans, they wish to transcend the constraints of status and instead work toward more egalitarian relationships, particularly within their families.

Chapter 4

Caribbean-American Women and Power

A MULTITUDE OF LANGUAGES AND CULTURES: A BRIEF HISTORY OF CARIBBEAN-AMERICAN WOMEN

The term *Caribbean* generally refers to the eastern and southern West Indies, a large group of islands located south and southeast of the mainland of the United States. This region includes islands such as Jamaica, Haiti, Dominican Republic, the Bahamas Islands, Trinidad, and even the Virgin Islands. This area is characterized by its many unique cultures, histories, and peoples. Immigrants from the Caribbean as a whole make up a significant minority population in the United States. In addition, more Haitians and Bahamians live in the South Florida area where we conducted our study than anywhere else in the United States, and the same region also hosts the nation's second-largest population of both Jamaicans and Trinidadians. According to Elliott (2001), Census 2000 data indicate that nearly half a million people living in Florida identify their ancestry as West Indian.

One particular segment of the Caribbean population has become a topic of increasing interest to sociologists and cultural researchers alike. Caribbean women are typically depicted as independent and dominant. What is less well known about these women, however, is their individual contributions to both American and Caribbean societies. On the surface, the majority of the women in this region are black, either of African descent or of mixed race. Yet Ellis (1986) reports that in Trinidad and nearby Guyana, South America, approximately 40 percent of the population is of East Indian descent. Smaller groups of Chinese, Syrian, Portuguese, and European immigrants settled here as well. Divisions of race, class, social and economic status, and residency affect the lives of Caribbean-American women and are responsible for significant differences in their roles in society and their contributions to their individual countries. Simply put, the population of the Caribbean is culturally varied, and this fact plays an important role in how women of these societies view themselves and how they are viewed by others.

Although ethnic diversity is one of the defining characteristics of the Caribbean region, the African descendants in the Caribbean, as in North America, inherited the legacy of slavery. African slaves were shipped to the Caribbean islands primarily due to "the growing European taste for sugar" (Mazrui, 1986, p. 159). The system of slavery in the Caribbean was somewhat different from antebellum slavery. On many Caribbean plantations, the owners remained in Europe and their Caribbean interests were protected by overseers. The paternalistic relationship between slave and master, romanticized in the antebellum South, was largely nonexistent on the islands. Slaves and property were often owned by absentee landlords (Patterson, 1967). The lives of slave and master, then, were generally isolated from each other, so that, for example, in Jamaica slaves turned to their own African traditions to reconstruct cultural practices relevant to their situation in the Caribbean (Johnson and Pines, 1982). This created an environment different from the slave/master relationship in the United States and led—to some degree—to the early development of a strong sense of self-determination and autonomy for former slaves in the Caribbean. Although certain aspects of slavery differed from island to island, slavery—as well as subsequent poverty—significantly influenced the roles of women in the Caribbean.

Women's Roles in Caribbean Cultures

The roles of Caribbean women are most often described in the context of the household. However, their place in society transcends the home and plays a large part in the structure of the working class. To better understand the Caribbean woman, both of these factors must be taken into consideration. Ho (1991) asserts that the dual roles performed for centuries by Caribbean women as workers and mothers blur the Western feminist distinction between the public world of work and the private domain of the home. Capitalist relations of production that have denied ample earning power to a large segment of the male population (making it unrealistic to expect them to be the main breadwinners) have necessitated the Caribbean woman's participation in the public workplace. Ellis (1986) states that women have always made up a significant percentage of the employed in the Caribbean. During slavery, women worked side by side with men in the fields. In fact, in the latter decades of slavery, women outnumbered male workers on the plantations. Women were denied the opportunities for training and advancement that were available to their male counterparts.

According to International Labor Organization (ILO) figures (Ellis, 1996), Caribbean countries are presently among those nations with the highest female activity in the workforce. It is estimated that over 20 percent of the female population are economically active. Despite this favorable fact, however, the truly unequal status of employed women in Caribbean countries is less appealing. For example, Ellis also cites statistics from the ILO that 70 percent of employed women are in low-paid, low-skilled, marginal jobs in domestic and other services. In addition, only a very small percentage of the jobs in administration and management are held by Caribbean women. Domestic work, which can be dated back to the postemancipation period, continues to be a common occupation for Caribbean women. Ellis states, however, that in recent years many more Caribbean women from all classes and ethnicities have been able to move successfully into nontraditional areas of activity. For example, a significant rise in the number of women in the teaching and nursing professions has occurred, and many senior positions are held in the public and private sectors. With increased involvement in the workforce, Caribbean women find themselves trying to cope with the pressures of maintaining a job and handling their personal domestic responsibilities.

In addition to this heightened role in the workforce, high value and status are attached to motherhood. This value has provided Caribbean women with considerable influence, authority, and respect in their communities, and it has helped to solidify their place in American society. Caribbean women of all races and classes, with no consideration for marital status, take on the responsibility of child care and child rearing. Although full-time motherhood and tending to the house might at one time have been considered ideal, for Caribbean women residing in the Caribbean and in the United States, this sole task no longer fits the changing environment. Ellis notes that over 75 percent of Caribbean women are mothers and the average number of children per mother is 4.5. Moreover, since slavery, Caribbean mothers learned to structure their homes and their families to fit economic conditions. In essence, a large percentage of Caribbean woman are engaged in a variety of economic activities outside the home while maintaining responsibilities inside the home. This well-maintained balance helps frame the discussion of the necessary adaptations Caribbean women immigrants have made in the United States.

Caribbean Immigration to the United States

Ho (1993) suggests that for the past 150 years, the Caribbean has been a significant exporter of people to North America and Caribbean women have had significant influence on social relationships in the United States. Furthermore, Deere et al. (1990) note that the Caribbean exports more of its people than any other region in the world. Although the sheer numbers are a fascinating subject for social science researchers, it is essential to evaluate the push-and-pull factors that lead to this constant flow of immigration. For example, a high population growth rate, a high unemployment rate, and a high literacy rate combine to constitute a significant impetus for those who choose to emigrate. Ho (1993) states that "migration is an enduring feature of the region, there being a migration tradition in the Caribbean for over a century and a half" (p. 33). In addition, social issues such as family values and educational advancement opportunities are some of the main pull factors that follow closely behind. Ho (1993) notes that, "Given the limits on opportunities in the Caribbean, it is hardly surprising that women would decide to migrate to improve their economic and social status" (p. 33).

Although agreeing with the information presented by Deere et al. (1990), Thomas-Hope (1992) posits that this influx of Caribbean immigrants to the United States generally has been undertaken in order to expand life choices and to help create a more affluent life for future generations. Basch, Schiller, and Blanc (1994) offer other reasons for this migration, some of which include the shortage of schools in the Caribbean that appeal to pupils in search of higher learning, the production of more skilled workers than the economy of the home country can absorb, and the impact of the relationship between transnationalism and global capitalism in the Caribbean region. Despite the significant contributions of the first two factors, it is the latter factor that grabbed the attention of Basch, Schiller, and Blanc. They suggested that as Caribbean governments responded to the changing structure of the global economy, the resulting salary cuts and declining standard of living sparked a mass exodus of all social classes in search of a better life. Ho adds that beginning in the mid-1970s, a major consequence of these changes in the global workforce was the disempowerment and discrediting of labor. This negative change transformed workers with set salaries, job security, and benefits into temporary workers with reduced standings. Regarding gender issues, however, Thomas-Hope suggests that the impact of global capitalism differs from class to class as well as changes according to gender.

Thomas-Hope (1992) believes "in contrast to the Caribbean elite, who tend to migrate as entire families, working-class women in the Caribbean not only migrate independently, but practice circular migration and often pave the way for the migration of others" (p. 4). In sharp contrast to the comfortable distribution of responsibilities that is characteristic in a nuclear family structure, it was common to find Caribbean women migrating on their own with the burden of assimilation at their heels—alone in a new world. However, despite the obvious incentive to emigrate, several factors inflict a great toll on these women during this transition. Henry (1994) suggests that one of the greatest burdens on Caribbean immigrants is marriage and relationship breakdowns. Bonnett (1990) also suggests that another consequence of migration is strained parent/child relationships. For example, as Caribbean mothers assert their authority and make decisions independent of Caribbean fathers, the children also begin to challenge their fathers, causing conflict between the parents. Thus the Caribbean mother faces challenges both at home and in the larger society. Although this additional challenge is an integral part of understanding Caribbean women's cultures, it is perhaps more important to discuss how their cultures actually changed and the shift in women's roles given their exposure to the United States.

The Effect of Immigration on Caribbean Women

Of interest, research indicates that the predominant roles of Caribbean women in their original cultures and in the culture of their host society are not vastly different. In fact, the traditional balance between home life and work life is just as characteristic in the Caribbean woman's native land as it is in her adopted Western home of the United States. Basch, Schiller, and Blanc (1994) suggest that one of the primary differences most of these women face in the United States is that of racial discrimination, which was not evident in their home culture; they state that "The social construction of race in the host society undermines class solidarity and strengthens transnationalism" (p. 234). Furthermore, despite their best efforts at improving educational levels and avoiding stagnant social status, Caribbean migrants battle glass ceilings that block their occupational advancement. Wiltshire (1992) posits that through painful experience Caribbean women realize that race and gender are closely tied to political, economic, and social domination in North America. It is the existence of these complex power relationships and their impact on Caribbean women that is examined in our study.

ANALYSIS OF ETHNOGRAPHIC FINDINGS

Demographics

Twenty-one women completed the survey and interview. The women ranged in ages from eighteen to sixty-five, with the majority falling under the age of forty-five. There were twelve married women and nine single women. Household incomes ranged from $15,000 to over $76,000, with ten falling between $15,000 and $35,000, and six between $36,000 and $65,000. Ten of the women had completed community college, three had completed an undergraduate degree, and three had completed a graduate or professional degree. In terms of race, fifteen identified themselves as black, two women said they are black/Haitian, two identified themselves as Spanish, one said she is mixed, and another simply said "other." As for ethnicity, nine of the women identified themselves as Caribbean Islanders, three as Jamaicans, two as Haitian Americans, and two as African American/Caribbean. One each identified herself as follows: Haitian, West Indian, Hispanic/Dominican Republic, and Caribbean Islander/Dominican. One woman did not respond to the survey question concerning ethnicity.

Analysis of Survey

On the survey statements that questioned the women's personal attitudes toward traditional power attributes, a majority agreed with the personal use of four of the fourteen power attributes (see Table 4.1). Specifically, eighteen of the women agreed with the statement, "I feel that if I have access to resources I can exercise power," fourteen of the women agreed that, "I feel that I must have authority in order to exercise power," and thirteen each agreed that, "Struggle is acceptable in order to exercise power" and "It is acceptable to compete with others in order to exercise power." The strongest level of disagreement (fourteen) was with the statements, "I feel that it is acceptable to use force in order to exercise power" and "I feel that domination over others is necessary in order to exercise power." Thirteen women disagreed with both winning and physical strength.

Conversely, when asked to respond to statements questioning their perception of society's use of traditional power attributes, a majority of the women agreed that society uses twelve of the fourteen attributes. Twenty of the women agreed with the statement, "Society teaches that the more resources a person has the more powerful they are." Nineteen of the women also agreed that society uses wealth, eighteen said society uses authority, and seventeen each said society associates sway over others and competition with traditional power. Although the women agreed that both they and society use the traditional power attributes of resources, authority, and competition, a majority of them personally disagreed with society on the use of domination and winning.

A majority of the women agreed with three of the five empowerment statements (see Table 4.2). For example, eighteen of the women agreed with the statement, "I feel that it is important to be compassionate regardless of whether or not it benefits me as long as I empower others." Seventeen of the women agreed with the statement concerning competence, and thirteen women agreed with companionship. The women were almost evenly split between agreeing and disagreeing with the statement, "I feel that it is important that I be willing to reach consensus whether or not it benefits me as long as I empower others." There was a virtual three-way split among "agree," "disagree," and "neither agree nor disagree" when it came to the statement ,"I feel that it is important to be a part of a collective regardless of whether or not it benefits me as long as I empower others."

TABLE 4.1. Caribbean-American Women: Personal Feelings Regarding Power and Society versus Power and Self

Traditional Power and Society				Traditional Power and Self			
Attribute	**Agree**	**Disagree**	**N A/D**	**Attribute**	**Agree**	**Disagree**	**N A/D**
Domination	16	5	0	Domination	5	14	2
Conflict	13	5	3	Conflict	9	9	3
Force	12	8	1	Force	6	14	1
Win	15	3	3	Win	5	13	3
Struggle	9	3	9	Struggle	13	5	3
Resistance	12	6	3	Resistance	9	8	4
Competition	17	2	2	Competition	13	4	4
Physical strength	9	9	3	Physical strength	7	13	1
Control-over	14	4	3	Control-over	8	12	1
Sway others	17	2	2	Sway others	8	9	4
Wealth	19	1	1	Wealth	9	10	2
Authority	18	1	2	Authority	14	6	1
Resources	20	0	1	Resources	18	1	2
Coercion	15	3	3	Coercion	4	11	6

$n = 21$
N A/D = Neither agree nor disagree

TABLE 4.2. Caribbean-American Women: Personal Feelings Regarding Empowerment

Attribute	Agree	Disagree	N A/D
Collectivity	6	8	7
Companionship	13	6	2
Compassion	18	1	2
Consensus	9	8	4
Competence	17	1	3

$n = 21$
N A/D = Neither agree nor disagree

As with the other groups, a majority of the Caribbean-American women agreed with all five statements related to personal authority (see Table 4.3). All but one of the women agreed with the statement, "I feel that having knowledge is important in order to gain and use personal power." Nineteen of the women agreed with the statements concerning both choice and independence, and eighteen agreed with self-determination and fifteen with ability to take action.

Similarly, a majority of the women agreed with all fourteen statements related to reciprocal empowerment attributes (see Table 4.4). Of note, the reciprocal empowerment statement that received the highest level of agreement (twenty) was about consensus; yet when consensus was framed as an empowerment attribute the women were split nine to eight in their agreement/disagreement. Nineteen of the women agreed with the reciprocal empowerment statement concerning compassion. In this case, they also overwhelmingly agreed with the compassion statement when it illustrated empowerment (see Table 4.2). Nineteen of the women also agreed with choice, self-determination, and knowledge. Independence and competence received eighteen and seventeen agreements respectively.

Analysis of the Interview

The analysis of the four power models, their relationship to the five introductory questions, and responses regarding perceptions of how power *is* and *should be* used in the areas of work, family, religion, and politics follows.

TABLE 4.3. Caribbean-American Women: Personal Feelings Regarding Personal Authority

Attribute	Agree	Disagree	N A/D
Ability to take action	15	4	2
Ability to choose	19	2	0
Self-determination	18	1	2
Knowledge	20	1	0
Independence	19	1	1

n = 21
N A/D = Neither agree nor disagree

TABLE 4.4. Carribean-American Women: Personal Feelings Regarding Reciprocal Empowerment

Attribute	Agree	Disagree	N A/D
Mutual responsiveness	15	5	1
Competence	17	3	1
Compassion	19	2	0
Independence	18	0	3
Ability to choose	19	1	1
Collectivity	13	4	4
Companionship	15	2	4
Ability to take action	16	0	5
Self-determination	19	0	2
Mutual engagement	13	2	6
Knowledge	19	1	1
Consensus	20	1	0
Mutual attention	16	1	4
Mutual empathy	16	0	5

n = 21
N A/D = Neither agree nor disagree

Introductory Questions

A review of the five introductory questions reveals that in all but one of these questions traditional power and personal authority were the models of power most frequently described by these Caribbean-American women (see Table 4.5). For example, regarding the meaning of the word *power* to them as individuals, sixteen of the twenty-one interviewees used words directly associated with the traditional power model. Terms such as control-over, authority, strength, and money were used in almost every response. One woman felt that, as an individual, power to her means "the ability to exercise control, gain respect, and have strength." Another felt power is "having the ability to act and react effectively and having the ability to exercise control and authority. I also feel that having financial security plays a very viable part in achieving power." One woman responded, "Power

TABLE 4.5. Caribbean-American Women: Responses to Introductory Interview Questions and the Relationship of These Responses to the Power Models

Introductory Interview Questions	Traditional Power	Empowerment	Personal Authority	Reciprocal Empowerment
What does the word *power* mean to you as an individual?	16	0	4	0
What do you think the word *power* means in American society today?	17	0	2	1
What do you think the word *power* means in your culture?	16	1	3	0
As a woman, what kind of power do you think you have in U.S. society?	0	0	1	1
As a Caribbean-American woman, what do you think the word *power* means in your culture?	10	0	5	0

$n = 21$

Note: Total numbers may not match *n* since in some cases responses could not be associated with a power model. Zero equals no responses or responses could not be associated with a model.

means strength. A powerful person is an authoritative one." Personal authority terms mentioned by the women included independence and education. For one woman, individual power meant being "independent, making up your own mind, and making your own decisions." For another woman, "personal power lies in educating yourself." Other words that emerged in response to this question included decision making, respect, status, giving orders, and skin color.

The meaning of power in U.S. society today elicited similar responses in terms of traditional power. Seventeen responses used traditional power attributes. As with the previous question, wealth, control, and authority were the terms most frequently used. For example, "The word power denotes having wealth, authority, and the ability to persuade in American society today. There is also a certain amount of control that comes along with exercising power." Personal authority again surfaced as the second model of choice for these women with their use of terms such as education and independence. Decision making and respect were also often used in response to this question.

The meaning of the word *power* in Caribbean-American culture also drew a large number of responses associated with the traditional power model. Wealth, control, and authority again topped the list. Personal authority was the second model of choice; however, unlike responses to the previous two questions, the empowerment paradigm was evident in one response: "In my culture, power tends to mean the person who represents the people the most. The powerful person is the one who speaks for the people and cares about their rights." Along with the additional words previously cited, politics/politicians and having a voice were frequently referenced in relationship to the meaning of power in Caribbean-American cultures.

None of the responses to the question asking the participants what kind of power they think they have as women in U.S. society could be deemed descriptive of traditional power. The women gave responses that indicated that twelve of the twenty-one felt they had a lot or some power; whereas, nine felt they had little or none. The only significant terms that emerged were equality and opportunity. This question also revealed one instance of reciprocal empowerment and one instance of personal authority. The reciprocal empowerment response was, "If [women have] enough money and fame, they can make a difference. They can be role models for girls and stay in school. In this country, it's not only about individual power, but power as a group." The personal authority response noted that power for women in U.S. society means "making your own decisions and being independent."

The final introductory question asked the women, "As a Caribbean woman, what do you think the word *power* means in your culture?" Traditional power was again the power model of choice, with money, control, and authority being the predominant terms. There were five women who used personal authority terms, with four of the five mentioning education.

Work

Nineteen of the twenty-one women indicated they were employed outside the household. All nineteen women also said that people have different kinds of power where they work. Only one, however, said that this demonstration of power had to do with the amount of money that the boss has. The only other kind of power mentioned had to do with personal authority, as one woman said that knowledge gives certain people power. The question regarding different kinds of power on the job was the second one that drew answers revealing skin color (white) as a form of power: "The power is with the vice presidents, directors, and managers. Most of them would not make it if they were not white. Educationally they are lacking—common sense stupid. They're all great talkers, unable to write or express themselves clearly."

Less than half of the women felt that they personally have any power on the job, and the few who mentioned power related it to traditional power with terms such as influence, control, and money. The respondent quoted previously mentioned color again, relating it to power: "I'm educationally superior. I have the power to let them know that they're only in the position they're in because they're white."

The next question sought responses giving more specific examples of how power *is used* on the job (see Table 4.6). For these women, traditional power seemed to be what they generally recognized at work. The majority of the examples given included authority, followed by money, and the power to persuade. Only one woman gave an example of personal authority as a type of power used on her job. Of interest, color was mentioned, but by a different respondent than previously discussed. She felt that power can be used to degrade others, but that

TABLE 4.6. Caribbean-American Women: Interview Responses to Questions About Work, Family, Religion, and Politics

How Power *Is Used*

	Traditional Power	Empowerment	Personal Authority	Reciprocal Empowerment
Work	10	0	2	0
Family	9	1	3	0
Religion	2	0	0	0
Politics	2	1	2	0

How Power *Should Be Used*

	Traditional Power	Empowerment	Personal Authority	Reciprocal Empowerment
Work	5	0	0	0
Family	2	0	1	0
Religion	1	0	1	1
Politics	0	0	0	0

$n = 21$

Note: Total numbers may not match *n* since in some cases responses could not be associated with a power model. Zero equals no responses or responses could not be associated with a model.

on her current job, as in Jamaica, color does not matter. Giving orders was also used as an example of power on the job.

The women's opinions did not differ significantly in terms of how they felt power *should be used* on the job. Again, those that responded using attributes from the power models referred to traditional power. Several statements that we could not associate with the models repeatedly discussed respect, equality, and decision making. One response that we interpreted as reciprocal empowerment included the notion of mutual respect.

Family

Fourteen of the twenty-one women described their families as nuclear, while six defined their families as extended. The position of head of household was split almost evenly among males, females, and both. For Caribbean-American women, power in the family meant both traditional power and personal authority, with traditional power attributes receiving slightly fewer references than personal authority attributes. One previously unmentioned term, understanding, appeared here: "It's [power] not a thing in the family. The word *power* doesn't play a role. It's mutual respect and understanding." Another woman said, "a mutual understanding that I am the mother."

The majority of decisions regarding children were either shared or left to the female in the household, whereas housework decisions were made primarily by the females. Unlike most of the other ethnic groups studied, the majority of Caribbean-American women made financial decisions. In only three of twenty-one instances did the male in the household make financial decisions.

Fourteen of the twenty-one women felt that people have different kinds of power in their immediate families, with finances being the deciding factor. Many of the women described power in terms of the division of labor in the family. Only five of the women felt that they have power in the family, and all five referred to traditional power by citing influence and money. These women all said their influence and financial abilities allow them to make family decisions. Specific examples of how power *is used* in the family included nine references to traditional power and three to personal authority (see Table 4.6). Other examples drew upon words that, again, we could not associate with the power models but that repeatedly surfaced throughout the interviews. Mutual understanding and equality topped this list.

In terms of how power *should be used* in the family, the only two references that we could associate with the power models were two traditional power attributes, one having to do with influence and one having to do with authority. The only other response contained a personal authority attribute which suggested that power should be used to educate and motivate.

Religion

Nine of the twenty-one Caribbean-American women interviewed belonged to a religious group, while eleven did not; one did not respond. Five of the women said they belong to the Catholic church (one of these women had previously said she did not belong to a religious group), two women simply identified their religion as Christian, and one each identified as Baptist and Episcopalian.

When asked if people have different kinds of power in their religions, eight of the women said yes and two indicated no, but those two also suggested that power in religion belongs to God. Of those who said they have some kind of power, five women gave answers that suggested they believe they have some or a lot of power. For example, one woman said, "I have the power of persuasion." Another said she has the "power to freely speak in the congregation." The remaining four women who responded to this question indicated they have little or no power. One woman said, "I'm a subservient person when it comes to church. I do what I'm supposed to and go home. I listen."

Specific examples of how power *is used* in their religion were sparse and referred only to decisions about financial matters and the authority of the church (see Table 4.6). In terms of the kind of power women have in their particular religious organizations, only four felt that they had some or a lot of power, and of these only one referred to this power as authority. She said, "Women's roles of power and authority have increased tremendously over the last decade in the Baptist/Protestant religious organization." The other five women who responded felt women have little or no power. One Catholic said, "Not any, because the value system is set up by the Catholic church."

The question, "How do you think power *should be used* in your religion?" elicited two responses that we associated with the power models. One woman described personal authority as she considered power a matter of choice. The other response included terms that could be associated with both traditional power and reciprocal empowerment. This individual saw power as a tool of influence and as the ability to have finances available to institute programs to assist the less fortunate. She also thought power should be used "to predicate change by making a difference in the community and to promote education by establishing educational scholarships."

Politics

Eighteen of the women were not affiliated with a political organization or cause. Of the three that were, two mentioned affiliation with the Democratic Party, and the third did not state an affiliation. All three women felt that people do have different kinds of power in their political organizations, but only one woman used terms associated with traditional power in her response. She said, "Politics is power. It's always putting people against people, ego against ego, and money against money. Politics and politicians possess greed, exert influence over others, and boast of what they are or can be."

When asked what kind of power they have in their political organizations, two of the women's responses matched the personal authority model and were both associated with action. One woman said she is actively involved in issues by voting, and the other woman said "staying knowledgeable and cognizant of political issues as they relate to me." When asked to provide specific examples about how power *is used* in politics (see Table 4.6), one woman said it is used to "sway individuals and voters." Another response, although not associated with any of the power models, follows: "Power has been used in an extremely positive perspective: to decrease the welfare roles, balance the budget, decrease the percentage of unemployment, promote racial harmony, increase minimum wage, and sign the Brady Bill into law." This same woman felt that power *should be used* in politics "To create diversity, create mobility, curtail homelessness, improve upon the epidemic of police and prosecutorial misconduct and incompetence in this country, and to continue to fight to uphold affirmative action." Another woman thought that power in politics should be used "for the benefit of all, not just for candidates or for them to get the votes."

The final question of the interview asked the women to discuss how they see the power roles of women who are affiliated with politics. A few of the women did not respond to this question. The responses given by eight of the women suggested that they felt women's roles in politics are important or that women are gaining more power. For example, "In the last century the power roles of women have changed drastically. We have made enormous gains in an extremely positive direction; yet there is room for improvement. For example, Christine Todd Whitman ([former] governor of New Jersey), Sandra Day O'Connor (Supreme Court justice), Dr. Joycelyn Elders (former surgeon general), and Janet Reno (former attorney general)." Another woman said, "When they get into politics, women are just as powerful as their male counterparts." And finally, "Women are getting more respect and becoming more predominant figures in politics." A few of the other women were not as optimistic about the power roles of women associated with politics: "They're mostly attached to their husbands. They get power because of their husband's affiliation or position and so become prominent persons," and "Very few [women get into politics], and for the ones that do their power will never be equal to men's power roles." One woman simply saw women's roles as very minimal, and another said that women are "still lacking the ability to achieve the highest level. We should look to other places, such as Europe, where women are able to ascend to top positions while still attracting respect, adoration, and camaraderie from men."

CONCLUSION

Our analysis of the survey results indicated that traditional power attributes were not personally popular with these Caribbean-American women, whereas a majority of the women agreed that society uses most of these attributes. The few traditional power attributes that did resonate with them were resources, authority, struggle, and competition. Reciprocal empowerment, personal authority, and empowerment fared better with this group, with the majority agreeing with all of the reciprocal empowerment and personal authority statements and with three of the five empowerment statements.

Conversely, our analysis of the interview statements revealed that the forms of power mentioned most frequently by these Caribbean-American women primarily included traditional power followed by personal authority. We surmised, based on contextual information about the history and culture of Caribbean-American women, that the interview responses in which the women were free to describe power in their own words were more telling than their responses to the predetermined survey statements. We speculated that something about the way the survey statements were framed led the women to disagree with the traditional power attributes contained in the survey statements yet use those same attributes in their interview responses. For example, in responses to the interview questions concerning what power means to them as individuals, what it means in U.S. society, what it means within their home culture, and what it means specifically as women in their Caribbean cultures, overwhelmingly the responses were associated with traditional power. It was only when asked about their power as women in the United States that no mention of a traditional power attribute occurred. Here, the few responses we could associate with any of the power models were related to personal authority and reciprocal empowerment. As for the remaining responses, two factors seem to be at play. First, some of the women who see themselves as having little or no power in the United States attribute this to their gender because men control society. For example, one participant said, "As a woman, I don't think I have much power. Not much from what I've seen. The U.S. is still dominated by males." Second, for the other women, having power appears to be a function of personal authority as we defined it. Although these women did not specifically use personal authority attributes such as self-determination, we were still able to interpret their responses in this way. For example, "[You have power] if you believe in yourself as a woman or as an individual, what you think of yourself and how you approach life . . . It's up to you how far you get," and "Women [in this country] have more of an opportunity to do what we want. You don't have to stay home and take care of babies."

Responses about how power *is used* at work and in the family followed the same trend. Most of the answers that we were able to interpret in relation to the four power models were directly associated with traditional power. A few other responses referred to personal authority. Although there were fewer responses regarding how power *should be used* in the family and at work, we were able to associate many of them with traditional power. In addition, we found the repeated use of words such as decision making, respect, and equality. Religion and politics were bereft of results that we could associate with any of the power models. This was due to the fact that the majority of the women chose not to respond to the questions, partly because of lack of affiliation and partly because of lack of active involvement.

As we have mentioned throughout this chapter, Caribbean-American women repeatedly used several words throughout their interview responses that were not directly associated with any of the power models. These words included respect, decision making, equality/sharing, and color.

Decision making as an attribute of power was used most often, especially in discussions about power in the family where the ability to make decisions gives them power. This was also revealed in the introductory questions, where the women associated power in both American society and Caribbean-American culture with decision making.

Respect was the second-most frequently used word, found particularly in the responses to the introductory questions and to the questions related to work. Respect was important to their individual perceptions of power and to the meaning of power in Caribbean-American culture. Respect was also paramount in terms of how these women believe power should be used on the job. One individual specified "mutual respect" in her response. Finally, respect was important to the meaning of power in their families.

Equality/sharing followed as a popular term, primarily as it related to work and family. With work, the women suggested that power on the job should be shared equally, and equality appeared as a description of what power means in their families. Skin color also appeared as a power attribute for these Caribbean-American women. Several examples of this included two women who responded to the question, "What do you think the word *power* means in American society today?" with "color; white is powerful" and "money and skin color."

Overall, the Caribbean-American women preferred reciprocal empowerment and personal authority when responding to the survey statements, but mentioned traditional power, particularly in terms of control-over and money, and personal authority in their interview responses. In addition, these women found skin color a significant factor related to power in the United States. Finally, this group of women was unique in that several of them described their preferred concept of power in the language of reciprocal empowerment by mentioning mutual respect, mutual understanding, mutual agreement, and mutual responsiveness.

Chapter 5

European-American Women and Power

EUROPEAN-AMERICAN WOMEN AND THE HISTORY OF "WHITENESS" IN THE UNITED STATES

When we first assigned labels to the ethnic categories that would constitute the organizational scheme of our study, we thought of European-American women primarily as a kind of catchall category for white American women. That is, we thought of European-American women as white women, whose families have lived in the United States for at least two generations, and who constitute the focus of the bulk of works one encounters in the women's studies sections of libraries and bookstores. We fashioned our study to focus primarily on women of ethnic and/or racial minorities living in the United States, those women who historically have been given less attention than white women in both scholarly and popular writings. A chapter on European-American women, then, would allow us to compare findings about "minority" women with white women. In addition, historical reasons exist for comparing women of European descent with women of color in America. As Jacobson (1998) notes, "It was the racial appellation 'White persons' in the nation's naturalization law that allowed the migrations from Europe in the first place" (p. 8). Further, when early European immigrants arrived in the United States, they found they could lay claim to the most valuable of all possessions—whiteness. Jacobson (1998) explains, "this history of whiteness and its fluidity is very much a history of power and its disposition" (p. 9). To determine variations in perceptions of power by women from different ethnic groups in the United States, then, it is important to include European-American women because whiteness and its significance in relation to other groups was forged by the dynamics of power. What we had not considered, however, is that since the breakup of the Soviet Union, the phrase "European-American immigrants" has taken on a more nuanced meaning. In our study, however, the majority of European-American women who participated fit our original conception of the category, with just a few participants identifying themselves as recent immigrants from Eastern European countries that had previously been under Soviet control.

Women in European Cultures

Much has been written about women in European cultures from antiquity to contemporary Europe, therefore we do not presume to offer an overview of the roles of women in particular European cultures or within particular time periods. To provide context to our analysis of ethnographic findings, we provide only a brief summary of the conditions experienced by European women during the time that migration from Europe to the United States was particularly significant.

A succinct way to offer this summary is to review the various themes and patterns concerning gender in Europe that Caine and Sluga (2000) discuss in their gender analysis of the history of Europe. Despite differences in the development of various parts of Europe during the eighteenth and nineteenth centuries, Caine and Sluga argue that four themes affected the lives of European women: citizenship and sexual difference, the ideology of separate spheres, gender and nationalism (as well as imperialism), and social Darwinism and racial ideologies.

As for the first theme, during the Enlightenment and the French Revolution, ideas about sexual difference and the rational nature of man framed major political activities and ensured that the "idea of female citizenship was constituted as fundamentally problematic" (Caine and Sluga, 2000, p. 4). For example, during the French Revolution a disdain for women's political expression led to subordination of women and their confinement to "the world of family and home under the supervision of a male household head" (p. 4). This configuration, of course, comprised the second theme, the classic ideology of separate spheres. The masculine public sphere afforded men economic opportunity and a valued role in the social order, while the feminine private sphere consisted of unpaid and often undervalued labor. As Caine and Sluga note, the different spheres of activity caused a gendering of work that, in turn, created significant class distinctions between men and women. The third theme, gender and nationalism, is a curious one. Caine and Sluga discuss that women as well as men embraced both nationalism and imperialism. For women, a resulting sense of patriotic duty afforded them some political identity, but because women often organized politically around so-called "women's issues," they were associated primarily with maternalism. The consequence of this was that often emphasis was placed only on their roles and responsibilities as mothers. The fourth theme constituted a debate about the health and survival of the European races that was tied to questions about sexuality, sexual difference, and concerns with homosexuality and venereal disease. These issues characterized European legislation and the development of sexology and psychoanalysis. These four conditions, although responsible in large part for the continued subordination of women, also often paved the way for change, growth, and expansion of women's roles through protest and alternative institutions such as the development of "a separate 'female' public sphere in which women undertook philanthropy, social work and cultural activities" (Caine and Sluga, 2000, p. 4).

European Immigration to the United States

Since much has been published covering the specific groups who have immigrated from Europe to America, in this section we provide a brief, general overview of European immigration. Kiser (1962) says that the origins of what he calls "intra-white" diversity in the United States are found in "multiple-power attempts at colonization" by the English, the Dutch, the French, and the Spanish (p. 23). Barron (1962) notes that historically Europe has been the major source of immigrants for the United States. In fact, Davie (1962) states that "of all the Europeans now living elsewhere, three-fifths are in the United States" (p. 231). The original settlers of the British colonies hailed from England as well as from northwestern Europe, most notably Germany. Kiser mentions that many examples of small numbers of non-English groups were also allowed and sometimes encouraged to immigrate to the United States. Until recently, European or "white" immigration to the United States was often divided into three distinction periods (Kiser, 1962). First, prior to 1882, immigrants arrived from Northern and Western Europe (many Chinese also immigrated during this period, as discussed in Chapter 3). These "older" immigrants came from Britain, Germany, Scandinavia, Ireland, and Canada (Kessler-Harris and Yans-McLaughlin, 1978). Second, between 1882 and 1923 immigration from Northern and Western Europe declined, but immigration from Southern and Eastern Europe increased. It was during this period that many Italians, Russians, and Poles arrived. Finally, scholars generally describe a third wave of immigration that included small numbers of immigrants from a variety of places. This wave included continued immigration from Northern and Western Europe, since United States immigration quotas favored this region, but it also included immigrants from various parts of the western hemisphere and some refugee populations.

According to both Barron (1962) and Davie (1962), because travel was difficult during the nineteenth century, immigration was mainly confined to populations driven to consider relocation for several reasons: (1) to leave a densely populated area, (2) to seek greater economic opportunities, (3) to seek lighter military burdens, and (4) to locate broader opportunities for social relations and religious expression. More specifically it was not until the 1840s, when legal obstacles were removed and an economic liberalism had set in, that immigration from Europe to the United States became a mass movement. Some of the reasons Davie cites for leaving Europe include the famine in Ireland in 1847, political and religious intolerance in Germany, anti-Semitic riots in Russia from 1881 to 1883, and failure of the currant crop market in Greece. These problems in the emigrants' home countries are typically called "push" factors by immigration scholars. But "pull" factors also existed, such as the deliberate targeting of Europeans for immigration by American employers.

Kessler-Harris and Yans-McLaughlin (1978) offer comparisons among three major immigrant groups: the Italians, the Irish, and the Jews (mostly German Jews). They note that "Many Italians, like some eastern Europeans, saw America as a temporary haven where they hoped to accumulate large sums of money and return home with their savings to buy land" (p. 109). However, those Irish and Jewish immigrants escaping economic discrimination and religious persecution considered their immigration permanent. Furthermore, differences in how these three groups fared in the United States offer one illustration of the nuances of immigration that cannot be discussed at length here. That is, although the Irish and Italians arrived unskilled, placing them at a disadvantage economically and relegating them early on to day labor and the like, Germans and German Jews entered the United States as a "labor aristocracy" (Kessler-Harris and Yans-McLaughlin, 1978, p. 111), becoming tradespersons and self-employed shop owners. Subsequent generations of Jewish immigrants, then, entered the middle class far more quickly than did either the Irish or the Italians.

The Effect of Immigration on European Women

Harzig and colleagues (1997) note that of the European immigrants entering the United States from the 1850s to the 1920s, 30 to 50 percent were women. These women left Europe voluntarily with a wealth of knowledge about earlier immigrant experiences, a clearly established set of developed migration networks, and generally with help from neighbors and relatives. Women left Europe to "escape gender constraints, to enhance their chances in the marriage market, and to fulfill family obligations" (Harzig et al., 1997, p. 4). During this time, immigration to the United States was a basic European reality and a predictable experience for both women and men.

Harzig and colleagues suggest that a three-phase assimilation process occurred for these women. The first phase was adaptation, consisting of the fulfillment of basic needs associated with work, food, and shelter. The second phase, acculturation, occurred as immigrant women "were significantly influenced by—and influenced—urban culture" in various ethnic communities in the United States (p. 21). The third part of the process, full assimilation, occurred as immigrants began moving out of ethnic communities and settling in various areas of urban America.

Although their previous lives in Europe were often rural and thus influenced by agrarian circumstances, social and economic institutions, and daily routines, the move to the United States was often also a move to urban life. The lives of immigrant women from Europe were then centered on factory employment, a consumer economy, and an urban neighborhood life. As with many other immigrant groups, this meant the loss of a support system usually supplied by an extended family. Instead, women were primarily faced with reclusive household activities. As Harzig and colleagues (1997) explain, "they had to discard much of what had structured their lives; it was no longer of use in a capitalist industrial economy" (p. 15). However, they also argue that "These women kept from their former lives what had value and discarded what did not work as they learned to function in their new situation" (p. 2).

One of the effects of the new situation for European-American women was a more complex and fluid class structure as well as some measure of self-determination and gradually changing gender relations. These changes resulted from the fact that a husband's income was rarely sufficient, so women found various ways to supplement the family income. By taking in boarders, doing washing, cleaning offices, and the like, women developed a wage-earning ability and had access to cash that, in turn, gave them some measure of control and choice. In addition, Harzig and colleagues note that although immigrants often chose to marry early (and generally from within their own cultural group), they also began to have smaller families.

Another result of immigration to the United States was further development of female activities in the public sphere. Wage-earning work provided some association with the public sphere; this also helped women to develop a sense of personal authority. Harzig and colleagues note that at least for German, Irish, Swedish, and Polish immigrants to the United States, women helped build their local ethnic communities, did important charity work, and engaged in vital fund-raising activities. In these ways, European immigrant women "shaped social relations in an urban American environment, affected gender relations, and helped to create a social network and charity system in which they both gave and received assistance" (p. 2).

Prior to the 1800s, however, the earliest female European immigrants to America (the Anglo-American colonialists of the 1600s) quickly lost equality even in the religious realm when their identities were legally submerged as married women through coverture, whereby the legal existence of a woman is suspended during marriage. Norton (1999) suggests that both women and men expected men to speak for women in numerous settings, even in relation to their religious beliefs and their individual consciences. When this subservience was codified in law, women's "independent identities were literally erased from society's consciousness" (p. 41). This situation set the stage for a return to the kind of clearly established separations between public and private spheres that women had been experiencing in Europe. However, by the nineteenth century, growing consternation arose about the "woman question"—a male concern with the increasing visibility of women in the public sphere.

Yet because of the configuration of race, class, and ethnicity in the United States, even women of European descent were not united in their efforts to transform gender relations. Harzig and colleagues describe the development of two movements that occurred parallel to each other in time, but which were otherwise almost entirely separate. On one hand, Anglo-American women instigated both the suffrage and the temperance movements. However, ethnic European-American women were concerned with Old World nationalisms and ethnic identities. The two groups did not find affinity with each other's concerns. Further, Newman (1999) explains that an additional split occurred between the suffrage movement and the abolitionists over emancipation and the ratification of the Fourteenth and Fifteenth Amendments to the U.S. Constitution. Newman (1999) states that "Where antebellum suffrage ideology often emphasized a common victimhood [between Black men and White women], postbellum suffrage ideology stressed White women's racial-cultural superiority to newly enfranchised male constituencies—not just black men, but also naturalized immigrant men" (p. 5). White proponents of women's rights, then, developed an unfortunate sense of superiority over blacks and other ethnic minorities (including non-Anglo-European Americans). This situation complicated racial and ethnic relations even further since black women could not share a sense of sisterhood with the suffragettes' criticism of the Fourteenth and Fifteenth Amendments. As Norton (1999) explains, black women generally saw black men as their "allies and protectors against a racist culture. Most Black women supported the Fourteenth and Fifteenth Amendments, which they considered advantageous to the Black race as a whole and thus to themselves, even though their own rights to citizenship went unaffirmed" (p. 6).

History indicates, then, that ethnic European-American women became alienated from Anglo-European-American women, who alienated themselves from black and other ethnic women in the United States (including Native Americans). The consequences of this early segregation of the women's movement are still being felt today (Moraga and Anzaldua, 1981). In addition, problematic race, class, and ethnic relations felt by both women and men in the United States today are the result of the early development of hierarchical power dynamics.

ANALYSIS OF ETHNOGRAPHIC FINDINGS

Demographics

Twenty European-American women ranging in age from eighteen to over sixty-six completed the survey and interview. Ten of the women identified themselves as married and ten as single. Nineteen women identified their race as white while one identified herself as Jewish/white. In responding to the question of ethnicity, five women indicated Italian descent while two also noted that they are Catholic. Two women identified themselves as German Americans, one as German Indian, and one as Belgian German American. Two women identified their ethnicity as European American. Nine women provided unique ethnic designations, each belonging to one of the following: Swedish, Romanian, Irish American, French, Russian, Polish, Jewish Russian, Spanish Jewish, and Jewish American Czechoslovakian Hungarian. Household income was spread across the board, with six respondents between $15,000 and $35,000 and nine falling between $36,000 and $55,000. In terms of education, seven indicated they had completed high school, nine had either a community college or a four-year degree, three had attained either a graduate or a professional level of education, and one did not respond.

Analysis of the Survey

Fourteen of the survey statements were designed to evaluate participants' level of agreement versus disagreement with society's use of traditional power attributes. These responses were compared with the responses to the fourteen statements designed to measure participants' level of agreement versus disagreement with their personal use of these same attributes (see Table 5.1). Results indicated that a majority of the European-American women felt society uses at least twelve of the fourteen traditional power attributes. The highest level of agreement (at least sixteen women) was with the attributes domination, wealth, authority, resources, winning, resistance, and competition. However, more than half the women personally disagreed with

TABLE 5.1. European-American Women: Personal Feelings Regarding Power and Society versus Power and Self

Traditional Power and Society				Traditional Power and Self			
Attribute	**Agree**	**Disagree**	**N A/D**	**Attribute**	**Agree**	**Disagree**	**N A/D**
Domination	16	1	3	Domination	6	14	0
Conflict	9	5	6	Conflict	5	11	4
Force	9	6	5	Force	1	18	1
Win	16	3	1	Win	4	14	2
Struggle	12	3	5	Struggle	11	4	5
Resistance	16	1	2	Resistance	11	4	5
Competition	16	2	2	Competition	12	6	1
Physical strength	10	5	5	Physical strength	7	12	1
Control-over	15	4	1	Control-over	5	11	4
Sway others	15	5	0	Sway others	5	11	4
Wealth	18	1	1	Wealth	5	12	3
Authority	17	2	1	Authority	11	6	3
Resources	18	2	0	Resources	17	1	2
Coercion	15	4	1	Coercion	7	10	3

n = 20
N A/D = Neither agree nor disagree
Note: Where totals equal less than *n*, there were instances of no response.

the use of eight of these power attributes: domination, conflict, force, winning, physical strength, control-over, sway others, and wealth. Force was considered personally undesirable by the largest number of women (eighteen). The attribute with which the highest number of women (seventeen) agreed was the use of resources, and a majority of women also agreed with the use of competition, struggle, resistance, and authority.

Only two statements highlighting the use of empowerment attributes received a majority of agreement from the women (see Table 5.2). These statements were, "I feel that it is important to be compassionate regardless of whether or not it benefits me as long as I empower others" and "I feel that my competence should be used to empower others regardless of whether or not it benefits me." In terms of the remaining attributes, collectivity, consensus, and companionship, the women were evenly split in their agreement and disagreement; however, in each of these cases, between three and five women neither agreed nor disagreed or chose not to respond. A vast majority of the women agreed with all of the personal authority attributes, with the largest number of women agreeing with the importance of having knowledge and the ability to make choices (see Table 5.3).

Half or more of the women agreed with all the statements highlighting the use of reciprocal empowerment attributes (see Table 5.4). The attributes with which the greatest number of women agreed included knowledge (twenty), self-determination (eighteen), ability to take action (seventeen), and consensus (sixteen). It should be noted

TABLE 5.2. European-American Women: Personal Feelings Regarding Empowerment

Attribute	Agree	Disagree	N A/D
Collectivity	7	7	5
Companionship	7	8	5
Compassion	13	5	2
Consensus	9	8	3
Competence	12	4	4

n = 20
N A/D = Neither agree nor disagree
Note: Where totals equal less than *n*, there were instances of no response.

TABLE 5.3. European-American Women: Personal Feelings Regarding Personal Authority

Attribute	Agree	Disagree	N A/D
Ability to take action	13	4	3
Ability to choose	17	2	1
Self-determination	15	1	4
Knowledge	19	0	1
Independence	16	1	3

n = 20
N A/D = Neither agree nor disagree

TABLE 5.4. European-American Women: Personal Feelings Regarding Reciprocal Empowerment

Attribute	Agree	Disagree	N A/D
Mutual responsiveness	10	5	4
Competence	13	4	3
Compassion	13	2	5
Independence	15	2	3
Ability to choose	15	3	2
Collectivity	12	2	6
Companionship	11	8	1
Ability to take action	17	1	2
Self-determination	18	2	0
Mutual engagement	14	5	1
Knowledge	20	0	0
Consensus	16	2	2
Mutual attention	15	2	3
Mutual empathy	15	2	3

n = 20
N A/D = Neither agree nor disagree
Note: Where totals equal less than *n*, there were instances of no response.

here that the attributes that received majority agreement mostly derived from the personal authority aspect of the reciprocal empowerment model.

Analysis of the Interview

To analyze the interview results we categorize and describe the responses given to the first five questions in terms of (1) what power means to them as individuals, (2) what power generally means in American society, (3) what power means in their ethnic culture, (4) whether, as women, they have power in American society, and (5) whether, as women, they have power in European-American culture (see Table 5.5). We then evaluate responses regarding their perceptions of power in the areas of work, family, religion, and politics, including how power *is used* and how power *should be used* in these areas (see Table 5.6).

TABLE 5.5. European-American Women: Responses to Introductory Interview Questions and the Relationship of These Responses to the Power Models

Introductory Interview Questions	Traditional Power	Empowerment	Personal Authority	Reciprocal Empowerment
What does the word *power* mean to you as an individual?	9	0	7	0
What do you think the word *power* means in American society today?	18	0	0	2
What do you think the word *power* means in your culture?	11	0	2	4
As a woman, what kind of power do you think you have in U.S. society?	1	2	9	2
As a European-American woman, what do you think the word *power* means in your culture?	8	0	4	0

n = 20

Note: Total numbers may not match *n* since in some cases responses could not be associated with a power model. Zero equals no responses or responses could not be associated with a model.

TABLE 5.6. European-American Women: Interview Responses to Questions About Work, Family, Religion, and Politics

How Power *Is Used*

	Traditional Power	Empowerment	Personal Authority	Reciprocal Empowerment
Work	17	0	1	1
Family	7	5	5	1
Religion	3	2	0	0
Politics	3	0	1	0

How Power *Should Be Used*

	Traditional Power	Empowerment	Personal Authority	Reciprocal Empowerment
Work	2	2	0	1
Family	1	1	0	3
Religion	1	2	1	0
Politics	0	1	0	0

n = 20
Note: Total numbers may not match *n* since in some cases responses could not be associated with a power model. Zero equals no responses or responses could not be associated with a model.

Introductory Questions

Our analysis of the interviews focuses on how the women's responses illustrate their attitudes toward the four models of power. Traditional power attributes surfaced most frequently in the women's responses when asked the question concerning what power means to them as individuals. Seven of the women said power means having "control over" or "giving orders to others." Other statements reflecting traditional power included: "Power means the ability to make others nervous" and "Power means being on top of the chain instead of below." Five of the women's answers focused on money and/or resources. Examples of these included: "Power is money. How can you have power if you don't have money?" and "Power means strength, wealth, ambition, knowledge, and having resources." Three women focused on strength. Four of the women's responses included the personal authority attribute "independence." Another word mentioned was "freedom."

In the case of U.S. society, eighteen women responded using traditional power attributes. A majority of the women (twelve out of twenty) identified money and/or resources as the primary source of power in U.S. society, while seven identified control as the primary source of power making statements such as, "control over others, wealth, taking control over everything, and politics" and "control over people, places, and things." Two respondents mentioned the personal authority attribute knowledge, and two talked about connections or titles of authority. Two mentioned politics, and one mentioned respect.

As with the previous question, the traditional power attribute money was the most popular response when asked, "What do you think the word *power* means in European-American culture?" This was followed by three mentions of control and four mentions of the personal authority attribute knowledge. Five women made statements using the words connections/status/prestige, three mentioned politics or government, and one woman stated, "It is the self-righteous attitude that the white race is superior."

When asked what kind of power they have as women in general in U.S. society, two women focused on the personal authority attribute of knowledge/education. We could interpret two of the responses as empowerment because they spoke of helping others and contributing to society. Fifteen of the women indicated that they have some or a lot of power. Specific responses included, "I have power to use my sexuality to get what I want," and "Society forces us to manipulate, to use sexuality to manipulate men." Five women said they have little or no power and gave responses which included: "None, as much as there's the idea of American women being independent, there's not as much power as people think [there is]—only power to vote, but they are limited in the way they can live their lives," "Very little, the woman bears the brunt of many conflicts," and "no power—I am retired, not working."

Five women did not respond to the question, "As a European-American woman what do you think the word *power* means in your culture?" Perhaps this lack of response occurred because the women saw no distinction between this question and the previous question, since, as European-American women, "their culture" and the American culture can be seen as one and the same. Of the responses we did receive, however, four women mentioned money, three referred to control or dominance, two used the personal authority attributes of choice or independence, and three mentioned status.

Work

Seventeen of the twenty European-American women indicated that they are employed outside of the household. When asked, "Do people have different kinds of power where you work?", sixteen of the women said yes. Of those who responded, the answers in one way or another referred to types of power in terms of positions and hierarchy in the workplace. For example, one woman said, "Yes, I work for a doctor, and he has all the power. The office manager runs the office and holds power." An attorney said, "Yes, some people are partners or associates, some people have clients, and some people don't." Another woman said, "Yes, the manager has power over the servers. The kitchen has power over the manager. The owner has power over us all." When asked to describe what kind of power they have on their jobs, ten women indicated by their responses that they feel that have a lot of power. An example of this type of response follows: "I have power over my employees. I receive the most respect and I have the ability to hire and fire my employees." On the other hand, some women felt they have some power even if of limited scope: "[I have] authority over the children; they are supposed to do what I say." Finally, some women felt they have a minimal amount or even no power and indicated this in statements such as, "I have no power, I follow rules, I do as I am told." Two respondents seemed to feel that power of any kind was not a consideration on their jobs. This was evidenced in responses such as, "I don't strive for power; I strive for teamwork for the mutual benefit of the company."

In responding to interview questions that asked the women to describe how power *is used* on the job, the women showed a strong unified opinion that the traditional power model prevails (see Table 5.6). Few women actually described specific instances of the use of power, but of those who responded, twelve mentioned the use of control, authority, title, and position. For example, one woman said, "The boss has the power to change your duties, increase or decrease your pay, and solve your problems." Another said, "I make the decisions as to what is ordered, as well as the inventory, delivering, etc., that will be coordinated for the VIPs checking into hotel rooms. I am in charge of my department." One woman stated, "It is used to ensure that people do their jobs right," and one said, "Through respect—we're all friends."

When asked how they think power *should be used* on the job, very few of the responses fit descriptions of any of the power models. Of the few that did, two described traditional power attributes, two described empowerment attributes, and one described a reciprocal empowerment attribute. Responses were spread over suggestions such as "just the way it is," power is needed "to keep things organized" and "to make sure people do their jobs to the best of their ability." One respondent said that leadership is needed, but there should be a limit to power. Several responses mentioned teamwork, equality, responsiveness, and accommodating everyone.

Family

Of the twenty respondents, twelve described their immediate families in terms of the traditional Western nuclear family with members consisting of parents, spouses, siblings, children, and grandchildren/grandparents. Eight described their families as extended and included in-laws, cousins, aunts and uncles, nieces and nephews, boyfriends, girlfriends, friends, and pets. When asked, "Who is the head of your household?", eight respondents identified themselves or some other woman, five identified their husbands, four said that both their husbands and themselves function equally as heads of household, two simply said "equal," one said she shares this role with her roommate, and one said that her entire immediate family functions as a unit in this capacity.

More women than men were cited as the major decision makers regarding children and housework. More specifically, nine women claimed responsibility for decisions concerning the children, six women said that both parents make these decisions, and five either did not respond or indicated that the question was not applicable to them. In terms of housework, fourteen responses identified a woman as the major decision maker, five respondents said "both," and one said "husband and wife."

Regarding financial decision making, half of the women said "both," referring to husband and wife, mom and dad, or roommates. Six women said they make the financial decisions and four women identified a man, either their husbands or fathers.

There was a variety of answers to the question, "What do you think the word *power* means in your family?" Four women responded in ways that focused on control, influence, or position. Examples include the following: "The ability to lead and have influence over family members," "Control, authority, being in charge, and being aggressive and assertive," and simply "Controlling." Three of the women once again referred to wealth or money. One of these women made this point quite clearly: "If you have the money, you have the power—without it, even in the family context, you can't do all that much." Two of the women referred explicitly to teamwork, love, and respect: "The word *power* in my family means having understanding, working together as a team, having respect for one another as well as for each individual's opinions, and love," and "In my family the word *power* means teamwork, love, respect, the right to an opinion, and gratitude." One woman referred to unity and another referred to equality.

When asked if people have different kinds of power in the immediate family, eleven women said yes and nine women said no. Although many of these responses were simply "yes" or "no," of those that gave extended answers at least three described, in one way or another, a division of labor in the family. For example, "My father takes care of finances and my mother takes care of cooking and cleaning," and "Everyone has his or her own responsibilities." Some other responses included the following: "Yes, some have the power to manipulate; others have the power of conviction" and "No, decisions have to be agreed upon." Of interest, a Polish woman said, "I strongly avoid power. I was born in a country where my grandfather died in a concentration camp. So power, I avoid it, the concept of it."

When asked what kind of power they have in their immediate families, only one woman felt that she has a lot of power; however, she did not indicate what kind of power she has. On the other hand, 75 percent of the women (fifteen of twenty) felt they have some power. The responses indicated that this realm of power exists in the arena of the children. This was demonstrated in statements such as, "The only power I need is over the children as far as safety is concerned"; "I hold my family members accountable and they listen when I speak"; "Decisions regarding the children"; and "The availability to make the right choices for my family." Some women found power in having the ability to take care of the home. Examples of these statements included "Decorating the house and [deciding] what is for dinner and cleaning" and "When visiting my parents I share power roles with my parents . . . cooking, cleaning, shopping." One woman felt her power in the family comes from her ability to make her own decisions. She and one other woman said their power comes from their ability to make choices. One felt that she has the power of education as she is the only person in her family to have graduated from college.

In response to questions about how power *is used* in the family, the women could easily identify with all four power models, with the traditional power attributes being mentioned the most (see Table 5.6). However, many statements indicated that power is used equally. These included statements such as, "The power is used evenly to benefit the family"; "We share our opinions and we both make decisions"; "Everything we do is together. [We] get each other's opinions and then make our decision"; and "We decide the areas of responsibility that suited each of us best." Several responses indicated that power is used to create and maintain "respect" and "order" and to benefit the family: "Power is used to maintain respect and order. If my little brother is disrespectful to my mom, I have the power to beat his butt"; "Rules—respect in relation to curfew and chores"; and "You have power when you become a parent, not to control but to maneuver your children to good decisions. I am in the driver's seat of the family. I talk to each family member individually regarding decisions; we talk things out to come to a consensus." Four women indicated that power is not used in their families, and one woman who resides at her parents' home said, "Dad does the finances, gives orders; he has the last say. Mom does the cooking, cleaning; she is the mediator, and she tries to compromise." Three responses indicated a negative perspective on the use of power. These included, "My brothers use the power of my mother's unconditional love to manipulate her," and "When leasing a car for our son I was never consulted. I wish they had because I am the mother. We disagree a lot on discipline of children."

Although all twenty of the women responded to the question of how power *should be used* in the family, few of the responses could be identified with any of the power models. In fact, traditional power attributes were described only once, empowerment once, reciprocal empowerment three times, and personal authority was not mentioned. Nine of the women who all agreed that power should be used equally and fairly in the family gave responses such as, "I think power should be used fairly and evenly. Each person has responsibilities," "I believe power should be used as teamwork—evenly throughout. No person should have more power than the other," and "Everyone's opinions should be heard and discussed." Five women said power should be used specifically for the family's well-being. They made statements such as "To keep the family in line. We need to look out for each other. To offer advice to someone—to watch them take it is powerful," "[There is] strength in unity, the ability to pull together. Power should be used in a constructive way," and "With love, understanding, passion, and giving up. It helps to facilitate communication to surpass obstacles." Two women said power in the family should be used for structure and support, while two said it should not be used at all.

Religion

On the subject of religion, twelve of the women said they belong to a religious group and eight said they did not. When asked about their religious affiliation, two identified themselves as Baptists, eight as Catholics, one as Christian, and two as Jewish. When asked if people have different kinds of power in their religion, most of these women simply stated "yes." However, in a few longer responses the women indicated mainly that power is held by men in their religion. Responses included, "Yes, [the] pastor has expertise to teach and guide congregation"; "Yes, men are capable of being priests and conducting services, but women are increasingly gaining power"; "Sure, the pope has the power, and the subsequent power that he delegates"; and "Yes, the rabbi has power; also, men and women have different types of power roles in the Jewish religion. The men and women are always separated in the religion." One woman seemed to put the power squarely in the organizational structure of her religion. She stated, "The Catholic religion is overpowering. There are a lot of hypocrites who don't understand the religion. It's a very aggressive religion. Religion is about respect. I don't like the word *religion* because it is associated with power." Two felt that, in religion, power should not be used at all, and two said it should be used for structure and support.

When asked what kind of power they personally have in their religion, the responses varied from those who feel that they do not need any power to those who feel that they have the power to give. One woman stated, "I require no power in my church. It is a place for unity, not pedestals." Another said, "I have the power to attend Mass and to participate. I also have the power to write a check each week to put in the gift basket." Another stated, "I have the power of convicting [sic] myself to repent." Several women said they find their power in their relationship with God. This was demonstrated in statements such as, "I believe it is a personal relationship with God that gives me complete power to have a relationship with God," and another said "to make wrong or right decisions—power to believe in God, power to steer me in the right directions." Five of the women felt they have no power in their religion.

The question of how power *is used* in religion received even fewer responses than the preceding questions about religion (see Table 5.6). Three people mentioned traditional power attributes, and two mentioned empowerment attributes. The women again alluded to men using the power. This was evident in statements such as, "It's a man's world, the pope and so on. Nuns can't do the Mass. Women can only sing, read, or take communion. We have no say"; "Priests have power to control their flock"; "Power is used by higher members of the church (pastor, deacons, etc,) to allow people to know their words are words of authority"; and "Men are priests; they conduct church services. Women are sisters in my religion and have power over churchgoers, but not over the church." Several women hinted at negative examples of the use of power: "It [power] used to be used in an aggressive way"; "My opinion is that religion controls the masses, and that is how the church survived throughout the centuries. The church is power"; and "It is used by certain people to be able to dictate to others."

In terms of the kind of power they feel women in general have in their religion, the majority of the women indicated that women either have no power, they have the power to support the religious organization with fund-raising and other philanthropic work, or they simply have the power to be a member of the religion.

Regarding how power *should be used* in religion, few women responded. Of those who did, one each described traditional power and personal authority, while two described empowerment. Two women referred to teaching or studying, one each mentioned equality and unity, one said, "I like it the way it is because it is based on Scripture," one said, "To get people to listen to others living their lives for the Lord," and one said, "To come down to earth, to be more approachable."

Politics

Only five of the twenty women indicated that they were affiliated with a political organization or cause, thirteen were not, and two did not respond. Of the five who did indicate political involvement, there were two Democrats, two Republicans, and one Independent. Of interest, of the six women who responded to the question, "Do people have different kinds of power in your political organization/cause?" all said "yes," but few elaborated. One did say that "Unfortunately, the one with the most money wins. That is the way our political system is." In response to the question asking the women what kind of power they have in their political organization/cause, four women said they have little or none, and the one woman who believes she has some power simply indicated that she has the "power to vote and make choices."

When asked how power *is used* in politics, three women described traditional power (see Table 5.6). One woman mentioned money, another described persuasion or swaying others, and the remaining two referred to a specific policy issue (Social Security) or bipartisan politics (referring to attempts to "dethrone" the Democrats). One woman described political power in terms of choice, a personal authority attribute.

Five women responded to the question, "How do you think power *should be used* in your political organization/cause?" One woman responded using empowerment attributes. Two of these five women referred specifically to the Constitution, as in, "It should be based on the Constitution, where every man has an equal vote." One referred to the common good; one said to elect "good candidates for education";

one wished to see adherence to Christian principles; and one said "Congress should have to vote how people tell them."

Only two of the women did not respond to the final question on politics: "How do you see the power roles of women who are affiliated with politics?" Of the eighteen women who did respond, twelve gave answers that, in one way or another, indicated they believe women are gaining more power. For example, one woman said, "You see more and more government positions filled by women. They work hard, stand up for what they believe in, and they accomplish their goals. We finally have women in power who represent other women"; and "It [power] is increasing. Women are underestimated, but I think they will take the political forum by storm one day." One woman explicitly argued that women should be on equal footing with men in politics, and another said that, "Women are not to be trusted. They are weaker. Men are stronger." Finally, one woman described the kind of power she believes women exert in politics: "I see women in the political arena utilizing their power in the way of emotions. In my opinion the plateau is starting to shift from a selfish, strictly business mentality to a more moral one."

CONCLUSION

In the survey, personal authority surfaced as the model of power preferred by European-American women. This was evidenced not only in the responses to the personal authority statements, but also in the responses to those reciprocal empowerment statements which were drawn from the personal authority model.

Results of the first part of the interview suggest that the European-American women interviewed believe that U.S. society views power according to the traditional power model. Only a few women indicated that, as women in U.S. society, they practice personal authority. These women see a distinction between how women in general in U.S. society use power and how they use power in their own culture. Although a few of the participants indicated that, as women in U.S. society, they practice personal authority, in their own specific culture (however they chose to define it, for example, Polish American, German American, etc.) they more often chose traditional power attributes. This suggests that perhaps they see their culture—and their practice of power within it—as somehow distinct from the public sphere. Finally, results also illustrate that empowerment and reciprocal empowerment attributes barely surfaced in any of the women's answers to the introductory questions. In fact, their descriptions never clearly addressed reciprocal empowerment at all.

Traditional power attributes surfaced most frequently in the responses to questions concerning how power is currently used in the workplace. However, when it came to family, the responses included attributes that were fairly evenly spread across three power models: power, empowerment, and personal authority. Although the women responding tended to use both empowerment and personal authority attributes, this did not carry over as an endorsement of reciprocal empowerment. That is, since reciprocal empowerment is a combination of empowerment and personal authority, we would have expected that these elements would appear together in individual responses.

Further, few of the responses concerning how power should be used on the job or in the family fit within the constraints of the four power models. What surfaced in many cases were terms that were not identifiable with any of the models. It was evident that the respondents had opinions about how power *is used,* but when the question of how power *should be used* arose, they had little to say that we could associate with the power models.

In the responses to questions about religion, few respondents indicated that women have or even should have power in religion, and when participants did describe power it was usually associated with the men involved in their religious organizations. There were so few responses concerning how power *is* or *should be used* in politics that we originally thought we could not draw any meaningful conclusions. However, it appears that the women's hopes and aspirations emerged in their responses to the question, "How do you see the power roles of women who are affiliated with politics?" This was demonstrated in responses such as, "I believe the power roles of women affiliated with politics are becoming very strong. They are great role models not only to Americans but to other societies as well. Women today are playing a bigger role in society, especially in my culture in Romania"; "We are going to have a lot more women in Congress, for example, Hillary Clinton, the president's wife, is moving on further than her husband. In years to come there will be a woman president"; and "They're much different than they were in my day. Women are much more active and powerful in politics today.

Look at Hillary Clinton, Janet Reno, and Dianne Feinstein as examples."

In examining the responses to the interview questions, several terms recurred that we could not easily associate with our original list of attributes of the four power models. We believe that these terms have some significance and that some of them can be associated with reciprocal empowerment. These words included decision making, equality, status, and respect. Contextually, both equality and decision making were spread throughout answers to the interview questions related to family. However, the areas of greatest concentration were in response to the questions asking how power *is* and *should be used* in the family. In response to the introductory questions, the women tended to use the terms status, position, prestige, title, or connections. This kind of response was given most frequently in answering the question asking the women what they think the word *power* means in their culture. These terms also arose in response to the questions asking them about power in U.S. society and about power as a European-American woman. Respect also appeared throughout the interview responses, but tended to cluster primarily in answers to questions about the meaning of power in the family and in examples of how power is used. The word decision making appears to relate to personal authority, while the cluster of terms status, connections, prestige, and title seems to relate to traditional power. Status and related words appeared to resonate strongly with these European-American women. This is perhaps a reflection of the position their heritage has afforded them in the United States.

Chapter 6

Latin American Women and Power

POLITICAL AND ECONOMIC INFLUENCES: A BRIEF HISTORY OF CUBAN-AMERICAN AND PUERTO RICAN-AMERICAN WOMEN

Of all the ethnic classifications used to organize our study, the term *Latin American* is perhaps the most troublesome. Our study included women of Latin American origin living in the United States; yet to call these women Latin American Americans sounds silly and reveals the ethnocentrism of the United States and our insensitive and inaccurate tendency to claim the term "American." Dictionaries describe the geographical name "Latin America" as Spanish America and Brazil, or more broadly as all of the Americas south of the United States. Jackson and Hudman (1986) define Latin America as "the American landmass south of the United States' border with Mexico" (p. 507). They go on to describe U.S. ethnocentrism concerning this region as follows: "For most residents of Anglo-America, and particularly those of the United States, the term America is synonymous with the United States or, generously, the North American continent. Rarely do Anglo-Americans recognize that Latin America is also America, and the people of Latin America are Americans" (Jackson and Hudman, 1986, p. 507). Even without this problem, *Latin American* is still a problematic term. For example, geographical maps of this area contribute to potential confusion about the term. These maps also highlight every geographical entity in the western hemisphere south of Mexico, including the British West Indies (Jackson and Hudman, 1986). But it would be rare, indeed, to find a Jamaican who considers herself Latin American! An alternative classification might be Hispanic, which—according to dictionaries—refers to anything related to the culture of Spain, Portugal, or Latin America. Since our study did not include American women from Spain or Portugal, we are left again with the precarious designation *Latin American.*

The Latin American population in the South Florida area in which our study was conducted is both significant and diverse, ranging from Mexicans and Guatemalans to Colombians and Brazilians. In fact, according to Viglucci (2001), Florida "is now home to one of about every 13 Hispanics in the country" (p. 1A). However, our introductory material in this chapter focuses on Cuban Americans and Puerto Rican Americans since nearly all the participants in our study identified themselves in one of these two ways. These two groups represent significant Latin American cultures in South Florida. Two-thirds of all Cubans living in the United States reside in Florida, with 52 percent of them living in Miami-Dade County (Viglucci, 2001, p. 22A). In addition, according to Viglucci, "So substantial was the growth in Florida's Puerto Rican population [based on 2000 Census figures] that it is now second only to New York's in size" (p. 22A).

Women in Cuban and Puerto Rican Cultures

Both of these islands were colonized by Spain. Cuba gained independence in 1895, but Puerto Rico has been a possession of the United States since 1898 (Jackson and Hudman, 1986; Stoner and Perez, 2000). In Cuba a traditionally strong relationship existed between women and the Catholic Church (Miller, 1991). In Puerto Rico, women's relationship with the church changed significantly in the nineteenth century when the Catholic Church moved from its earlier view of women as dangerous and sinful to viewing them as virtuous and innocent (Rodriguez, 1998). In addition, the traditional roles of both Cuban and Puerto Rican women were associated with the family. As Perez y Gonzalez (2000) describes traditional Puerto Rican roles, women were assigned responsibilities related to housekeeping and child rearing. Both Cuban and Puerto Rican women have transcended these stereotypical roles, but for somewhat different reasons.

For Cuban women, the political system first established after independence inadvertently affected gender roles in its attempts to distance itself from its Catholic colonizer, Spain. Consequently, early in the twentieth century Cuba gave women property rights, created a no-fault divorce law, and provided public secular education to all children, including girls (Stoner and Perez, 2000). Laws were passed guaranteeing rights to working women, and Cuba legislated equal pay for equal work long before any of its neighbors in the western hemisphere even considered such actions. Later, with the Cuban Revolution in 1959, Castro's revolutionary reforms as a matter of course included women. That is, broad economic, political, and social reforms enacted as part of the socialist worldview necessarily also affected the lives of women in relation to literacy, health, employment, and the like (Stoner and Perez, 2000).

It should not be assumed from the occurrence of all these reform efforts in the twentieth century that Cuban women enjoy equal opportunities. According to Randall (1974), until the Cuban Revolution, women were victims of Spanish machismo and the Western objectification of women. At the beginning of the twentieth century, women were guided into so-called "feminine" occupations, with 70 percent of working women functioning as domestic servants, while most others labored in the tobacco industry. Even by World War I, 50 percent of Cuban working women were maids. And although the Boleshevik Revolution influenced Cuban women to join militant, left-wing, and feminist groups, even then, Stoner and Perez indicate, feminists came primarily from the upper classes and failed to address class and race issues. Of interest, despite Marxist influences at this time as well as during the Cuban Revolution of 1959, Cuban feminists focused on gaining power in the home.

Stoner and Perez (2000) argue that "inequities between men and women were not necessarily resolved. Because Cuban feminists did not directly attack the patriarchy, machismo continued unchecked" (p. 33). The Cuban revolution affected the lives of women in that improved economic standing was meant to result in their liberation: "Thus, women came to be viewed as workers, housewives, students, members of the militia, and revolutionary leaders, not as women with gender-specific problems" (Stoner and Perez, 2000, p. 118). The challenge for women after the 1959 revolution was the juggling of work and family obligations. It took some time for the government to understand that reforms related specifically to gender issues were needed. Hence, in 1974, the Family Code was revised: "Based on the ideal of complete equality between women and men in marriage, divorce, and family, it stated that both partners have the same obligations and duties concerning the protection, upbringing, support, and education of their children" (Miller, 1991, p. 190). In addition, according to Randall (as cited in Miller, 1991), paid housework legislation and a campaign to degender work roles ensued. Even Castro (as quoted in Miller, 1991) has said that "the work of the Revolution is not complete—there must be real equality for women" (p. 189). As a result, although some disadvantages are still felt by women, Dominguez (1978) reports that Cuban women are well represented in medical schools as well as in other professional and academic areas. Similarly, Stoner and Perez (2000) suggest that Cubans have come to expect that some of the country's political leaders will be women.

As for the roles of Puerto Rican women, Perez y Gonzalez (2000) notes that traditionally the Puerto Rican family structure was based on absolute male authority. *Marianismo,* which anchors women's roles securely in the private sphere, includes "obedience, submission, fidelity, meekness, and humility" (Perez y Gonzalez, 2000, p. 19). However, this traditional "ideal" may be far from reality. Whalen (1998) reports that contrary to stereotypes about Puerto Rican families "women are not completely subordinate to their husbands. . . . It was observed that they make as much of a contribution as do their husbands" (p. 221). Historically, Puerto Rican women forged strong roles for themselves out of economic necessity. Morales (1998) argues that the

> female head of household is not a new thing with us. The men left for Mexico and Venezuela and Peru. They left every which way they could, and they left us behind. We got our own rice and beans. . . . We were never still; our hands were always busy. . . . Ours is the work they decided to call unwork. The tasks as necessary as air. Not a single thing they did could have been done without us. (p. xxxii)

Although Morales's comments focus on the unpaid labor undertaken by Puerto Rican women by necessity, they also became part of the paid labor force, at least by the time that Puerto Rico was colonized by the United States in 1898. In addition, although the absence of men created a vacuum that Puerto Rican women adeptly filled, this does not mean that women found themselves on an equal footing with men. To the contrary, according to Rodriguez (1998) and Ortiz (1998), in the nineteenth century Puerto Rican women labored primarily in stereotypically "female jobs" as maids, laundresses, and seamstresses. The U.S. program Operation Bootstrap that intended to bring industrial jobs to the island also had the effect of bringing more Puerto Rican women into factory jobs. In addition, women played a significant role in both the tobacco and needlework industries. By 1935, three out of four tobacco workers were women (Baldrich, 1998). According to both Ortiz (1998) and Baldrich (1998), many of these women organized, becoming involved in trade unions and in the socialist party. Baldrich also notes, however, that as more women entered the tobacco industry, wages for women cigar makers went down and male cigar makers earned more than their female counterparts.

Similar to their Cuban sisters, Puerto Rican women face the challenges of two jobs: full-time work outside the home as well as full-time work as homemakers. According to Ortiz (1998), this situation led Puerto Rican women to expect, in their families, a "greater participation in decision making and information sharing" (p. 52).

Cuban and Puerto Rican Immigration to the United States

Although we generally tend to associate Cuban migration to the United States with the Cuban Revolution of 1959, the first Cuban immigration to Florida dates back to the 1830s. According to Masud-Piloto (1998), Cuban cigar manufacturers relocated to Key West to avoid high tariffs. In addition, once the war in Cuba for independence from Spain began in the 1860s, over 100,000 Cubans sought refuge in the United States, settling in New York, Philadelphia, and Boston, but mainly in Florida.

During the first half of the twentieth century, small groups of Cubans moved to the United States for various political reasons. Some opposed President Gerardo Machado y Morales in the 1920s and 1930s, and between 1940 and 1958 a few Cubans immigrated to the United States because of political disagreement with Cuban presidents Batista y Zaldívar, San Martín, and Carlos Prío Scocarrás.

A series of waves of immigration from Cuba to the United States began in 1959, when revolutionary forces overthrew Batista and Castro became president of socialist Cuba. According to Masud-Piloto (1998), the first of these immigrants were people who had worked for Batista and feared political reprisal. These were followed by Castro's own defectors. However, the largest group of immigrants at this time was the elite class of businesspeople and professionals who were essentially nonpolitical. Due to the U.S. government's cold-war policies toward all things communist, the United States reacted to this situation by developing an open-door policy toward Cuban immigrants. As long as someone claimed he or she was fleeing from communist oppression, the United States waived requirements for a visa and granted refugee status. According to Masud-Piloto (1998), the U.S. government even offered free airlifts from Cuba during the early 1960s. More than 215,000 Cubans entered the United States at the time, with more than 33,000 settling in Miami in 1961 alone.

Gonzalez-Pando (1998) reports that a second wave of Castro-era immigration occurred from 1965 to 1973. Competing arguments exist as to what caused this wave of immigration. Some scholars contend that economic woe, not politics, was the culprit; others cite reasons related to government policies under Castro: obligatory military service, government confiscation of private farms larger than 167 acres, and a system of standardized wages for all nonagricultural workers. Added to these factors was Castro's announcement in 1965 that he would open the Port of Camarioca for all Cubans who wanted to leave the country because they had family in the United States. Gonzalez-Pando notes that immigrants of this area were primarily of the middle class, but included some working-class and peasant Cubans. Nearly 270,000 Cubans left the island during this time period.

The Mariel boatlift of 1980 is probably one of the most well-known moments in Cuban immigration. After armed Cubans wanting to leave the island forced their way into the Peruvian embassy and killed a guard, 10,000 Cubans entered the embassy grounds and Castro responded by opening up the Port of Mariel to Cubans at the embassy as well as to any Cubans whose relatives in the United States came to claim them. The large influx of Cuban immigrants led the United States to change its policy, ending the era of granting automatic refugee status. Masud-Piloto (1998) reports that nearly 100,000 Cubans entered the Miami area. Then in 1985, the United States issued visas to 3,000 political prisoners, their families, and an additional 20,000 Cubans.

Finally, the most recent wave of immigration from Cuba to the United States is typically explained by the collapse of the Soviet Union and withdrawal of its economic support to Cuba. Thus, the 1990s is known for the many Cuban rafters attempting to reach the United

States. Currently, 20,000 visas to the United States are issued annually to Cubans wishing to relocate in the United States. Dominguez (1978) argues that "The exiles had left partly of their own will, partly induced by the government, and partly enticed by the United States" (p. 140).

The history of immigration from Puerto Rico to the United States is perhaps less overtly political, but nevertheless is closely related to U.S. policies and to economics, both on the island and in the United States. Although some writers claim that migration from Puerto Rico was the result of overpopulation on the island, others such as Muniz (1998) reject this interpretation and note that the colonial relationship between the island and the United States must be considered. Muniz argues that a dramatic move toward capitalism in Puerto Rico was initiated by the United States, and that although some elite Puerto Ricans benefited from this change, it resulted in poverty for most Puerto Ricans. After World War II, U.S. electronic media enticed many Puerto Ricans who had served during the war and were already familiar with the United States. In short, migration from Puerto Rico is linked to the U.S. economy. If opportunities on the mainland rise, immigration to the United States increases; in tough economic times, Puerto Ricans often return to the island.

Three basic time periods are generally associated with immigration from Puerto Rico to the United States. First, from 1900 to 1945, what Perez y Gonzalez (2000) calls the Pioneer Migration occurred. Approximately 2,000 Puerto Ricans arrived in the United States each year, most settling in New York City. According to Perez y Gonzalez, the majority of first-wave immigrants were urban, well educated, and were skilled workers. In addition, more men and whites immigrated than women and blacks. The second wave of immigration is often called the Great Migration, occurring between 1946 and 1964. During this time, over 34,000 Puerto Ricans entered the United States every year. Perez y Gonzalez (2000) notes that this second wave of immigrants had fewer skills, were younger, and were less educated. More of the immigrants during this period came from rural areas, were poor, and were darker skinned. The ratio between men and women was nearly even. Finally, the third and ongoing wave of immigration is called the Revolving Door. This wave of immigration started in 1965 and still continues. The revolving door describes a pattern of Puerto Ricans traveling back and forth between Puerto

Rico and the United States caused, at least in part, by economic conditions. By 1973, 40 percent of the island's population was living in the United States (U.S. Commission on Civil Rights, 1976).

The Effect of Immigration on Cuban and Puerto Rican Women

As might be expected, prerevolution-Cuban women immigrated to the United States for different reasons than did postrevolution-Cuban women. According to Doran, Satterfield, and Stade (1988), before 1959 Cuban women sought education, careers, and extended visits to the United States, but above all they wanted freedom and independence from restrictions imposed by their families and by traditional Cuban culture. These women usually came alone, but often with help from wealthy relatives. Due to their poor English skills, many of these women ended up doing factory work, primarily in the garment industry. Doran, Satterfield, and Stade (1988) suggest that first-generation Cuban-American women developed a dual identity—a more traditional one in the home than the one they adopted in their more public roles as students and workers.

After the revolution of 1959, Cuban women immigrated to the United States under very different circumstances. They came as part of a family unit, rather than alone, and their reasons for immigrating had little to do with self-determination and more to do with their new identity as political exiles. Doran, Satterfield, and Stade (1988) note that although the first generation of postrevolution immigrant women were from the wealthy and upper-middle classes, later immigrants were of the working class. Women left Cuba to preserve the family unit and to escape the island's new communist ideology. Of interest, although prerevolution immigrant women sought independence, postrevolution immigrant women were comfortable with their traditional roles as wives and mothers; hence, they were uneasy about the changes in gender roles socialism promised to produce.

Ironically, once they arrived in the United States, most Cuban women quickly realized that they would need to work to help support their families. Fox (1973) reports that in traditional Cuban culture work by women in the public sphere had been considered tantamount to the destruction of the family. Yet in the United States, if women's earnings could help raise the status of the family, then paid labor outside the home was justified. In addition, according to Prieto (1987), unlike the jobs women would be expected to do in revolutionary Cuba, in the United States women originally worked in industries typically associated with women and the private sphere. Garcia (1996) says they worked as seamstresses, domestics, cooks, dishwashers, waitresses, and cashiers. In addition, they developed businesses that helped working women in their communities, starting day care centers and housekeeping, delivery, laundry, and dry-cleaning services.

Although entry into the paid labor force may have been one of the most significant changes Cuban women faced in the United States, Garcia argues that they did not reject their cultural background, but instead adapted old customs and traditions to new situations in order to meet their needs. As Garcia puts it, cultural compromises were forged. Boone (1989) further explains that new roles were added to their traditional roles as wives and mothers. Boone uses the phrase *feminine assertion* to describe the dual character of the lives of Cuban-American women. At the same time that they maintained their passionate devotion to family, Cuban-American women sought to enhance their potential through education and work. In this way, they could more effectively protect and improve the lives of their families. According to Boone, although machismo still exists, its value system includes more than just the male expectation of being the king of his castle. A Cuban-American woman receives support from her husband to develop her own life, as this is thought to reflect well on him. Finally, although Garcia notes that Cuban-American women traditionally did not play central roles in politics within their communities, they did provide community support to political campaigns started by Cuban-American men. As might be expected, then, Cuban-American women painted political banners, made telephone calls, fed protesters, wrote letters, and marched in demonstrations. Furthermore, they established a number of women's political organizations that functioned as auxiliaries to their male counterparts.

Somewhat similar to women from prerevolution Cuba, both Aranda (1997) and Ortiz (1998) explain that Puerto Rican women immigrated to the United States independently from men. That is, they did not follow their husbands to the United States, but had become part of the colonial economy in Puerto Rico, were accustomed to working outside the home, and came to the United States to pursue potential economic opportunities. Ortiz indicates that from the outset Puerto Rican women faced discrimination on the job in the United States based on both gender and ethnicity. Yet according to Perez y Gonzalez (2000) Puerto Rican women were more likely than men to find work in the United States. Whalen argues (as quoted in Delgado and Rodriguez, 1998) that "Migration changed the context within which they did this work, but it was not a novelty to balance the reality or possibilities of paid employment with the other responsibilities of home" (p. 222). As did their Cuban counterparts, many of these women performed factory work. Ortiz (1998) notes that Puerto Rican women in the United States worked in the garment, tobacco, and meatpacking industries. They also provided domestic and clerical services, and some of these women worked in professional sectors.

Puerto Rican women played a significant and vital role in developing and supporting their communities in the United States. Ortiz (1998) reports that Puerto Rican women in New York City functioned as teachers for young Spanish-speaking children, helping to develop a bilingual and bicultural school curriculum there. Along with this, Puerto Rican women started local community organizations in an effort to empower Hispanic communities, particularly in relation to education and to teaching opportunities. Rodriguez (1998) notes that Puerto Rican women have been "crucial mobilizing forces" in major cities such as Boston and New York (p. 31). He further notes that Puerto Rican professionals in New York City gathered important social and economic information useful to their communities, and they participated in volunteer, social, and religious organizations. They have played important community leadership roles.

Although the circumstances that led to immigration for Cuban and Puerto Rican women may have been different, both groups had to adapt to their new host country, and both groups of women played significant roles in supporting and building their communities in the United States.

ANALYSIS OF ETHNOGRAPHIC FINDINGS

Demographics

Twenty-five women completed the survey and interview. The women ranged in age from eighteen to over sixty-six, with the majority falling between twenty-six and fifty-five. Two women were over the age of sixty-six. Fourteen of the women were married, and eleven were single. Household incomes ranged from $15,000 to over $76,000, with six earning from $26,000 to $35,000 and six earning over $76,000. Six of the women were high school graduates, six of the women had completed community college, seven had undergraduate degrees, four attended graduate or post-graduate school, and two did not indicate their level of education. Of the twenty-five women, fourteen responded "white" to the question of race, two identified themselves as Puerto Rican, two gave no response, and one each identified themselves as follows: Hispanic, Cuban American, white Cuban American, Spanish, white Spanish, and "multi." In terms of ethnicity, fourteen women identified themselves as Hispanic, five as Cuban American, and one each as Cuban, Cuban Puerto Rican, Cuban Irish, Spanish, Puerto Rican, and American.

Analysis of Survey

On the statements that were designed to evaluate participants' level of agreement versus disagreement regarding their personal use of traditional power attributes, only four attributes received majority agreement (see Table 6.1). These attributes included resources (twenty-one), competition (twenty), struggle (eighteen), and authority, with which seventeen women agreed. Although the women identified with only four of the traditional power attributes, the majority agreed that society overwhelmingly uses most of the traditional power attributes. For example, twenty-three of the women said society uses authority, twenty noted the use of resources and sway over others, nineteen believed society uses wealth, competition, and control-over, and seventeen named domination. In fact, the only traditional power attribute that the women felt society did not use was force.

It was clear that the women identified with the general society in using resources, competition, and authority, all traditional power attributes, and they agreed that neither they nor society use force. However, a major disconnect was felt with the use of the attributes domination, winning, resistance, physical strength, control-over, coercion, sway others, and wealth. In each case, a majority of the women agreed that society uses these traditional power attributes, but they personally disagreed with their use.

TABLE 6.1. Latin American Women: Personal Feelings Regarding Power and Society versus Power and Self

Traditional Power and Society				Traditional Power and Self			
Attribute	**Agree**	**Disagree**	**N A/D**	**Attribute**	**Agree**	**Disagree**	**N A/D**
Domination	17	6	2	Domination	5	16	4
Conflict	12	6	7	Conflict	11	9	5
Force	7	15	3	Force	7	16	2
Win	15	6	4	Win	5	18	2
Struggle	13	7	5	Struggle	18	4	3
Resistance	13	9	3	Resistance	2	18	5
Competition	19	2	4	Competition	20	3	2
Physical strength	15	8	2	Physical strength	4	14	7
Control-over	19	3	3	Control-over	7	16	2
Sway others	20	3	2	Sway others	6	14	5
Wealth	19	5	1	Wealth	8	16	1
Authority	23	0	2	Authority	17	5	3
Resources	20	2	3	Resources	21	1	3
Coercion	14	4	7	Coercion	1	18	6

n = 25
N A/D = Neither agree nor disagree
Note: Where totals equal less than *n*, there were instances of no response.

In the survey statements that examine empowerment, a majority of the women agreed with three of the five attributes: compassion, companionship, and competence (see Table 6.2). Of interest, twelve of the women neither agreed nor disagreed with the statement "I feel that it is important to be a part of a collective regardless of whether or not it benefits me as long as I empower others." We believe this ambivalence toward the idea of a collectivity may be explained by the fact that the majority of women valued independence (twenty-two) when asked to respond to statements concerning that personal authority attribute (see Table 6.3). The only two personal authority attributes that received higher levels of agreement than independence were knowledge, with which twenty-four of the women agreed, followed by the ability to choose (twenty-three). Self-determination received

TABLE 6.2. Latin American Women: Personal Feelings Regarding Empowerment

Attribute	Agree	Disagree	N A/D
Collectivity	6	7	12
Companionship	15	6	4
Compassion	17	1	7
Consensus	10	5	10
Competence	15	4	6

n = 25
N A/D = Neither agree nor disagree

TABLE 6.3. Latin American Women: Personal Feelings Regarding Personal Authority

Attribute	Agree	Disagree	N A/D
Ability to take action	19	4	2
Ability to choose	23	2	0
Self-determination	22	1	2
Knowledge	24	1	0
Independence	22	2	1

n = 25
N A/D = Neither agree nor disagree

twenty-two agreements, and the ability to take action received nineteen agreements.

The women overwhelmingly agreed with all of the reciprocal empowerment statements: knowledge, competence, independence, the ability to choose and take action, and self-determination all received twenty-two or more agreements (see Table 6.4). The attribute receiving the lowest level of agreement, consensus, still received fourteen. This was not surprising considering the fact that when responding to the traditional power statements, the women agreed with the idea of competition—an attribute which can be seen as the antithesis of consensus.

Analysis of the Interview

The following is an analysis of the relationship of the five introductory questions to the four power models. We then discuss the in-

TABLE 6.4. Latin American Women: Personal Feelings Regarding Reciprocal Empowerment

Attribute	Agree	Disagree	N A/D
Mutual responsiveness	18	3	4
Competence	22	1	2
Compassion	20	2	3
Independence	22	1	2
Ability to choose	22	1	2
Collectivity	19	2	4
Companionship	20	0	5
Ability to take action	22	1	2
Self-determination	22	1	2
Mutual engagement	20	2	3
Knowledge	23	0	2
Consensus	14	1	10
Mutual attention	21	0	4
Mutual empathy	17	2	6

n = 25
N A/D = Neither agree nor disagree

terviewees' responses regarding how power *is used* and *should be used* in the areas of work, family, religion, and politics (see Tables 6.5 and 6.6).

Introductory Questions

In responding to the first question regarding the meaning of power to them as individuals, thirteen of the women used terms that could be directly related to the traditional power model: strength, wealth, money, force, persuasion (sway-over), and control. These statements, though generally brief, were direct. They included the following: "[Power is] control and strength, control over my life, my job, my family, my project"; "Power very coldly means control and order to a certain place and relates to productivity of other individuals"; "Using force on other people"; and "Power means strength."

TABLE 6.5. Latin American Women: Responses to Introductory Interview Questions and the Relationship of These Responses to the Power Models

Introductory Interview Questions	Traditional Power	Empowerment	Personal Authority	Reciprocal Empowerment
What does the word *power* mean to you as an individual?	13	1	7	0
What do you think the word *power* means in American society today?	18	0	0	0
What do you think the word *power* means in your culture?	11	0	3	1
As a woman, what kind of power do you think you have in U.S. society?	4	3	7	0
As a Latin American woman, what do you think the word *power* means in your culture?	2	1	3	0

n = 25
Note: Total numbers may not match *n* since in some cases responses could not be associated with a power model. Zero equals no responses or responses could not be associated with a model.

TABLE 6.6. Latin American Women: Interview Responses to Questions About Work, Family, Religion, and Politics

How Power *Is Used*

	Traditional Power	Empowerment	Personal Authority	Reciprocal Empowerment
Work	10	2	1	0
Family	11	0	4	0
Religion	0	0	1	0
Politics	2	0	0	0

How Power *Should Be Used*

	Traditional Power	Empowerment	Personal Authority	Reciprocal Empowerment
Work	1	0	1	1
Family	1	2	0	0
Religion	0	1	0	0
Politics	0	1	0	0

$n = 25$

Note: Total numbers may not match *n* since in some cases responses could not be associated with a power model. Zero equals no responses or responses could not be associated with a model.

Personal authority attributes surfaced as the second-highest form of power described by these women. Seven women used terms such as independence, choice, and knowledge. Statements included "to have the knowledge to help others," "to be independent, secure, and safe," and "having the right to do, say, and choose." Only one individual made a statement that could be associated with empowerment. She said, "It has a lot to do with consensus." However, within the same statement she also associated her individual power with control. Attributes specifically related to reciprocal empowerment did not emerge in response to this question.

Other terms that emerged but were not associated with any of the four power models included decision making, intelligence, and equality. For example, one woman said that for her power means "the ability to make changes or decisions on my own," and another said, "achievement, the power to make decisions for yourself as well as the corporation you represent." One response was, "If you are intelligent, you can obtain power," and another associated power with "equality in society [that is] necessary to reach the income potential that I know I am qualified for."

The second question asked the women what they think power means in U.S. society today. Eighteen of the women chose attributes associated with the traditional power model. As in their response to the first question, control and wealth or money surfaced. They made statements including the following: power is "who has control over whom, like in government, the workplace, or the family"; "greed and money"; "wealth, it seems only rich people are powerful"; "I think power is related to wealth; it's also related to how much you've got in terms of what you drive and what you wear"; and "Power is viewed as a tool for control. It has direct correlation to controlling people and events, sometimes without a lot of thought or compassion behind it. [It is] sometimes used for personal gain, political gain, and things of that nature." One woman said power in American society is "to be white and to have money." None of the women described power in U.S. society in terms that we could associate with empowerment, personal authority, or reciprocal empowerment. As with the previous question, however, other terms surfaced, including equality, self-sufficiency, and politics.

Again, traditional power attributes appeared most frequently when the women were asked what the word *power* means in Latin American culture. Several women made statements using the terms money, wealth, and control, and many individual statements contained terms such as competition, strength, and resources. The following are some examples: "To be of high class, have studied in a good private school, and to come from a wealthy family"; "having absolute control"; "playing a strong role in your family and church"; and "being a Puerto Rican woman, power means control."

Two statements could be associated with the personal authority model. One woman said, "[Power in the culture means] to be independent, make decisions, and give the best to your family." However, the second response combined both personal authority and traditional power. This individual said, "[Power in our culture is] being independent and having control over others." Although no statements specifically related to the empowerment model, one statement combined personal authority and empowerment, illustrating reciprocal empowerment: "In my culture, it [power] means financial stability, being well educated, and having the appropriate resources to be able to empower others." Other terms that arose which we could not associate with the existing power models included politics, freedom, respect, and decision making.

A dramatic change in the perceptions of power occurred when the women were asked about themselves in terms of the kinds of power they have as women in U.S. society and as women what they think power means in their own ethnic culture. In the question concerning women, power, and the United States, only four of twenty-five used terms associated with traditional power, making statements such as, "I think I have just as much power as anyone else. My power comes from the people who surround me, the people who help to mold me and my ideas and psyche. In my circle of influence I believe I have a strong voice and a strong opinion," and "If I utilize all resources available, I believe I have enough power to get what I need."

In response to this question, personal authority surfaced more strongly with seven women making statements such as, "I have the power to make my own decisions and choices," "power to make changes so that I can live differently from my family. I think women are more independent," and "independence, freedom of speech, democracy. I do whatever I want with myself." Two statements that we associated with empowerment follow: "[I have] the power to help and teach people," and "I feel that the majority of my power lies in my ability to help the less fortunate." We could relate no response to reciprocal empowerment. However, the terms freedom, voice, and decision making again surfaced as indicators of power.

In the question concerning women, power, and Latin American culture, traditional power attributes appeared only twice and both times the reference was to money or wealth. Three of the women, all Cubans, provided responses having to do with personal authority. In two cases women made reference to independence: "What power means to me is independence and more equal rights for women versus communistic beliefs and no rights," and "Power in Cuba is about abuse. The one who has the power is the one who abuses us. For Cuban Americans power is independence." Only one statement utilized an empowerment attribute, consensus. In addition, freedom was mentioned more than once.

Work

Seventeen of the women said they were employed outside the household, seven were not, and one woman did not respond. When asked if people have different kinds of power where they work, sixteen said yes, and one said no.

Only three women used traditional power attributes when asked what kind of power they have on their jobs. One woman said, "I have the power to communicate; that is my strength," another woman, indicating a position of authority, said, "It's kind of a powerful position because it entails looking at other people's work, pointing out other opportunities, and telling them whether they can release this product or not depending on the quality of their work." Another woman, although not indicating the specific kind of power she has, said she has power over the children she takes care of.

There was one reference each to empowerment and personal authority: "I have power because I help people at work, and I get what they need," and "I have the power to set my own hours, make my own decisions, and determine my income with the hours I choose to work." We could not attribute any of the statements here to reciprocal empowerment. However, other terms that emerged were decision making and respect.

When we asked the women to give specific examples of how power *is used* where they work, ten women provided answers related to traditional power (see Table 6.6). For example, one woman said, "Some people use it aggressively. It's a personality thing; they think if they scream louder you can hear them better. Some people take little issues and make big issues out of them because that makes them feel powerful." Another woman said, "Many opportunities come across my desk, and I secure those resources so I can be with influential people of affluence. Along with that comes the perception of power." A third woman said, "You listen to whatever your boss tells you to do. He has control over what is going on, and you have to do what he says or you will lose your job."

In response to the question asking the women how they think power *should be used* on the job, we could associate only a few of the responses with any of the four power models. One could be associated with traditional power: "I believe if you don't have some kind of authority people tend to slack off." One statement each could be associated with personal authority and reciprocal empowerment. For example, one woman said, "to accomplish things for the benefit of the common good of mankind."

Family

Eighteen of the women described their immediate families as extended, and five as nuclear. Two of the women chose not to describe their immediate families. Ten of the women indicated that men were the heads of their households, while seven identified a woman. Four women described the head of the house as a shared position, two did not respond to the question, and two identified other people (such as an ex-boyfriend).

When the women were asked what they think the word *power* means in their family, they gave six examples of traditional power, three examples of personal authority, and one example of reciprocal empowerment. The traditional power terms included money and control, whereas personal authority terms had to do with independence and education. The single reciprocal empowerment statement follows: "[In my family power means] independence and helping others. They feel empowered when they are in a position to help others and also to be completely independent as I am." Again, the terms freedom and decision making appeared several times. The next set of questions asked the women to identify who makes the major decisions concerning children, housework, and finances. In terms of children, thirteen of the women identified a female, only one woman mentioned a male, and seven of the women indicated that this responsibility was shared. Two women indicated that the question was not applicable, and two women did not respond. As for housework, seventeen women identified a female, no males were mentioned, and five said this responsibility was shared. One woman said her husband had hired the maid. Two of the women did not respond. In terms of household finances, five women identified a female, eight mentioned a male, ten said this was a shared responsibility, and two did not respond.

Twenty of the women responded "yes" to the question of whether people have different kinds of power in the family. Of these, five women elaborated with responses that indicated the traditional power model was demonstrated in their families, and they mentioned that this power had to do with money.

When asked to discuss the kind of power they think they have in their immediate families, six women used traditional power attributes mostly having to do with strength, control, and money. For example, one woman said, "I help with the bills even though I'm not in charge of them, and I am strong." Another said, "I have the power to make financial as well as domestic decisions," while a third said, "A lot—what I say goes, except my husband has power over the monetary issues." Two women indicated personal authority attributes, both having to do with education. Other terms mentioned by the women which we could not clearly associate with any of the power models included decision making, equality, and respect. In addition, one woman referred to the power to protect her family, one said she derived her power from her age, and one said of her children that she has the "power to love and care for them."

Five of the women chose not to respond to the question seeking specific examples of how power *is used* in their families (see Table 6.6). Four women responded using traditional power attributes, again having to do with strength and money. One woman indicated personal authority when she said "Choosing the right education and helping my children learn right from wrong." The other fifteen women who responded did not actually offer specific examples, but rather made general statements such as, "The Puerto Rican culture has patriarchy—where the men make all decisions, except in San Juan where there's more liberation due to Americanization." Decision making topped the list of descriptors mentioned in response to this question. Nine of the women spoke of making decisions in the family, although some referred to male decision making and some to their own ability to decide.

When asked to describe how they believe power *should be used* in the family, only one woman used a term related to traditional power. That term was strength. However, although saying that everyone should be strong, she also felt that power should be used equally. Two women described the way they believe power should be used in terms that can be associated with empowerment: "Power should be used to help family members become better people," and one wanted to empower her children through education. Eight of the women talked of equality or of sharing equally. Five of the women said that how power is currently being used is fine. One woman said, "I think it [power] shouldn't be used in the family. I don't see why someone has to have power over somebody else."

Religion

Thirteen of the twenty-five women said they belong to religious groups. When asked what religious group they belong to, twelve of the women said they were Catholic, and one said, "I was a Buddhist for five and a half years. This is unusual for an Hispanic woman. I've created an inner religion for myself."

When asked if people have different kinds of power in their religions, twelve of the women replied "yes." Of those who gave more extensive answers, seven mentioned priests in relation to power, and a few mentioned the pope or other religious leaders. One specifically described religious power as hierarchical. Two women associated power with God, as in, "I just believe in God's power." Descriptions associated with the traditional power model surfaced only twice in response to this question, in both instances having to do with money. One woman, for example, suggested, "People who give a lot think they have a right to more power and influence over matters."

When asked what kind of power they have in their religions, eight of the women indicated they believe they have little or no power. One simply said "zero," and another said, "I personally have no power." Six of the women replied in ways that suggest they believe they have some power. One woman said, "I am my religion! I think that everyone has power, even though we are each only single grains of sand. If there were no grains there would be no desert. You have the ability to be everything, so of course you have total power." We were able to associate one of the women's responses to personal authority. This woman said, "I think I have the power of choice. I choose to be an active member and to take my son there and participate." Other answers included talk of belief and prayer, and one woman mentioned the ability to teach her students about God (she is a Catholic preschool teacher).

In describing specific examples of how power *is used* in their religions, seven of the women referred to their priests (priests giving communion, interpreting the word of God, and listening to confession) (see Table 6.6). Traditional power references were made when two of the women talked about donating money to the church. Other descriptions of traditional power included the following: "The priest is the authority figure at that level. He gives us permission to eat meat on Friday." One example of empowerment emerged with one woman's statement "to serve instead of to lead."

When asked what kind of power they, as women, have in their religions, nine of the women indicated they have little or none: "None, it's a man's world," and "I do not believe women have power because they are not allowed to do what men do." None of the responses were directly related to any of the four power models.

Little agreement occurred when the women responded to the question, "How do you think power *should be* used in your religion?" The only type of power evident in their responses was empowerment when one woman said, "The more powerful should help the people more. I'm talking about helping the children, giving money out to organizations. We should do a lot more, and the person with the most power should be in charge of it." Three women spoke of equality, two talked about using power to attract people to the church, and one each mentioned love, justice, liberation, and actualization. One woman said, "They should allow women to become priests." Three women responded that they do not think power should be used in religion. As one of them put it: "I believe strongly there should be no God when it comes to God."

Politics

When it came to politics, Latin American women generally had little to say. When asked if they were affiliated with a political organization or cause, only four said yes. These four included three Democrats and one Republican. When asked if people have different kinds of power in their political organizations, three of the women said yes, and one of the women who earlier had said she is not affiliated with a political organization commented: "Yes, I dislike it because people manipulate things for their own purpose. All issues come down to finances and money. If you pay enough, those in power will push your cause. There is very little ethical power behind political power." This traditional power reference was the only one that matched any of the four perspectives of power.

Voting was the response given by three of the women when they were asked what kind of power they have in their political organizations or causes. When asked for specific examples of how power is used in their political groups, one woman again mentioned voting, two women made reference to traditional power when they talked about the role of money in politics, and one of these also mentioned resources (see Table 6.6). When asked how power *should be used* in politics, the few women who responded used empowerment references by talking about helping people. One woman said, "I think we need a group of people to truly represent the needs of their constituents, and more power needs to be given back to the constituents."

In response to the final interview question asking how they see the power roles of women who are affiliated with politics, eight of the women seemed optimistic with statements such as, "The future is very bright," and "There is tremendous potential." One respondent was more specific: "More people are referencing women when it comes to political issues; they are no longer left in the dark. Women are now seen as having a voice. The role of women should be to show their strength in voting. Be strong in their beliefs and back down for no one." Yet nine of the women cast a less optimistic picture of the political landscape. These responses included the following: "I feel there is still a great lack of female competition and success in politics. There is a great disparity. Look at the numbers in Congress and the Senate"; "There is no way a woman would be President . . . maybe in four years or a hundred years"; "Women seem to have very little power in politics"; and "I think women in politics are not considered as important as men." One woman suggested that "power is not the best word to describe women's politics. Women are becoming more educated and then go on to get jobs involved within politics," and another respondent said, "Women are more sensitive than men. Women are affiliated in or involved with politics because they are fighting for something, because they really feel it, and not because of personal interests. Women are becoming more powerful than before—in politics, in society, in family, and in everything. On the other hand, it's very different to see a lot of women in politics with complete power." Although some of the women were optimistic and others were not, these last two responses suggest that political power, in relation to women, needs to be cast in a light different from that of traditional power.

CONCLUSION

We begin by discussing the forms of power preferred by the Latin American women and by comparing the survey results to those obtained from the interview. Finally, we discuss terms or statements that emerged in the interview which we could not clearly associate with our original descriptions of the four power models.

Results of the survey indicate that the Latin American women who participated overwhelmingly agreed with the reciprocal empowerment statements, with its combination of personal authority and empowerment attributes. These women agreed with all the personal authority statements, but empowerment statements on their own did not receive as much agreement.

On the other hand, in response to the interview questions concerning what power means to them as individuals, both within society and within their ethnic culture, the women made statements overwhelmingly associated with the traditional power model. This was followed by personal authority. In answering the questions about what power means to them as women in U.S. society and their own culture, personal authority terms took precedence, followed by traditional power, and then empowerment.

Regarding both work and family, a large number of the women saw traditional power attributes being utilized. This evidently was incongruent with their ideas of about how and what kind of power *should be used.* Here, attributes clearly associated with the four perspectives of power were barely evidenced. Our analysis of the data on religion and politics provided little to no information either on how these women felt power *is* or *should be used.* This could clearly be a result of the fact that only thirteen of the twenty-five women were affiliated with a religious group, and nine of these thirteen felt they have little or no power. As far as politics was concerned, only four of twenty-five were affiliated, and their only involvement was with voting.

Although some areas of the interview did not garner responses from the women that were directly linked to our descriptions of the four power paradigms, we did notice that three other descriptors were mentioned repeatedly within specific areas of the interview. Decision making was clearly in the lead as an attribute of choice for the women, particularly in how it relates to the use of power in the family (decisions about children, the home, and finances). Decision making as an example of power was also spread throughout the rest of the interview. Equality, equal, or sharing also appeared frequently, most strikingly in the women's discussions of how power should be used in the family, for example, "I believe both parents should share the power; everyone serves a purpose in all the decisions. In my family, I want more equality because my husband's Cuban ways have caused problems in our relationship. He can't comprehend American ways." Finally, freedom was another word that we noticed in both the introductory questions to the interview and in the question asking what family means. Of interest, all but one of the references to freedom were given by Cuban-American women. For example, in response to the question asking, as women, what they think the word *power* means in their culture, one participant said, "Two extremes: in Cuba, a doctrine; as a Cuban American, freedom." We believe freedom is particularly important to the South Florida community of Cuban Americans, many of whom consider themselves members of an exiled population.

Chapter 7

Middle Eastern-American Women and Power

FACT AND FICTION: A BRIEF HISTORY OF MIDDLE EASTERN-AMERICAN WOMEN

Similar to many other writers who have attempted to "name" this group of people, we are not entirely at ease with the label *Middle Eastern,* and discuss here various alternatives and why we have chosen to use it. Some writers, such as Kadi (1994), reject the term *Middle Eastern* in favor of *Arab.* Her argument is certainly compelling, as she notes that *Middle Eastern* is merely a label given to the Arab world by European colonizers "who named the region only as it related to their particular worldview" (p. xix). Understandably, she finds the term offensive and too much like "adopting the oppressor's language" (p. xix). In the introduction to her book, *Food for Our Grandmothers: Writings by Arab-American and Arab-Canadian Feminists,* Kadi outlines two other possible labels. Along with *Middle Eastern,* she also considers and then rejects the term *West Asian/North African,* which includes both Arab and Middle Eastern people, but makes Arabs invisible to Americans who would fail to consider Arabs as West Asians. She finally settles on the term *Arab American,* even though it excludes Armenia, Turkey, and Iran. She does so primarily because she wants to reinstate the word *Arab* to counteract negative connotations of Arabs. Kadi (1994) defines Arabs as

> Semitic people who originated on the Arabian Peninsula. The nineteen Arab countries on the west part of the Asian continent and the northern part of the African continent are: Lebanon, Palestine, Jordan, Syria, Kuwait, Saudi Arabia, Yemen, Oman, Bahrain, Tunisia, Algeria, Egypt, Sudan, Qatar, Mauritania,

> Iraq, Libya, Morocco, and the United Arab Emirates. (pp. xvii-xviii)

Abraham and Abraham (1983) offer essentially the same list of countries, but they omit Mauritania. Kadi (1994) goes on to point out that the nineteen Arab countries, "along with the non-Arab nations of Turkey, Armenia, and Iran, are often referred to as the Middle East. In some contexts, Somalia and Djibouti are also considered part of the Middle East" (p. xviii).

In considering the geographical, cultural, religious, and political implications of these various choices, we have chosen the term *Middle Eastern American,* not because it is a perfect fit or for its colonialist origins, but merely because it is a term broader than Arab and allows inclusion of all the women originating from this region that we had the opportunity to interview. Our participants claimed a variety of Middle Eastern ethnicities, including Palestinian, Lebanese, Omani, and Israeli.

Women in Middle Eastern Cultures

To talk about women from the Middle East is certainly a daunting task, one which we outline only briefly here. It is important to note that what is included here is a broad brush stroke that, although necessary to provide some context for our ethnographic findings, unfortunately does little to characterize distinct cultures, let alone distinct women within the region.

We begin with a brief discussion of Middle Eastern culture in general, with an emphasis on traditions found primarily in Arab cultures. To understand the role of Middle Eastern women requires an understanding of Middle Eastern values, particularly in terms of the family and, in some women's cases, its relationship to Islam. According to Abraham and Abraham (1983), a central feature of the culture is the position held by the extended family and the primary importance of family honor and status. As they explain: "in return for protection, identity and status, the family demands conformity and the subordination of individual will and interests. The honor or dishonor of an individual reflects on the entire family" (p. 15). This theme reverberates in Kadi's (1994) statement that the family and self are really one and the same in Arab cultures.

According to Abraham and Abraham (1983), Middle Eastern family values include a competitive spirit, an ethic of hard work, thrift, perseverance, shrewdness, and conservatism. Fear of shame and of dishonoring the family generally prevents crime and indulgence. Although much of this value system remains intact, modernization and exposure to the Western world—even for those remaining in the Middle East—has had a significant effect on the traditional extended family. Even though recent anti-Western sentiments resulted in some cases in attempts to return to purely Arab or Islamic traditions, Minces (1984) argues that urbanization has broken the original structure of the extended family.

As one might expect, since family is of primary importance to the traditional Middle Eastern family and since women are often associated primarily with the domestic sphere, the role of Middle Eastern women is inexorably tied to family life. Minces notes that the experience of Arab women is really not exceptional in that, historically, women's roles have not differed much from women of nearly any other culture worldwide. In pre-Islamic times, women were considered chattel. Despite what Shukri (1996) calls gender equality in the sacred text of Islam, the Quran, Minces argues that women in the Muslim world remain fundamentally subordinate.

We believe it is important to distinguish here between the words of the Quran and actual Muslim practices. Wadud (1999) examines the Quran carefully in order to argue that no gender inequalities are contained within it. Minces (1984) agrees that the arrival of Islam to Arabia in the seventh century led to social reforms that improved the status of women. Under Islamic law, women were entitled to inherit and own property without an intermediary, and women could be guardians of minors. The Quran did not prevent women from engaging in a public life, and women were entitled to an equal education. However, old customs and beliefs die hard, and pre-Islamic traditions almost immediately began to permeate Islam. The culture remained patriarchal and patrilineal, and, according to Shukri (1996), the continued subordination of women was based on the belief that men needed to be protected from women due to women's power to distract men from religious piety.

Shukri (1996) argues that gender roles in Middle Eastern—and particularly Islamic—cultures are pronounced, including the segregation and seclusion of women. Gender segregation, however, does not exclusively apply to women. Cultural spaces can be allocated to either sex. It is possible that such segregation can be both constraining and liberating. The family functions as both an arena from which to control women as well as a source of power for women. The maintenance of family pride, in large part, is based on its members' conformity to norms of behaviors, and Shukri believes that an integral part of the men's honor is dependent upon the behavior of the women in the family. Likewise, the role of wife, mother, the required deference to one's mother-in-law, and restrictions on freedom of movement and association may be stifling. But although the pressures to conform may be great, Minces (1984) notes that the important roles of mother, teacher, and guardian of traditions offer women a rich and rewarding source of power. Both Minces (1984) and Shakir (1997) state that Arab women gain considerable power in the family as they grow older. Once a woman has given birth to sons she becomes more powerful. Likewise, in her postmenopausal years an Arab woman may impose her will on the entire family until eventually, as Shakir (1997) puts it, "her word becomes absolute" (p. 8).

Middle Eastern Immigration to the United States

In 1983 Abraham and Abraham estimated that there were around two to three million Arab Americans. In Orfalea's (1988) study of Arab immigration to the United States he indicates that during the first wave of immigration (1878-1924) over 106,000 people, mostly from Greater Syria (including present-day Syria, Lebanon, and Palestine) and mostly Christian, came to the United States. During the second (1948-1966) and third (1967-present) waves of immigration combined, over 309,000 Arabs, mostly Muslim, arrived in the United States. The reasons for these periods of significant immigration are important.

Although the first Jews came to New York in 1654, Orfalea (1988) says it was two hundred years later that the first Arab immigrants settled in the United States. The first wave of Arab immigration, from 1878 to 1924, occurred for five reasons identified by Orfalea (1988): "the wooing and salubrious role of American missionaries in Syria; the shattering of the religious mosaic in 1860; economic uncertainties exacerbated by overpopulation and the land squeeze; the death throes of the Ottoman Turkish empire and ensuing lawlessness, taxation, and conscription; and the starvation of one-quarter of Lebanon's population during the Great War" (p. 53). The impetus for the second wave of immigrants, from 1948 to 1966, is less complex, however, as the forced removal of Palestinians due to the establishment of Israel in 1948 led to the arrival in the United States of numerous refugees and exiles. This immigration wave was, unlike the first one, primarily Muslim. It also marked the beginning of what has been called the "brain drain" from Egypt, Syria, Iraq, Jordan, and North African Arab countries. Orfalea explains that well-educated, professional Middle Easterners fled their homes due to political instability or their desire to seek better standards of living, or as political exiles. Finally, Orfalea identifies a third wave of Middle Eastern immigration from 1967-1985, primarily by Palestinians and largely due to intensified Israeli aggressions, intra-Arab warfare, increased Islamic fundamentalism, and the loosening of U.S. immigration restrictions. The third wave, as with the second, consisted mostly of well-educated professionals, but the third wave was three times larger than the second, and these later immigrants have become more politically active in the United States. Orfalea (1988) characterizes the situation as follows: "They were leaving societies wracked by abysmal violence. . . . More angry with America [because of its pro-Israeli foreign policy], the Third Wave paradoxically made more enthusiastic Americans" (pp. 177-178).

The Effect of Immigration on Middle Eastern Women

Traditional values and customs were inevitably influenced by American culture once Middle Eastern families settled in the United States. Yet perhaps the most significant challenge to Middle Easterners—both at home and in the United States—has come from Western myths about Arabs. According to Shakir (1997), Edward Said's groundbreaking 1978 work, *Orientalism,* explains that these myths are more than simple xenophobia, but have been used as "convenient justification for the political, economic, and cultural exploitation of colonial lands" (Shakir, 1997, p. 2). Shakir (1997) describes Said's concept of Orientalism as a "habit of mind that divides the world into polar opposites, East and West, them and us, and assumes that those exotic others are so benighted, depraved, or genetically disabled that they cannot run their own affairs or be trusted to know what is in their own best interests" (pp. 2-3). Hamilton (1994) explains that these stereotypes extend back to the time of the Crusades, and she describes the Western caricature of the Arab as an alien, an enemy, a fanatical terrorist, or simply a crazy Muslim. Collier (1994) notes that these age-old stereotypes resurfaced with a vengeance during the Oil Embargo of 1973 and then again during the Persian Gulf War of 1990-1991. During this time period, and certainly since the terrorist attacks of September 11, 2001, the Western world has made scapegoats of Arabs for numerous world problems.

Middle Eastern immigrants to the United States, then, have had to face the deleterious effects of Orientalism, including, as Majaj (1994) reports, a fear that claiming one's heritage will open you up to suspicion and hatred. In addition to prejudice fueled by virtually timeless negative stereotypes, Middle Eastern families have had the task of adapting to a culture whose values often conflict with their own. In particular, Majaj explains that the values of the Middle Eastern extended family are in direct opposition to the U.S. emphasis on individualism. Life in a rather hostile environment has, however, had some positive effects. For example, Abraham and Abraham (1983) note that Middle Eastern immigrants have developed a certain level of community cohesiveness in response to the U.S. government's traditionally pro-Israeli stance.

The effect of immigration on Middle Eastern women has, in large part, been the consequence of a twofold traditional Western stereotype of Arab women: the veiled woman (either as bewitching or oppressed) and the exotic whore in the form of harem beauties such as Scheherazade (Kadi, 1994; Hamilton, 1994). Shakir argues that equally pernicious is the more recent stereotype of Arab women by Western feminists. Unfamiliar with Middle Eastern customs, traditions, values, and religious practices, Kahf (1999) notes that Western feminists have made the sweeping proclamation that Muslim women are victims.

Although Middle Eastern-American women are confronted with distorted images from virtually all sides, they try to take control of their own identities, defend their heritage, and adapt to new roles in America. There have been both negative and positive effects. For example, Abraham and Abraham (1983) explain that although Middle Eastern extended family structures are significantly fractured by the American experience, this has given way to nuclear families in which the father's role of authority is somewhat reduced. Similarly, women's increasing role in the economic goals of the family has extended their freedoms substantially. As we shall soon see, the value of education for Middle Eastern-American women may be a catalyst for diversifying women's roles even further.

ANALYSIS OF ETHNOGRAPHIC FINDINGS

Demographics

Twenty-one women completed the survey; however, only nineteen completed the interview. The women ranged between the ages of eighteen to sixty-six with the majority (thirteen) falling in the eighteen to twenty-five age range. There was one woman who was sixty-six. Fourteen of the women were single; seven were married. The majority of the women's household incomes ranged from $15,000 to $35,000, and six households earned over $66,000. Eight of the women had completed community/junior college, five had undergraduate degrees, and two had graduate or professional degrees. The women represented myriad ethnicities, and several combined their nationality with their religion when responding to the question about ethnicity. Four women identified themselves as Jewish, two identified themselves as Arabic, two as Middle Eastern, two as Muslim, and two as American. There was one each who identified herself as follows: Palestinian, Lebanese Armenian American, Armenian, Omani Muslim, American Egyptian, Palestinian American Muslim, Arabic Muslim, Jewish Israeli, and Arab American. In relation to race, fifteen identified themselves as white, two said they belong to the human race, one identified herself as Asian, and one woman did not respond.

Analysis of the Survey

On the statements that were designed to evaluate participants' level of agreement versus disagreement regarding their own use and society's use of traditional power attributes, the majority of the women agreed that society uses all but two of the traditional power attributes (see Table 7.1). These two were physical strength and force. The at-

TABLE 7.1. Middle Eastern-American Women: Personal Feelings Regarding Power and Society versus Power and Self

Traditional Power and Society				Traditional Power and Self			
Attribute	**Agree**	**Disagree**	**N A/D**	**Attribute**	**Agree**	**Disagree**	**N A/D**
Domination	13	3	5	Domination	7	12	2
Conflict	13	3	5	Conflict	7	7	7
Force	10	9	2	Force	3	15	3
Win	16	2	3	Win	6	11	4
Struggle	16	1	4	Struggle	15	3	3
Resistance	13	4	4	Resistance	4	11	6
Competition	19	2	0	Competition	14	4	3
Physical strength	8	9	4	Physical strength	5	14	2
Control-over	17	1	3	Control-over	5	12	4
Sway others	16	3	2	Sway others	8	6	7
Wealth	18	1	2	Wealth	12	7	2
Authority	19	2	0	Authority	12	6	3
Resources	20	1	0	Resources	17	1	3
Coercion	14	1	6	Coercion	5	7	9

n = 21
N A/D = Neither agree nor disagree

tributes receiving the highest levels of agreement were resources, authority, competition, and wealth.

On the other hand, the majority of the women agreed with their personal use of only five of the fourteen traditional power attributes. The highest levels of agreement were with the attributes resources, struggle, competition, wealth, and authority. The majority of women disagreed with four of the attributes. Fifteen of the women disagreed with the use of force, fourteen with the use of physical strength, and twelve with the use of both dominance and control-over.

A high level of neither agreement nor disagreement occurred with the personal use of the attribute coercion. Similarly, seven of the women neither agreed nor disagreed with the personal use of conflict and sway over others, and six neither agreed nor disagreed with the personal use of resistance.

The analysis indicates that when comparing their personal use to society's use of these attributes, the women agreed that they use at least three of the same attributes that society uses. These included resources, with which at least seventeen of the women agreed, struggle, in which at least fifteen of the women agreed, and competition, with which at least fourteen of the women agreed. In two instances, the women's personal feelings were clearly divergent from their feelings about society. That is, although they felt that society uses the attributes domination and control-over, they personally disagreed with the use of these two attributes.

In the survey statements that examined empowerment, a majority of women agreed with only two of the five attributes (see Table 7.2).

TABLE 7.2. Middle Eastern-American Women: Personal Feelings Regarding Empowerment

Attribute	Agree	Disagree	N A/D
Collectivity	11	7	3
Companionship	10	8	3
Compassion	12	4	5
Consensus	10	5	6
Competence	13	5	3

n = 21
N A/D = Neither agree nor disagree

These attributes, competence and compassion, received majority agreement, but only by a narrow margin. There were two empowerment attributes with which five or more women neither agreed nor disagreed. As for personal authority, a vast majority of the women agreed with all of the five attributes (see Table 7.3). The attribute knowledge received unanimous agreement, while nineteen of the women agreed with both choice and self-determination.

In terms of reciprocal empowerment attributes, the majority of women agreed with all of the statements (see Table 7.4). The attributes that received the highest level of agreement were all related to personal authority. Twenty women agreed with the importance of knowledge, ability to take action, and self-determination. Fifteen of the women agreed with the other two personal authority attributes, independence and ability to choose. Of the empowerment aspect of reciprocal empowerment, sixteen of the women agreed with competence. This was followed by compassion, mutual engagement, and mutual empathy, which each received fifteen agreements. Fourteen of the women agreed with the empowerment attributes companionship and consensus, and thirteen agreed with mutual responsiveness. Mutual responsiveness and the ability to choose turned out to be the attributes that received the highest level of "neither agree nor disagree." Of interest, although the attribute ability to choose received no disagreements, it received six "neither agree nor disagree."

In comparing the responses to the statements associated with results of the four power models addressed in the survey, we noted that a large majority of the women agreed with all of the personal author-

TABLE 7.3. Middle Eastern-American Women: Personal Feelings Regarding Personal Authority

Attribute	**Agree**	**Disagree**	**N A/D**
Ability to take action	17	3	1
Ability to choose	19	0	2
Self-determination	19	0	2
Knowledge	21	0	0
Independence	17	2	2

n = 21
N A/D = Neither agree nor disagree

TABLE 7.4. Middle Eastern-American Women: Personal Feelings Regarding Reciprocal Empowerment

Attribute	Agree	Disagree	N A/D
Mutual responsiveness	13	2	6
Competence	16	2	3
Compassion	15	1	5
Independence	15	3	3
Ability to choose	15	0	6
Collectivity	12	6	3
Companionship	14	2	5
Ability to take action	20	0	1
Self-determination	20	0	1
Mutual engagement	15	1	5
Knowledge	20	0	1
Consensus	14	2	5
Mutual attention	14	2	5
Mutual empathy	15	2	4

$n = 21$
N A/D = Neither agree nor disagree

ity attributes. The model that received the next highest level of agreement was the reciprocal empowerment model. Generally, the women did not favor the empowerment or the traditional power models, with a majority of the women agreeing with only two of the empowerment attributes. However, when these same empowerment attributes were framed in the context of reciprocal empowerment, a majority of the women agreed with all of them. This probably resulted from the fact that the statements related to empowerment in the reciprocal empowerment part of the survey were written differently from those in the part of the survey that dealt specifically with empowerment. This was done deliberately since the original conception of empowerment lacks the reciprocity emphasized by reciprocal empowerment. The following is an example of a statement regarding compassion and empowerment: "I feel that it is important to be compassionate regardless of whether or not it benefits me as long as I empower others." In comparison, the reciprocal empowerment statement about compassion reads as follows: "I feel that by being compassionate I empower myself and others."

Analysis of the Interview

To analyze the interview results we categorized and described the responses. We did this by first looking at the five questions in terms of (1) what power means to the women as individuals, (2) what they think power generally means in U.S. society, (3) what power means in their culture, (4) whether as women they have power in U.S. society, and (5) whether as women they have power in Middle Eastern cultures, and we examined the responses in terms of their relation to the four power models (see Table 7.5). We then evaluated responses

TABLE 7.5. Middle Eastern-American Women: Responses to Introductory Interview Questions and the Relationship of These Responses to the Power Models

Introductory Interview Questions	**Traditional Power**	**Empowerment**	**Personal Authority**	**Reciprocal Empowerment**
What does the word *power* mean to you as an individual?	7	1	5	2
What do you think the word *power* means in American society today?	16	0	1	0
What do you think the word *power* means in your culture?	7	2	4	1
As a woman, what kind of power do you think you have in U.S. society?	1	1	4	0
As a Middle Eastern-American woman, what do you think the word *power* means in your culture?	3	1	4	1

n = 21

Note: Total numbers may not match *n* since in some cases responses could not be associated with a power model. Zero equals no responses or responses could not be associated with a model.

regarding their perceptions of how power *is* and *should be used* in the areas of work, family, religion, and politics (see Table 7.6). We complete our analysis by discussing terms or statements in the responses that could not be clearly associated with our original descriptions of the four power models.

Introductory Questions

All nineteen participants answered the question asking them what power means to them as individuals. Seven of the women used terms associated with traditional power. Three each associated power with control-over, domination, and money or wealth, while others referred to authority. Five women used personal authority attributes. All five of the women focused on learning, education, or knowledge in brief

TABLE 7.6. Middle Eastern-American Women: Interview Responses to Questions About Work, Family, Religion, and Politics

How Power *Is Used*

	Traditional Power	Empowerment	Personal Authority	Reciprocal Empowerment
Work	7	1	1	0
Family	5	0	4	0
Religion	1	0	6	0
Politics	5	2	2	1

How Power *Should Be Used*

	Traditional Power	Empowerment	Personal Authority	Reciprocal Empowerment
Work	1	1	1	0
Family	1	3	1	0
Religion	1	0	1	0
Politics	0	1	0	0

$n = 21$

Note: Total numbers may not match n since in some cases responses could not be associated with a power model. Zero equals no responses or responses could not be associated with a model.

statements such as "power of learning." Three women mentioned independence and one mentioned choice when answering this question. Only two women made statements related to reciprocal empowerment, and one identified with empowerment. Two women referred to God, as in, "a deep-seated trust in God," and three women also mentioned freedom.

In response to the question asking them what they think power means in U.S. society, there was more agreement among the women. Sixteen of the women described traditional power and only one associated it with personal authority. Ten of the women described power in the United States as money or wealth, while five of the women specifically referred to "control over other people," "control by any means," or simply "controlling." Two of the women described power here as authority, and one each referred to strength, competition, and physical power. In addition, one woman mentioned independence, one referred to technology, and another referred to appearance.

The responses were quite different, however, when the women were asked what power means in their own culture. Here their characterizations of power varied. Only seven women used words associated with traditional power. Six of the women believed that money or wealth is closely associated with power in Middle Eastern cultures. Four women used personal authority attributes, and one each used words associated with empowerment and reciprocal empowerment. Several women referred to knowledge, learning, or education. One of these women went so far as to say that "power should be knowledge in any culture." Of interest, five of the participants referred to either religion or God when describing power in their own ethnic culture, as in, "Power is left to God." Two of the women identified children and two identified family as sources of power in their own ethnic culture, and one each referred to independence and freedom. Two of the women referred specifically to men having power. One of these women who identified herself as Jewish American said that "men are the ones with greater power." The other, an Israeli Jew, said that, "He can do whatever he can do; he can have whatever he wants also." Two women also mentioned the importance of having a voice. One said that, in Islamic culture, power is "to have a strong say in the community." A Palestinian-American woman said, "to have a voice and be recognized as a people. In Palestine none have that right—women or men." Decision making and influence were other descriptors used by some of the women.

In characterizing their sense of power as women in U.S. society, the overwhelming majority of the participants felt that they have some power. However, it is evident that this is not traditional male-oriented power. For example, a Jewish-American woman said, "being able to contribute to others in a way that I wasn't able to in my country—being more open-minded . . . more open than in Israel." Only six of the women indicated they believe they have a lot of power as women in the United States. For example, one woman said, "You can do what guys can do and it's up to you." Only one of the women responded that she feels she has no power: "I don't believe I have any; even though women are a majority of the population, society says males dominate over women." Within their answers to this question, four of the women identified with personal authority attributes, one identified with empowerment, and one with traditional power. These women associated power with education and knowledge, the ability to speak up or speak out, and choice. Of note, two women also indicated that physical appearance or looks are important. For example, one woman said "less than men . . . the prettier I am the farther I'll get." One woman suggested that power in U.S. society means freedom.

A number of the responses to the question, "As a Middle Eastern woman, what do you think the word *power* means in your culture?" could not be interpreted in terms of the four power models. Of those that could, four women described personal authority attributes and one each described power in their culture in terms of traditional power and empowerment. Three of the women chose not to respond to this question, and two of these women indicated that they did not feel comfortable speaking for their entire culture. Only two of the women responded in ways that indicated they think they have a lot of power in Middle Eastern cultures, and one woman who identified herself as Arabic said, "women have no power." The words the women used to characterize power and its relationship to women in Middle Eastern cultures emphasized education. Five women discussed education (or more specifically higher education) and one referred to knowledge. In addition, three women associated power with men, with two of these women being of Egyptian descent. They said, "After they [Egyptian women] marry, their men are their power," and "power of guys over women; a battle between the sexes—men attempting to control women and women not making it easy." An Omani woman made a connection between education and the struggle of women to gain equality: "education, otherwise the husband does everything—the more education, the more power—education equals higher position." Two of the women mentioned freedom.

Work

Twelve of the nineteen women were employed outside the household. Of the seven who were not, one identified herself as a college student and one volunteered at a local hospital. In responding to the question, "Do people have different kinds of power where you work?", all twelve of the employed women said "yes" in one way or another. Of the more extended answers, they generally discussed different forms of power on the job in terms of status, position, and hierarchy. For example, one woman said, "Yes, directors are in charge of everything, dispatchers are the boss for the night, and senior escorts also have authority" (this woman works at a local university escorting students safely to their cars at night). Another simply said, "I guess so because I'm in charge. There is a hierarchy."

In response to the question about what kind of power they think they have on the job, five women described traditional power using terms such as authority and influence. The women also described power according to control, the ability to persuade or influence, or the ability to reprimand others. Another, a cardiovascular specialist, said, "I'm in charge. I seek counsel for my main decisions, but the Quran has the last word. . . . A person never has absolute power; it is always completely governed by the Quran." One woman described empowerment, and one described personal authority. Seven of the women, while giving responses not associated with the power models, indicated they think they have a lot of power, two believe they have some power, and three believe they have no power.

When asked to give specific examples of how power *is used* where they work, most of the women gave responses that could not be associated with the four power models (see Table 7.6). Two women did mention the traditional power attributes authority and influence. A number of the women described examples in ways that were suggestive of authority and control-over. The actual terms associated with traditional power were not mentioned; however, they did provide more general descriptions of power relationships. Four of these descriptions focused on the process of giving instructions to other employees, while two dealt with correcting or reprimanding employees. For example, one woman said, "The boss tells me to do things," and another said, "She [boss] likes to give orders and scold me." Other characterizations included respect, decision making, and the right to speak.

Similarly, in response to the question, "How do you think power *should be* used on your job?", few of the women used terms we could identify with the models. Only one woman each used terms associated with power, empowerment, and personal authority. Three of the women referred to equality or working together. For example, one woman said, "Everyone should work together and do equal amounts of labor," and another said, "All should have the same power." Two of the women said they were satisfied with the way power is currently used. Respect and knowledge were also used in the responses to this question.

Family

When asked to identify who they include in their immediate families, ten of the women described a nuclear family while nine described an extended family. Seven of the participants identified a woman as the head of household, five identified a man, and six of the women described the position of head of household as shared. More specifically, four women identified themselves as head of the house, three identified their mothers as the head, four identified their fathers, and one identified her husband. Of the responses that suggested this role is shared, two pointed to their father and mother, two named themselves and their husbands, one said, "There is no one head," and another said, "There are two heads in my house and both count equally."

With regard to the meaning of power in the women's families, seven women described traditional power, three women described personal authority, one described empowerment, and one woman did not respond. Of the eighteen who did, the answers were varied. Control and strength were each mentioned three times, and education, religion, independence, and struggle were each mentioned twice. Three of the women focused on decision making, as in, "being able to make decisions which involve everyone." Sharing, influence, and collectivity were also mentioned.

In response to the question, "Who makes the major decisions with regards to children?" ten of the participants identified a woman, one identified a man, and six indicated that this responsibility is shared by husband and wife or mother and father. In terms of who is responsible for decisions concerning housework, seventeen respondents identified a woman, one identified a man, and two said these responsibilities are shared by various family members. As for family finances, eight women indicated that a female is responsible, five identified a male, and six said this responsibility is shared by mother and father or husband and wife.

When asked if people have different kinds of power in their immediate families, eleven of the women said yes while six women said no. Among the extended "yes" answers were statements such as, "No matter your age, you must comply to parents' wishes in Islam," and "Yes. It's okay for the men to have girl friends, travel, and live alone. Women can't do these things. It's all sexism." As for those women who responded to this question by saying "no," one said, "we share equal power" while another simply said, "no, equal."

In answering the question that specifically asked the women what kind of power they have in their immediate families, the responses were not indicative of a particular type of power; however, of the nineteen women who responded to the question, eight indicated that they have some power. For example, one woman said, "The same as everyone. I don't pretend to have more or less, just different types of power." Five of the women indicated they felt that they have a lot of power. For example, one participant responded, "Women can be run around by male relatives but not in this case." Three of the women said they have little or no power in the family by giving very simple statements such as, "I don't think I have any power."

Questions that asked the women to indicate how power *is used* in their families resulted in five descriptions using traditional power attributes and four descriptions using attributes associated with personal authority (see Table 7.6). Four women gave clear indications that power is used in the form of control or influence. An example of power as control follows: "Mom has influence and control over her children. We don't have to do what she says, but then we'll never hear the end of her lectures and yelling. We don't like to cook so if we really piss her off, she stops cooking. She also stops doing her part of the cleaning. My father is hardheaded so he never takes her advice, but she makes sure she always yells at him and tells him how dumb he is and that he is a loser." Several attributes of traditional power were combined with decision making: "Making certain decisions about particular issues happening in certain instances—for example, who's going to let me stay out past curfew, Mother or Father? They have power in what they say more than what they do." "The father has financial power. I make the everyday decisions. For example, if the children want to go out they have to ask me." "Both parents seek the other parent's verification of decisions." "I suppose when decisions are made about finances, buying a new house, car . . . things like that . . . that is power." Six women suggested that power is used mainly for decision-making purposes. Only one mentioned that power is used to gain respect.

When asked how they think power *should be* used in their families, three women identified empowerment attributes such as cooperation and consensus, as in, "Everybody should give their opinions and cooperate on final decisions," and "Parents make decisions until the child is mature. Parents must come to a common consensus." One woman gave a response that used the words respect, money, and compassion:

> Mother deserves the most respect and first consideration; she works harder and worries about her children and family more so it is understandable if she wants things to go her way. My father's the one who brings money in and that's important, but my mom's the one who does everything else and it is harder than his job. In Islam you don't have to obey your parents if they are asking you to do something that goes against God's law, but you must always—no matter what—respect them. In return, children are a gift from God that God is entrusting you with and so you have to be compassionate toward them, and child abuse is a sin. Power is not supposed to be about dominating and abusing, although in reality it is; it is a responsibility, something God is entrusting you with a duty you have unto others.

One woman each described traditional power and the personal authority attribute choice also appeared: "Power should be used in making choices about how to run the household." Two women felt power should be used equally while three said it should be shared. One felt that it should be used to gain respect while two mentioned the use of power for decision-making purposes.

Religion

Eleven of the women said they currently belong to a religious group, three did not, and three of the women indicated that they were not sure what we meant by the term *group.* Although only eleven of the women gave indications of current affiliation, when asked the follow-up question, "If yes, would you care to tell us which religion?" several of the women who had not claimed an affiliation responded. Nine gave Muslim or Islam as their response to the question. Five said they were Jewish. Three women identified themselves as Christian, and one specifically as Catholic.

When asked if people have different kinds of power in their religions twelve of the women said yes and two said no. Four did not answer. Some of those who responded "yes" went on to elaborate, giving examples of who they felt held power. Six said that men had power while two specifically indicated the rabbi, and one said God. Two felt that the person with the most knowledge had the most power.

In response to the question, "What kind of power do you have in your religion?" the women said the "power to pray," "the power to make decisions whether they are in accordance with religious teachings or not," the "power of conviction," and "the power of speech."

When asked to give specific examples of how power *is used* in their religions one woman used the term *force,* a term associated with traditional power, and five used attributes associated with personal authority (see Table 7.6). Regarding knowledge as power, one woman said, "The person with the most knowledge has power. [One] must understand the Arabic language. If there is an equal amount of knowledge then the older will preside. It's not about money or power, but wisdom. One can't put oneself forward for a position of power. It eliminates greedy, power-hungry people." Another woman said,

> Real power is something only God has. The Hadeeth (prophetic tradition) says "heaven lies at the feet of mothers." Also in regard to who you should listen to, the Hadeeth says, "Your mother, then your mother, then your mother, then your father,"

> and "The man who is closer to heaven is the one who is more loving and compassionate toward his wife." Also, according to Islam, the only difference between a man and a woman in God's view is the one who is more righteous. That one is favored. The difference between a black and a white person is the one who does more good.

Two mentioned the use of religion to cure some people.

The question, "What kind of power do women have in your religion?" elicited several lengthy and seemingly passionate responses from the women, and knowledge again surfaced as an apparent indicator or symbol of power to several of the women. Examples of responses in which the word *knowledge* was used included: "[Women have] the power to spread their knowledge," and "Islam respects women. Women have a place. Women were active in the Prophet's time. For example, in war, knowledge is required by both men and women." One woman who said she did not belong to a religious organization seemed very adamant in her belief that power meant having some form of "rights":

> In speaking of the religion itself, Islam is the only religion that guarantees specific rights to women, such as the right to own or sell property, the right to an education, to work, to initiate a marriage contract or choose a partner, to abort before the fortieth day (before the fetus develops a beating heart), to divorce. Also, if a woman wants to go out and work for money, the men in her family *must* support all her needs. Islamic tradition also allows women in business and politics.

This woman went on to state that many Muslim countries today deny women their "God-given rights." She and several of the other respondents also made a distinction between what Islam says regarding women and the present conditions for some women. Some other responses included: "Women are equal to men. Women have a lot of power too because they are educated. Women are rabbis, teachers, etc. Women have power roles in government and religion," and "I think they have somewhat equal power to men. They are respected, but men are macho and speak over religion. Religion itself is equal, but interpreted unequally."

When asked how power *should be used,* only two women mentioned terms associated with the models, one woman used a term associated with personal authority, and one used a term associated with power. Although the women did not use the terms associated with the models, several other terms occurred repeatedly enough to warrant closer attention. These terms include "equally," which surfaced four times along with "fairly," "as is," and "only by God," which appeared twice. For example, "Power is something both men and women should share equally. Power should be based on knowledge and capabilities of an individual, not sex," "Women should have a little more power and should be equally represented," "Equal rights, equality between men and women," and "Women and men should be equal and they are—except Orthodox, where women must get permission from men for everything."

Politics

The next questions focused on politics. Only four of the women said they were affiliated with a political cause/organization. Thirteen said no; however, of these thirteen a few added explanations. One said that she is not involved, "however, I feel passion toward politics in Palestine." One said her cause is Islam, because "Islam fights oppression." One said "No, and I don't care," and one woman responded, "I am a strong advocate against domestic violence."

It is interesting that in responding to the follow-up question that asked if they would care to tell what political cause/organization they were affiliated with, at least two of the women seemed to equate politics with religion: "Islam is your political life, your family life, your way of life; there is no separation . . . not secular," and "I am a Republican who belongs to the Jewish Federation." One other woman identified herself as Republican, and one indicated she is a Democrat.

When asked if people have different kinds of power in their political organizations/causes, all four women who were affiliated said yes. One said, "There is a committee of women who each hold different positions so that things get done. There isn't one woman who dictates except when it comes to finance. If the accountant says it can't be done, then there is no debate." Another woman said, "Yes, I think the more wealth and experience you have, the more power you have." In terms of their own power in the political organizations/causes, however, that seemed to be limited. One woman responded, "I can be involved in discussions. I respond to action alerts and get people to sign petitions. I write or contact people in high positions/offices with our grievances and educate the public about our legitimate grievances and our cause." One said, "I don't really have power. I don't belong to any [political] group, but I belong to the Jewish organization and they work together." One woman said, "I submit my opinion and empower others through lectures and workshops."

The issue of how power *is used* in their political organizations/causes received even more responses that could not be associated with the models under examination (see Table 7.6). Five women used terms associated with power, two used terms associated with empowerment, two with personal authority, and one with reciprocal empowerment. These responses included, "The power of our cause is strong. The power of our message gets to people and may just change their minds. To empower people to take action against violence is a great example of the way the organization uses power." Another respondent said, "[My] organization serves as an advocate. Their power is to give a voice to those who don't have a voice. Others use power to blacklist me in Jerusalem." One woman, a Democrat, used the former President Bill Clinton and Monica Lewinsky affair as an example of power being used in politics. She felt that had it not been for publicity, Clinton's position as President would have let him get away with the affair. However, having been caught, had he not been President, he would have received greater punishment.

The women, however, were not willing to associate with power attributes when discussing how power *should be used* in politics. Only one response could be associated with the power models and that respondent used an empowerment term. Other responses, however, included "respectfully," "equally," "to help," and "to better people." Two more extensive answers gave a deeper insight into the strength of the feelings of two of these women regarding the use of power in politics. A Palestinian woman said, "Injustices makes us go on. The fight gives us hope. There's power through persistence. Rape didn't stop me; killing my family didn't stop me. [It] should be used for collective good. I don't believe in the concept of majority rule. I don't believe in democracy. Democracy leads to tyranny. Majority rule is illusory; what if majority is all wrong? Islam seeks for an equal chance for everyone." Another woman responded, "No one person should get too much power because power corrupts people. Besides, I don't think of those people or governments as powerful; what they are is corrupt . . . there's a big difference. To say they are powerful is to deny a higher authority, whereas God has real power that can't be taken away."

The final question asked, "How do you see the power roles of women who are affiliated with politics?" Of the nineteen women, only three chose not to respond. The other sixteen gave extensive answers and the one with the shortest answer got her impression across with one word, "Bitchy!" One woman said, "Ever increasing. We have come a long way, and I hope it doesn't stop now. As long as there are women to be governed, then their voices need to be equally commented upon in our government." The rest of the answers varied from being supportive of women in politics to being totally unsupportive of the idea: "I don't see women as having any power because the society never gave them a chance to become strong political leaders, such as President." "Madeleine Albright has lots of power, so does Hanan Ashrawi. If women in politics aren't puppets and are taken seriously, then they are powerful; however, for the most part women are given positions to avoid confrontation with women's issues. Also, women have to have strong personalities to hold political power." Some of the more negative responses included the following:

> Most Muslim women who have gone that way are traitors to their religion. They try to be like men to exist in politics. We have the right to be women and all that it entails. Being veiled doesn't mean you sit around at home—just the opposite. I feel pressure from my community because I am judged harshly and treated with suspicion because I am very political.

> I think some seem to be powerful but they don't use their positions to advance the less fortunate. They are no different than male politicians—sneaky and driven by self-interest. Madeleine Albright is a control freak. . . . She talks just like a man and doesn't care what her actions do to people as long as it's supposedly in the best interest of the American people.

This same respondent also indicated a liking for Janet Reno and Palestinian politicians/human rights activists such as Hanan Ashrawi.

One woman simply said, "I don't like women in politics, they are too aggressive and rude."

CONCLUSION

The overall results of the survey indicated that the Middle Eastern women who participated in our study preferred personal authority over the other power paradigms. The women generally had a favorable response to the reciprocal empowerment model as well. They also responded favorably to empowerment attributes, but only within the context of reciprocal empowerment. Explanations for the women's lack of a stance about some of the traditional power attributes could lie in the religious and/or political history of these groups, where these attributes could very well serve a purpose depending on the religious or political climate. For example, the attribute conflict received seven agreements, seven disagreements, with seven neither agreeing nor disagreeing. Given the current political and religious conflict between the Israelis and the Palestinians in the Middle East, these results are not surprising. First, conflict and resistance have become a way of life for the people from an area that has historically been in turmoil. Furthermore, persuasion (sway others) and coercion are strategies common to revolutionary movements and are often utilized by both the "enemy" and by one's own rank and file.

In the interview, when answering questions concerning their perceptions of power as individuals and the meaning of power within their own culture, about the same number of women identified with traditional power as with the three alternative models combined, and the women agreed that power in the United States is characterized by the traditional power paradigm. There was a shift in perception, however, when the women were asked to describe the power they have as women in both American and Middle Eastern societies. In both cases, personal authority attributes were used more frequently than attributes from any of the other models. In fact, the traditional power attributes were least frequently used.

In response to interview questions focusing on the meaning of power in both the workplace and the family, the women most often used traditional power attributes. It was more difficult to make a determination regarding how they think power *should be used* on the job since the resulting descriptions could not be associated with the power models. However, when asked about how power *should be used* in the family, a few of the women favored empowerment attributes. In answering the interview questions concerning both religion and politics, the women typically gave responses that could not be associated with any of the four power models. This was not the case when the women discussed how power *is used* in religion. Here, several women used personal authority attributes, and when describing how power *is used* in politics several mentioned traditional power attributes. When discussing how power *should be used* in religion and politics, the women did not use statements that could be associated with any of the power models.

In general, we noticed that throughout the interview the Middle Eastern women often seemed to think of power in terms different from those we associate with traditional power, personal authority, empowerment, and even reciprocal empowerment. Terms that did emerge frequently in their discussions included equality and sharing, decision making, freedom, respect, and voice or power to speak. Equality and sharing appeared most frequently, and the terms were generally used when the women discussed family and religion. They were particularly prevalent in response to the question asking them how power *should be used* in the family. For example, one woman said, "Power is something everyone in a family should share equally," and another said, "Equally! No one person needs to make all decisions. I really believe in the idea of equality." Equality/sharing also surfaced in response to how power *should be used* in religion. The analysis indicated that Islam plays a significant role in the lives of many of these women; therefore, it is not surprising that they think their families ought to be structured in the way they believe their religion is structured. This finding is further supported by researchers such as Wadud (1999) and Minces (1984), who, as noted earlier, argue that no gender inequalities are contained within the Quran. This was also asserted by several of the women whose responses placed great emphasis on demonstrating that Islam is a religion of equality and is nonsexist. These women also went to great pains to make a distinction between how Islam is practiced and the tenets of the religion as stated in the Quran. Earlier we noted the works of scholars such as Kadi (1994) and Hamilton (1994) who discussed Western myths about Middle Eastern women. We believe their findings suggest that the women we interviewed made a point of explaining the original intentions of Islam to the interviewers in an effort to overcome some of the Western stereotypes about women in Islam.

Another term that emerged frequently was decision making, which was discussed most often in relation to how power is conceived of and used in their families. Their descriptions suggest that these women believe power in the family is determined by who makes decisions.

Freedom was also mentioned several times. It first surfaced when the women were asked what power means to them as individuals. For example, an Egyptian American mentioned that freedom to her means independence and the "freedom to do whatever you want." It surfaced again when they were asked what kind of power they have as women in U.S. society. A Lebanese woman said that as a woman in the United States power means "freedom, the right to speak and equality between men and women." It is apparent, therefore, that individual freedom is of importance to them and that they believe that the United States affords them some level of freedom. While freedom was mentioned as a key term for the individual, the term respect brought us back into the arena of the family. This term was used most frequently when asked what power means and how it should be used in the family.

Finally, two other related terms surfaced throughout the interview: voice and power to speak. These terms were used in relation to individual power, power within Middle Eastern cultures, and how power is perceived and used in the workplace, in religion, and in politics.

To conclude, then, although the Middle Eastern-American women preferred personal authority and reciprocal empowerment, their conception of desirable notions of power did not necessarily match our predetermined list of attributes.

Chapter 8

Native American Women and Power

"IMMIGRANTS" IN THEIR OWN LAND: A BRIEF HISTORY OF THE SEMINOLE NATION AND ITS WOMEN

Although we had originally intended to speak with women from two of the most well-known Native American tribes of contemporary South Florida—the Seminoles and the Miccosukees—we were granted access only to the Seminole reservation. Therefore, this chapter focuses on that Native American group. The original indigenous peoples of Florida were the Apalachee, the Timuccua, and the Calusa. According to Garbarino (1972), the Seminole Indians are a post-Columbian group whose name does not appear widely until 1750. They are descendants of the Yamassee of the Carolinas and the Oconee of Apalachicola. Kersey and Bannan (1995) explain that those people, who now make up the Seminole Nation, are actually descendants of the Creek Indians who left Georgia for Spanish-governed Florida in the 1700s.

Due to historical circumstances, the Seminoles are rather like immigrants even though they are Native Americans. The Seminoles claim South and Central Florida as their current homeland primarily as a result of Andrew Jackson's policy to move all Indians of the Southeast westward to Oklahoma. The Seminoles of Florida are those Native Americans who resisted Jackson's policy by fleeing into the Everglades. As Garbarino (1972) explains, "The term 'Seminole,' indicating a social or political unit, was . . . applied to various people who were descendants of a number of different southeastern tribes which had mingled with one another and with the remains of the earlier Florida groups" (p. 9). When the United States acquired Florida in 1819 and began the process of taking what had been Seminole land and at the same time relocating Native Americans to reservations in

Oklahoma, a minority escaped, resisting the U.S. government in a series of Seminole wars from the 1830s through the 1850s (Kersey and Bannan, 1995).

The surviving Seminoles established lands and tribal recognition within Florida. The Seminoles now hold reservation lands both west (Brighton Reservation) and south (Big Cypress Reservation) of Lake Okeechobee, in Immokalee, Hollywood, and in Tampa. The related Miccosukee tribe holds reservation lands along the Tamiami Trail in South Florida. Most of the Seminoles speak Mikasuki, and members of the Brighton Reservation speak Muskogee. Big Cypress is the largest of the Seminole Reservations (covering 42,700 acres with over 2,000 enrolled members) and was established in 1911 (Garbarino, 1972; Kersey and Bannan, 1995). Since no paved roads into Big Cypress existed until the late 1950s, the Seminoles had little contact with the outside world and were able to preserve many of their traditional ways. Certainly, this has changed in the past few decades, given the advent of modern roads and Seminole economic ventures, including ecotourism. In 1957, the Seminoles voted to incorporate under the Indian Reorganization Act, giving rise to their contemporary political structure. Similarly, in 1965, the Miccosukee incorporated, becoming an entity distinct from the Seminole Nation (Garbarino, 1972).

Women in Seminole Culture

LaFromboise et al. (1990) note that the traditionally male-centered bias of social science research led to inaccurate depictions not only of Native American social systems but also of the role of Native American women in their societies. Historical and anthropological accounts of Native American social structures have, for the most part, been filtered through the values of white Western culture. In addition, in some tribes (including the Seminole Nation) it is the men who traditionally deal with outsiders (LaFromboise et al., 1990; Kersey and Bannan, 1995), perhaps further skewing outsider research about Native American life.

In general, Western culture has fabricated dual stereotypes about Native American women that closely parallel the "whore/madonna" dichotomy of stereotypes about white women. Klein and Ackerman (1995) argue that the Native American equivalent of this dichotomy is that of "squaw/Indian princess" (pp. 5-6). In popular culture, the Native American woman has been characterized either as a dumpy, subservient squaw or as a royal princess who rejects her own culture in favor of European-American values and romantic love (e.g., Pocahontas).

The reality of Native American women's lives, however, is quite different. LaFromboise and colleagues (1990) note that in Native American cultures a high frequency of egalitarian relationships exists between men and women. Traditionally, in Native American cultures women were well integrated into their societies. They were treated with sincere respect and were called upon often for advice (Klein and Ackerman, 1995). In various tribes a tendency exists toward a reciprocity of gender roles. Researchers often talk of this phenomenon as "complementary roles" (LaFromboise et al., 1990; Kersey and Bannan, 1995; Klein and Ackerman, 1995). That is, although distinctions are often made between men's and women's roles, no hierarchy is usually attached to these distinctions (men's roles are not valued more than women's roles). Furthermore, gender in many Native American cultures is tied to one's behavior, not to biology or even to sexual preference (Klein and Ackerman, 1995).

The complementary nature of these gender roles means that Native American cultures typically maintain a sense of the public and private spheres, just as non-Native cultures do. The difference is that in Native American cultures the private or domestic sphere is not devalued. Generally speaking, Native American women play a significant role in the life of their culture in at least three ways: (1) in religion, since women are often viewed as an extension of the great Spirit Mother, (2) in protecting, fostering, and maintaining the extended family and tribe, particularly in terms of the value of mothering, and (3) in conserving the traditional cultural ways of the tribe, since women function as educators and transmitters of cultural knowledge (LaFromboise et al., 1990).

The roles of women within the Seminole Nation are similar to LaFromboise and colleagues' (1990) general findings about Native American women. Kersey and Bannan (1995) report that Seminole women exist within a matrilineal and matrilocal society with a gender-based division of labor and a sense of the public and private spheres, but where men's and women's roles are complementary. Traditionally, Seminole men were responsible for dealings with the outside world while women, valued as cultural conservators, owned and ran everything related to the family camps (headed by the clans' grandmothers). Similarly, Sattler's (1995) study of the Muskogees in Oklahoma (who include Seminoles and Creeks) indicates that although men tend to dominate official roles of authority (in tribal government and the like), women exert considerable influence through indirect and informal access to power. Sattler (1995) describes the Muskogee woman's status in her society as a picture of "limited self-determination" (p. 218). Although Sattler goes on to note evidence of the subordination of Muskogee women, the contemporary situation for the Seminole women of Florida, as we discovered, is much more positive.

The Effect of the White Man's World on Seminole Women

LaFromboise and colleagues (1990), as well as Klein and Ackerman (1995), agree that Western colonialists—in the form of the U.S. government and Christian missionaries—worked consciously to influence gender roles within Native American cultures. Traditional Native American gender roles that exhibit a degree of flexibility and latitude were viewed by outsiders as subversive to European culture. Patriarchal religions and social systems, therefore, were imposed upon America's indigenous peoples to "correct" this situation.

According to LaFromboise and colleagues (1990), for Native American cultures the main result of these efforts has been a "breakdown of the complementary nature of male-female relations and a general increase in Indian male dominance and control over Indian women" (p. 461). In addition, contemporary U.S. life confronts Native American women who live off the reservation with a set of conflicting values. That is, although the majority culture in the United States privileges individual achievement, competitiveness, and accumulation of property and titles, traditional Native American society promotes cultural traditions, responsibility for extended family and friends, and the values of cooperation and group identification.

For the Seminole women of Florida, however, association with the outside world has not had entirely negative consequences. In the early twentieth century, white farmers began extending their settlements into the interior of Florida. At the same time, the state of Florida began to drain many parts of the Everglades to increase agricultural development. These actions decreased the wildlife population, effectively diminishing the hunting-trapping-trading economy which had given Seminole men prominence in associating with the outside world. As men's roles in the Seminole economy decreased, Seminole women stepped in and developed new commerce in arts and crafts, picked crops for wages, worked part time in the commercial tourist attractions, and began sewing and selling patchwork clothing. All of these endeavors were extensions of the tasks they were already fulfilling within their tribal culture. Kersey and Bannan (1995) report that by 1930 many Seminole families were headed by women, creating the need to bend the boundaries of established gender roles within the Seminole Nation. Increased association with the outside world quickly led to the development of more overt forms of power for Seminole women. Women became enfranchised into the Seminole electoral process, played leading roles in establishing Christian churches on the reservation, and young women were more apt to pursue formal education than were their male counterparts. In addition, from the outset of Seminole incorporation in 1957, Kersey and Bannan (1995) argue that "there was no overt discrimination against women holding tribal offices, and they were well represented in tribal government during the first decade" (p. 205). Numerous Seminole women, including the legendary Betty Mae Jumper, served on the tribal council. And although more recent evidence exists of resentment by men of women in prominent tribal roles, during the 1950s and 1960s women were very active in tribal governance.

Kersey and Bannan (1995) note that public service to the tribe is a natural extension of Seminole women's caretaking roles and strong commitment to serving their people. Likewise, LaFromboise and colleagues (1990), in their more general account of contemporary Native American women, argue that despite cultural conflicts between Native American society and mainstream U.S. culture, Native American women have engaged in what they say is a process of

> Retraditionalization—or the extension of traditional care-taking and cultural transmission roles to include activities vital to continuity of Indian communities within a predominantly non-Indian society—[which] represents a major current attempt on the part of Indian women to integrate traditional and contemporary demands in a positive, culturally consistent manner (Green,

> 1983). The structure of the cultural system remains intact, but the specific jobs are modernized in accordance with social change. (p. 469)

Despite European-American attempts to distort Native American value systems, association with the "white man's world" has inadvertently encouraged Native American women to extend their traditionally vital private sphere roles into the larger public sphere. Our discussions with Seminole women on the Big Cypress Reservation further support this notion of retraditionalization.

ANALYSIS OF ETHNOGRAPHIC FINDINGS

Demographics

Eighteen Seminole women completed surveys and interviews that were conducted at the government office in the headquarters of the Seminole Tribe in Southeast Florida. The interviews were facilitated by the tribe's communications director. Many of the respondents worked for the tribe and completed the interviews during breaks in their workdays over a period of several consecutive days.

The women ranged between the ages of eighteen and sixty-five with the majority falling between eighteen and forty-five. Fourteen of the women were single. Ten women had household income levels ranging from $15,000 to $35,000, and two averaged above $76,000. The vast majority of the women (sixteen) were either high school graduates or had completed community college. In terms of race, one woman identified herself as Indian, fourteen women identified themselves as Native American, two women identified themselves as American Indian, and one woman identified herself as Seminole. In terms of ethnicity, four classified themselves as American Indian, eight identified themselves as Native Americans, one identified herself as Orerdaga/Six Nations, one Native American/black, one Seminole, and three participants did not respond to this question.

Analysis of the Survey

The fourteen survey statements, designed to evaluate participants' level of agreement versus disagreement with society's use of traditional power attributes, were compared with the fourteen statements designed to measure participants' level of agreement versus disagreement with their personal use of these same attributes (see Table 8.1). In eight of the fourteen statements regarding society's use of power, more than half of the women agreed that society adheres to the attributes of the traditional power paradigm, with the statements "Society dictates that power usually involves the domination of others" and "Society teaches that in order for one to be powerful one needs wealth" getting the greatest number of agreement from the women. The women disagreed with the statement that society feels that physical strength is important in order to be powerful.

On seven of the fourteen statements evaluating the participants' personal use of traditional power, nine or more of the women disagreed with the use of these attributes, including force, winning, resistance, physical strength, swaying others, wealth, and coercion. An interesting contrast occurred in the results between the two statements concerning wealth and resources. Regarding wealth, eleven women disagreed with the statement, "I feel that wealth is necessary in order to be powerful." However, regarding resources, eleven women agreed with the statement, "I feel that if I have access to resources I can exercise power." The women apparently made distinctions between the attributes of wealth and resources in terms of their own personal use. In contrast, when evaluating society's use of these two attributes, fourteen of the women agreed that "Society teaches in order for one to be powerful one needs wealth," and thirteen agreed that "Society teaches that the more resources people have, the more powerful they are." One possible interpretation of this result is that although some people might interpret wealth as a potential resource, for these women the term *resources* may have a broader connotation, and they may not consider wealth itself necessary to gaining or using power. Another attribute with which a majority of the women agreed was the use of struggle. However, an equal number of participants agreed as those that disagreed with the personal use of the attributes domination, conflict, and competition.

In the portion of the survey that highlighted empowerment attributes, half or more of the participants were in agreement with all five statements (see Table 8.2). Even more of the women agreed with the use of personal authority attributes (see Table 8.3). We note two points of interest here: (1) there was an overwhelming positive response (seventeen of eighteen) to the statement "I feel that having the ability to

TABLE 8.1. Native American Women: Personal Feelings Regarding Power and Society versus Power and Self

Traditional Power and Society				Traditional Power and Self			
Attribute	Agree	Disagree	N A/D	Attribute	Agree	Disagree	N A/D
Domination	16	1	0	Domination	7	7	4
Conflict	11	5	2	Conflict	8	8	1
Force	8	7	3	Force	1	12	5
Win	11	5	2	Win	3	9	6
Struggle	9	5	3	Struggle	11	3	4
Resistance	10	5	3	Resistance	5	9	4
Competition	11	3	4	Competition	8	8	2
Physical strength	4	9	4	Physical strength	3	10	3
Control-over	9	6	2	Control-over	6	8	3
Sway others	9	5	3	Sway others	3	10	4
Wealth	14	3	1	Wealth	3	11	3
Authority	12	1	5	Authority	8	5	5
Resources	13	2	3	Resources	11	1	6
Coercion	9	4	5	Coercion	3	9	6

n = 18
N A/D = Neither agree nor disagree
Note: Where totals equal less than *n*, there were instances of no response.

TABLE 8.2. Native American Women: Personal Feelings Regarding Empowerment

Attribute	Agree	Disagree	N A/D
Collectivity	9	4	5
Companionship	9	6	3
Compassion	10	5	2
Consensus	9	4	5
Competence	9	3	5

n = 18
N A/D = Neither agree nor disagree
Note: Where totals equal less than *n*, there were instances of no response.

TABLE 8.3. Native American Women: Personal Feelings Regarding Personal Authority

Attribute	Agree	Disagree	N A/D
Ability to take action	16	1	1
Ability to choose	17	0	1
Self-determination	14	3	1
Knowledge	15	1	1
Independence	14	0	3

n = 18
N A/D = Neither agree nor disagree
Note: Where totals equal less than *n*, there were instances of no response.

choose is important in order to gain and use personal power" and (2) although fourteen of the women agreed that independence was important in gaining and using power, three of the women neither agreed nor disagreed, and one did not respond.

With regard to the use of reciprocal empowerment attributes, half or more of the women agreed with twelve of the fourteen statements (see Table 8.4). The statements that received the most agreement included "I feel that by being independent I empower myself and others," and "I feel that by being competent I empower myself and others." Other statements with high levels of agreement included those concerning the ability to choose and to take action and those that focused on having knowledge and self-determination.

TABLE 8.4. Native American Women: Personal Feelings Regarding Reciprocal Empowerment

Attribute	Agree	Disagree	N A/D
Mutual responsiveness	11	3	5
Competence	15	1	2
Compassion	12	1	5
Independence	16	1	1
Ability to choose	13	2	3
Collectivity	10	5	2
Companionship	9	5	4
Ability to take action	12	4	2
Self-determination	12	2	3
Mutual engagement	8	4	5
Knowledge	13	1	3
Consensus	8	4	5
Mutual attention	10	6	2
Mutual empathy	9	2	6

n = 18
N A/D = Neither agree nor disagree
Note: Where totals equal less than *n,* there were instances of no response.

Analysis of the Interview

To analyze the interview results we categorized and described the responses given to the first five questions in terms of (1) what power means to them as an individual, (2) what power generally means in U.S. society, (3) what power means in their ethnic culture, (4) whether, as women, they have power in U.S. society, and (5) whether, as women, they have power in Seminole culture. We then evaluated responses regarding the women's perceptions of how power *is* and *should be used* in the areas of work, family, religion, and politics. Finally, we examined the responses in terms of their relation to the four power models under examination.

Introductory Questions

All eighteen Native American participants responded to the question, "What does the word *power* mean to you as an individual?" Eight of the women identified with models other than the traditional power paradigm (see Table 8.5). Six identified with personal authority, two identified with reciprocal empowerment, six identified with power, and none identified with empowerment. In six of the eighteen cases, participants described their views of power as coming from within. For example, women gave statements such as, "You have inner strength and self-determination to do whatever you can as an individual," "independent, not relying on others," and "power comes from within." In contrast, six women responded with statements such as, "to be able to take control of others and have them listen to you," or "having control, being above everybody."

TABLE 8.5. Native American Women: Responses to Introductory Interview Questions and the Relationship of These Responses to the Power Models

Introductory Interview Questions	Traditional Power	Empowerment	Personal Authority	Reciprocal Empowerment
What does the word *power* mean to you as an individual?	6	0	6	2
What do you think the word *power* means in American society today?	9	1	0	0
What do you think the word *power* means in your culture?	5	3	4	3
As a woman, what kind of power do you think you have in U.S. society?	0	0	0	0
As a Native American woman, what do you think the word *power* means in your culture?	7	2	5	2

n = 18

Note: Total numbers may not match *n* since in some cases responses could not be associated with a power model. Zero equals no responses or responses could not be associated with a model.

In terms of the women's perception of what power means in general in U.S. society today, the overwhelming majority used terms associated with the traditional power model. Five of the eighteen women associated power in the United States with money, while five associated it with control. Statements reflecting these attitudes included "someone that has the money" and "control over others—power is having control over someone else, having money, and being in control of others in the worst way." Three women described power as an overtly negative attribute. Examples of these descriptions included "manipulation—negative meaning" and "negative connotation—provokes dark, evil, using people in a bad way."

In describing their perceptions about what power means in their own culture, the majority of women used terms associated with alternatives to the traditional power model. As a matter of fact, only two made references to traditional power by mentioning money. Unlike responses to previous questions, the women also noted empowerment attributes within their culture. In addition, thirteen of the respondents referred to family, customs, or tradition. Statements included "I would say family, values, traditions, knowing your culture and history seems to be important among us here [on the reservation]," "speaking our language—caring for or teaching our traditional beliefs to our children so they can pass them on to their future families or clans," and "knowledge of traditions and customs." Two respondents specifically referred to the "medicine man" as the focus of power in Seminole culture, one referred to religion, and one stated that "power is a word not in our culture."

The question of what kind of power they, as women, have in U.S. society elicited no responses that we could interpret in terms of the four power models. In fact, eleven of the respondents said that, as women, they thought they had little or no power in U.S. society. The majority of these responses were extremely brief: "little to none," "I don't think I have any," "not much at all," and "none really." Two of these women indicated that their only power was in numbers: "no power, unless in numbers; it's a man's world." Five of these women said they have little or no power because, in the United States, men have the power. Two women felt they had some power while one felt she had a lot.

The corresponding question, "As a Seminole woman, what do you think the word *power* means in your culture?" elicited a majority of responses associated with attributes of the other power paradigms. Five women used terms associated with personal authority and two each offered descriptions associated with empowerment and reciprocal empowerment. Seven of the respondents indicated that Seminole women have a significant amount of power in their culture with one identifying the Seminole tribe as matriarchal. She stated that "The Seminole culture is matriarchal. Women have power. Although men hold the positions on the council, they always come to a woman for advice." Of the eighteen respondents, nine associated family, traditions, and customs with power in their culture. For example, one woman said, "immediate care and responsibility of myself, my family, and my clan. Children are the future so we pass on our heritage, culture, and language," while another woman said, "Indian society, language, culture—having our own government."

Work

Seventeen of the eighteen Native American women were employed. All of these women worked on the reservation for the Seminole tribe in businesses such as the smoke shop, government offices, and the newspaper office. In responding to earlier questions on the influence of power in their Seminole culture, many women indicated that power does not play a major role. However, when discussing a specific area such as work, three of the women stated that people have different kinds of power on the job. Responses included "Some people believe they have power that they don't. Everyone feels powerful, but not really," "I work for the secretary of the treasurer's office; I work for the most powerful woman in the tribe," and "Yes—the level of position they hold determines the power they have." Two stated that the chairman has the final say and is answerable only to the council, who, in turn, is answerable to the people.

Nine of the eighteen women felt that they personally have some kind of power on the job. Of that group most seemed to associate power with "getting the job done right," and at least three of them attributed their power to their special knowledge or expertise. Their responses ranged from having the ability to "speak the language when most people don't" to "having the power to get things done." Six of the women felt, however, that they have little or no power.

When asked to give specific examples of how power *is used* where they work, ten women said that traditional power prevailed, and a large number also mentioned personal authority attributes (see Table 8.6). Four women, without giving specific examples, gave indications of the negative use of power as in, "People who think they have power use it to get what they want (individual benefits). It should be for the benefit of the department and tribe, but egos run high." Another statement given indicating that power is used negatively on the job follows: "People use power to coerce, intimidate, dominate . . . [to make people] afraid of them." Five of the women indicated that a power hierarchy existed on their job. This was evidenced in statements such as "There is a power structure that we all have to follow," ". . . answer to whomever is above me—give directions," and " have all the power—make all the choices."

TABLE 8.6. Native American Women: Interview Responses to Questions About Work, Family, Religion, and Politics

How Power *Is Used*

	Traditional Power	Empowerment	Personal Authority	Reciprocal Empowerment
Work	10	1	10	1
Family	11	6	1	2
Religion	2	0	4	1
Politics	2	2	0	2

How Power *Should Be Used*

	Traditional Power	Empowerment	Personal Authority	Reciprocal Empowerment
Work	2	6	0	4
Family	2	1	0	1
Religion	0	1	0	0
Politics	0	0	0	1

n = 18

Note: Total numbers may not match *n* since in some cases responses could not be associated with a power model. Zero equals no responses or responses could not be associated with a model.

The women's responses to questions about how power *should be used* on the job clearly indicated a desire to shift from the power and personal authority paradigms to empowerment and reciprocal empowerment paradigms. Six women responded with statements such as "not for personal use," "trying to help others, not trying to dominate, being there for them and giving them the information and access that they need, not saying 'no' but saying 'why don't you try it this way?' " and "to make positive changes within the community and assist others' needs. I am responsible for my own needs." All of these statements suggested a desire to use power in a manner that would benefit others. Four of the women, although not directly speaking of using power overtly to benefit others, still mentioned power positively. For example, "[power] should not be used to get above. It should be used positively, people working together," or ". . . positive way—people shouldn't manipulate others."

Family

When asked to identify their immediate families, three women described a nuclear family. These three women mentioned "husband and children," "son," and "my mother and father, my children." On the other hand, fifteen of the women described their families as extended. Six of these women mentioned the clan as members of their immediate family. Their responses included "husband, son, brothers and their family, mom, dad, and clan members (seventy-five people)." Other responses included "goes all the way to aunts, uncles, cousins, whether by marriage or by bloodline, I don't differentiate even my entire clan," and "Clan is thicker than blood, uncles, brothers, aunts, children, husband." Nine of these women, however, did not include the clan, but included aunts, uncles, brothers-in-law, grandchildren, and even some close friends.

Fourteen women said that a female is the head of the household. It was evident that, in at least one case, the female was a grandmother. Three indicated that a husband or father was head of the house and one associated that responsibility with a brother. Nine of the respondents indicated that a female made the major decisions with regard to the children. Four said the decisions were equally shared while one mentioned her father and two mentioned a grandparent. Twelve gave the major decision-making role regarding housework to a female.

Three indicated that the decision making was shared equally, one associated the responsibility with her father, and two mentioned a grandparent. With regard to financial decisions, eleven women indicated that a female made the major decisions whereas four indicated both a male and a female.

The responses to the question asking what the word *power* means in their families were quite varied, and included money, income and finances, or being in charge or in control. The women gave statements such as "control of oneself and knowledge of the culture," "being in charge," and "I would say control." Others said, "having an education and being able to make it up the income ladder," "I am the boss of the finances and the family," and "the boss of money, spending, and buying." On the other hand, several women spoke of unity or equality, mother, and tradition in statements such as "teaching kids the customs, language, the culture"; "keeping together in celebration, ceremonies, and anniversaries—extended families"; "when united all in one"; "keeping the customs and traditions alive"; and "Any mom! That's power, she guides me—tells it like it is."

Five of the eighteen women interviewed claimed they have a lot of power in their immediate families. This was evident in statements such as "I make all the decisions. I ask my husband, but I make the final decision," "I have control of everything," and "I have all of the power, I make all of the choices." Ten of the women felt they have some power as in, "The family looks to me to run the house smoothly. I give chores to the children to keep up their rooms and pick up the house," "giving the children the direction to be responsible in their future—old way, new way, future. For example, my daughter knows her history/roots." The women who indicated that they have a lot of power did not state the source of their power. However, of the thirteen women who felt they have some power, two felt their financial positions give them power, while six said that their role as mothers in charge of their children and teachers who pass on the culture and traditions gives them whatever power they do have. Three felt that they have no power.

Responses by eleven of the eighteen respondents to questions about how power *is used* in their immediate families showed evidence of traditional power (see Table 8.6). In some cases it was the women who wielded this power and in some cases it was the men. Six women responded using empowerment attributes, mostly referring to caregiving. The women mentioned one personal authority attribute and two reciprocal empowerment attributes.

In response to the question about how power *should be used* in the family, few responses related to the four power models. However, eight women said power, if used, should be equal, and one woman said it should not be used at all.

Religion

In terms of interview questions related to religion, eleven of the eighteen women responded. Nine gave Christianity as their religion (five identified themselves as Baptists, three as Catholics, and one simply said "Christian"). Two women identified themselves as Traditionalists, referring to traditional Seminole spiritual beliefs and practices.

Many of the responses were so vague that we could not draw any obvious conclusions. Of the more specific responses, the results were spread across the board with women seeing power as traditional power, empowerment, and personal authority. Seven of the women recognized different kinds of power in their religious practices while three replied that they did not. Of these three, the woman who had simply identified herself as a Christian said, "No—all are equal in the eyes of God." Of those who perceived different forms of power, some cited positions of authority as the source of power, such as "yes, the priest/pope leads and guides with spirituality" and "they think they do . . . pastor, deacon, Sunday school teachers." The two Traditionalists answered this question as follows: "everyone—each person has different duties" and "yes, tradition, history, knowledge of culture." Finally, a woman who had earlier identified herself as Baptist referred to the Seminole Green Corn Dance in answering this question: "yes, Green Corn Dance—men are only allowed to go into the sweat lodges. Men and women eat at different times." All three who referenced Seminole spiritual practices provided answers that reflected clear delineation of duties and responsibilities within the group.

Six of the women believed that they have some power within their religion, and two of these women explicitly identified the power to pray as a form of individual religious power. Three women, however, believed that they have little or no power in their religion, which they stated simply: "I don't really think that I do."

Two women said they could provide no examples of how power *is used* in their religion, while two of the women referred specifically to money: "don't think they use it except they're always collecting money" and "Money . . . the church has the power to help those in need" (see Table 8.6). Several women described power in terms of personal authority, mentioning knowledge and the power to act. Other answers were quite varied, but some of the participants mentioned counseling, praying, or referred, once again, to specific positions of authority such as "The pastor is the teacher to the congregation." One of the Traditionalists did not answer this question while the other said, "determining who will get knowledge to do certain things within the religion—determination is learned also."

When considering the role of women and power in their religion, these women responded in a variety of ways, with no particular response claiming the majority. Two of the women said they simply did not know. Two women believed that women have little or no power, stating that, "I don't think that women do because it is dominated by men" and "not too much—participating in song and Sunday school." In contrast, two women believed that they have a great deal of power. One of the Traditionalists said that "Women are the backbone. They get men going to do things they need to." The other woman who believed women were powerful simply said that "Women always handle the males." Two women also believed that women are equal to men in their religion. One stated that "[women are] seen as equal to men," while the other—also a Traditionalist—said that "They [women] can be equal to men, but all of it is earned and determined."

In terms of how they think power *should be used,* we could relate virtually no responses to any of the power paradigms; however, there was a good deal of variety in the responses. Two of the answers were worded to indicate that power should be used for the good: "family, work, spirituality—to help, not hurt" and "for good, not bad." Two women indicated that power in religion should be used equally, and three women thought that power should be used as it is now. The two Traditionalists answered in this way: "equal, but it's the way it has been for years and years" and "The way it is now—nothing wrong." Two women believed that power should be used in ways indicated by the Bible. One woman explicitly indicated that power should not be used in religion, and one of the women, who identified herself as a Baptist, responded that the "Seminole tribe does not use power. Other tribes do, but not the Seminole tribe."

Politics

In responding to questions on politics, thirteen of the eighteen women said they were not affiliated with a political organization or cause. Of the five women who indicated some involvement in politics, three did not identify a political affiliation (although in answering the previous question, one of these women said she was a Republican who votes Democratic), one identified herself as a Republican, and one identified herself as Seminole.

Two women who had indicated some association with politics did not respond to the question of whether people in political organizations have different kinds of power. One woman, a Republican, said that she does not vote, and two women indicated that they believe people do have different kinds of power in politics. One of these two women simply said "yes" to the question, while the woman who identified her political affiliation as Seminole said "yes—what they have as being a part of it—office—power and control provides choices to benefit the tribe and the community."

As in the previous questions on politics, two women chose not to respond to the question regarding what kind of power they have in their political organizations. Two of the women indicated that exercising their right to vote constituted the main form of power that they have in politics. The woman who identified with Seminole politics stated that she had a "voice in the community—I know the needs and areas of concern, [I] can resolve them by being involved with the needs of people."

Two women did not provide examples of how power *is used* in their political organizations, but of the three women who did, two specifically mentioned the role of money in politics: "use power and money to get what they want" and "Clinton-Lewinsky taking in money when it was wrong." The woman involved in Seminole politics said, "Power is the choices that are made to benefit the community. Needs are filled in regard to health, education, and welfare."

Three women chose to respond to the question of how power *should be used* in politics. Two of these three women responded in ways that reflect a desire for equality. One woman simply said "equally," while the woman active in Seminole politics said, "being used in the right way for the people. The whole tribe, every individual has a say like a shareholder—have the same backgrounds and beliefs." The woman who identified herself as a Republican who votes Democratic said that "power should be used very lightly because it is a very volatile arena and finding things like Hillary [Clinton] making money on stocks is pure luck. Because she is who she is, they thought 'Oh wow, she did something wrong.' "

Although the vast majority of these women chose to remain silent concerning the previous questions about power and politics, all eighteen women responded to the question, "How do you see the power roles of women who are affiliated with politics?" In sum, the responses were generally hopeful. These individuals indicated that women can do the job if they are given a chance, and many participants believed that women's roles in politics will be stronger in the future. One woman focused on women having to fight for power: "Women have to fight for every inch they get, while men seem to get it on a silver platter. Women have to fight just to keep what we got. It's not equal, they say it is, but it's not." Two women indicated specifically that women are often not taken seriously: "More women should be taken seriously and be heard." Five of the women desired to see more women in politics and indicated this by saying things such as "I like having women in politics—I want there to be more." One woman said that women's power in politics should be equal to men's, and a couple of the women interviewed seemed to give decided preference to women over men: "Women are more logical," "Women are caretakers and they will relay that to the whole community. In the future we will benefit from this," and "Janet Reno, [she] does not listen to the public. She does her job by the law; she is strong."

CONCLUSION

The overall results of the survey indicated that the Native American women preferred all of the alternatives to the traditional power paradigm, and it is obvious that of these alternatives they identified most strongly with the personal authority attributes. Although the women generally agreed with aspects of empowerment, their level of agreement was noticeably weaker than with personal authority and reciprocal empowerment. In examining the results concerning reciprocal empowerment, we noticed that the women agreed most frequently with the reciprocal empowerment elements that derive from personal authority. Conversely, they agreed less often with those reciprocal empowerment elements that derive from the empowerment model. It appears, then, that the Seminole women surveyed are comfortable in expressing the importance of developing personal authority in order to be powerful, and they seem quite willing to take this personal power into the community to help others, but they are not quite as eager to practice the traditional form of empowerment that emphasizes helping others with little attention to the self.

In terms of the traditional power attribute with which a majority of the women agreed (struggle) and those with which the women were evenly divided (domination, conflict, and competition), one possible conclusion could lie in the historical situation of Native Americans who have been the victims of force and coercion, who have had to struggle to maintain an identity, and who survive in a society which has afforded them few resources. In addition, for those who agreed with the use of domination, conflict, and competition, at least two possible explanations exist. It may be that these attributes are inherent to Seminole culture and do not carry negative connotations, or it could be that the half who agree with these aspects of traditional power believe that they are necessary in order to gain power in "the white man's world."

Two major themes emerged from the women's responses to the first interview question asking them what power means to them as individuals: (1) an inner directedness, indicating a source of power coming from within, and (2) an outer directedness which, while not necessarily pointing to the control-over aspect of the traditional power paradigm, does suggest the drawing of power from external sources.

In addition, in the interview responses, personal authority surfaced frequently along with traditional power in relation to the women's personal perceptions of power as well as the perception they have of themselves specifically as women in the Seminole culture. This tendency for the women to identify with the attributes associated with personal authority is contrasted sharply by their perception of U.S. society's notion of power and their place as women in that society. The participants most strongly identified U.S. society with traditional power and they believe they have little or no power in that society.

For both work- and family-related questions the participants indicated that traditional power is currently used. Along with traditional power, the women indicated that empowerment attributes are used in the family. They also indicated that personal authority attributes are evident in the workplace. This may be because personal authority and power are connected, or because the women associate job positions with authority. In terms of family, the vast majority of responses centered on traditional power, but more often than not, the power was wielded by women.

Particularly in the area of work, there was a noticeable difference between how these women see power being used and how they think it should be used. The women indicated a desire for the attributes of empowerment and reciprocal empowerment on the job. That is, rather than the hierarchical structure they currently see, the women preferred an equitable environment in which peers work together to achieve shared goals. In terms of family, the women simply preferred equality.

The fact that the Seminole women we interviewed described power in the family in terms of equality rather than according to any of the attributes of the power models we identified correlates with the secondary literature discussed earlier in this chapter. Historically, Seminole gender roles have been distinct and have adhered to public and private sphere categories. Yet unlike white Western cultures, the Seminoles value both spheres equally. We believe the significant recurrence of the term "equal" or "equally" in our interviews affirms the Seminole practice of complementary gender roles indigenous to their culture.

The women also associated their culture and its traditions with power. These terms arose primarily within the introductory questions of the interview, particularly in relation to individual perceptions of power, perceptions of power in Seminole culture, and in response to the question about what power means as a woman in the Seminole culture. The women also mentioned teaching as an important part of power in reference to passing on their culture and traditions. In addition, these Seminole women mentioned respect in relation to the questions about power in their culture and about power in the family, the workplace, and in politics.

Although the majority of these women indicated preference for power of personal authority, the small number of women who identified strongly with traditional Native American culture were those who had a strong sense of both personal authority and reciprocal empowerment. To determine who these women were, we scoured the interview for respondents who continuously referred to their clans, culture, and traditions. For example, in responding to questions on work, one of these women said, "power should be used positively, not to manipulate each other, but to communicate and empower each other instead of overpowering others." Another woman, in responding to a question on family, said, "providing a sense of responsibility and understanding, being fair and nonjudgmental. Power is what you make of it, it's your choice determining the path you will take."

Finally, in terms of the questions on politics, two women responded to the question, "How do you see the power roles of women who are affiliated with politics?" as follows: "Roles of women will be stronger and more dominant in the future. Women are caretakers and they will relay that to the whole community. Women are more sensitive to the needs of society. In the future we will benefit from this," and "Women in politics here [on the reservation] are women who are educated both culturally and through college and school. Within our culture they are treated equally as the men in politics."

These last two quotes indicate a preference for reciprocal empowerment, which is related to LaFromboise and colleagues' (1990) discussion of retraditionalization. These Seminole women hold tightly to their traditionally important roles of protecting and maintaining the family and tribe, and they extend these roles to the public sphere within the reservation, perhaps even outside it, in their style of maneuvering within the larger U.S. culture. For Seminole women who closely identify with their indigenous culture, then, retraditionalization is reciprocal empowerment.

Chapter 9

Conclusion

We began this project in an effort to discover whether women from the seven racial/ethnic groups under investigation preferred or practiced reciprocal empowerment rather than the other forms of power being evaluated. We were also interested in revealing what differences might surface in relation to the women's perceptions of power. Our results were mixed. Survey results indicated that when the women were asked to indicate their level of agreement versus disagreement with statements embodying the attributes of traditional power, empowerment, personal authority, and reciprocal empowerment—overwhelmingly and without exception—they chose those statements which represent personal authority and reciprocal empowerment. Survey results also indicated that although they rejected empowerment, they embraced its attributes when they were stated in a form consistent with reciprocal empowerment. Also without exception, and as anticipated, the women generally rejected traditional power. Yet results from the interview presented a rather interesting turn. At first glance it appeared that the women did not describe reciprocal empowerment; however, a more careful examination of the power attributes used by these women in their responses suggested that many of our participants found affinity with what we now propose as a revised form of reciprocal empowerment.

Our final discussion begins with a more detailed comparison of results from the survey and the interview. We then introduce a revised form of reciprocal empowerment suggested by the participants' interview responses. In conclusion, we present our recommendations, both in terms of future scholarly studies as well as practical action that should extend beyond the academy.

DISCUSSION OF SURVEY AND INTERVIEW RESULTS

Our survey consisted of fifty-two statements using attributes representing the four power paradigms. The women were asked to indicate how they felt about each statement by agreeing or disagreeing with the statements. The women's responses supported much of the literature presented in Chapter 1, which suggested that women, in general, do not espouse the attributes associated with traditional power (see Table 9.1). Except for the Asian-American women who participated in the study, the women were generally in disagreement with most of the attributes associated with this model of power. However, a majority of women in all seven groups personally agreed with the traditional power statement about resources, and a majority of women in six of the seven groups personally agreed with the survey statements about competition and struggle. Although empowerment was also rejected by many of the women, a majority of women in all seven groups personally agreed with the statement about compassion. In addition, a majority of women in six of the groups agreed with the statement about competence.

The interview was divided into two main sections for analysis: (1) a discussion of responses to the five introductory questions and (2) a summary of answers to questions of how power *is used* and *should be used* in the areas of work, family, religion, and politics. In the women's responses to the introductory question asking about their individual perceptions of power, all groups most often described traditional power followed by personal authority (see Table 9.2). This question did not, however, ask them what form or kind of power they preferred. Next, when asked about the meaning of power in U.S. society, without exception the women described traditional power. When the women were asked about the meaning of power in their specific culture, they spoke of personal authority attributes, but these characterizations were secondary to traditional power. An obvious change in the responses occurred when the women were asked about their perceptions of power—specifically as women—both within U.S. society and in their particular culture. In responding to questions about their perception as women in U.S. society, four groups identified with attributes associated with personal authority. These women were African American, Asian American, Latin American, and Middle East-

TABLE 9.1. Survey Results Indicating the Women's Preference Among the Four Power Models

	African-American Women	Asian-American Women	Caribbean-American Women	European-American Women	Latin American Women	Middle Eastern-American Women	Native American Women
Traditional power							
Empowerment							
Personal authority							
Reciprocal empowerment							

Note: Shadings indicate levels of preference

1st preference =

2nd preference =

3rd preference =

TABLE 9.2. Power Paradigm Associations from the Five Introductory Interview Questions

Introductory Interview Questions	**African-American Women**	**Asian-American Women**	**Caribbean-American Women**	**European-American Women**	**Latin American Women**	**Middle Eastern-American Women**	**Native American Women**
What does the word *power* mean to you as an individual?	TP/PA	TP	TP/PA	TP/PA	TP	TP/PA	TP/PA
What do you think the word *power* means in American society today?	TP	TP	TP	TP	TP	TP	TP
What do you think the word *power* means in your culture?	TP/PA	TP	TP	TP	TP	TP/PA	TP/PA
As a woman, what kind of power do you think you have in U.S. society?	PA	PA	O	O	PA	PA	O
As a/an [insert appropriate ethnic group] woman, what do you think the word *power* means in your culture?	TP/PA	TP/PA	TP/PA	TP	PA	PA	TP/PA

TP = Traditional power; E = Empowerment; PA = Personal authority; RE = Reciprocal empowerment; O = No responses or responses could not be associated with a paradigm.

ern American. Caribbean-American, European-American, and Native American women provided some responses to these questions that we could not associate with any of the four power models. Their responses, however, were indicative of certain positions these three groups of women chose to take. For example, the Caribbean-American women saw men, not women, as power brokers. For European-American women, power in U.S. society was associated with freedom of expression, sexuality, and decision making. Some of the Native American women felt it was a man's world, others simply felt that they had no power, and still others did not see themselves as part of U.S. society.

When participants were asked about the meaning of power for them as women specifically in their culture, traditional power followed by personal authority resurfaced as the forms of power most often described. In two groups, Latin American and Middle Eastern American, the women chose only personal authority attributes. In only one case, European American, did the women select traditional power terms exclusively.

Responses to interview questions about work and family followed the same pattern as the five introductory questions in that traditional power was the model all the women described most often (see Table 9.3). This was particularly evident in response to questions asking how power *is used* in these arenas. Only the Native American women described additional attributes, indicating that personal authority attributes along with traditional power attributes are used in the workplace. In regard to family, the groups using attributes in addition to those associated with traditional power were the European Americans, Latin Americans, and Native Americans. Both European Americans and Latin Americans saw evidence of personal authority attributes in the workplace, whereas the European American and Native American women both said empowerment attributes are used in the family.

Of note, only two of the seven groups of women had much of anything to say in relation to the four power models when asked how power *should be used,* and then only in relation to work. These two groups were Caribbean-American and Native American women. Caribbean-American women felt that traditional power attributes should be used on the job, whereas Native American women desired empowerment and reciprocal empowerment attributes on the job.

TABLE 9.3. Power Paradigm Associations from the Interview Questions Regarding How Power *Is Used* and How Power *Should Be Used* in the Areas of Work, Family, Religion, and Politics

Interview Questions	**African-American Women**	**Asian-American Women**	**Caribbean-American Women**	**European-American Women**	**Latin American Women**	**Middle Eastern-American Women**	**Native American Women**
Work							
is	TP	TP	TP	TP	TP	TP	TP/PA
should be	O	O	TP	O	O	O	E/RE
Family							
is	TP	TP	TP	TP/E/PA	TP/PA	TP	TP/E
should be	O	O	O	O	O	O	O
Religion							
is	O	O	O	O	O	O	PA
should be	O	O	O	O	O	O	O
Politics							
is	O	O	O	O	O	O	O
should be	O	O	O	O	O	O	O

TP = Traditional power; E = Empowerment; PA = Personal authority; RE = Reciprocal empowerment; O = No responses or responses could not be associated with a paradigm.

It must be made clear here that just because we were not able to associate the women's responses with a power paradigm does not mean that they had nothing to say. To the contrary, they had many opinions. In the case of work and family, many of the women's responses simply were not phrased in ways related to the four models. Instead, several other attributes emerged and were used repeatedly by a majority of the groups, especially in response to how power should be used in the family. These terms included decision making, respect, and equality, which we will discuss at length later. To a lesser extent, these same terms were used by the women in the few responses we received regarding how power *should be used* at work.

In terms of religion and politics, the women had virtually nothing to say in relation to our original list of attributes related to the four power models. Furthermore, unlike the areas of work and family, the women made very few additional comments we could interpret as descriptors of power. In fact, Native American women were the only group whose responses to the question asking how power is used in religion suggested evidence of personal authority attributes.

These results raised one major question: why did these women demonstrate such a marked disinterest or disassociation with the areas of religion and politics, particularly in terms of how power should be used in these arenas? In the few responses concerning religion, five major themes emerged across the seven cultures interviewed. In general, the women felt that men held all the power in religion, God held the power, power was not associated with religion, power should not be used in religion, or the women indicated that the only power they had was the power to pray. As one woman said, "I have the power to watch all the priests and other men conduct a Mass. It's been that way since the beginning of time. Why make a fuss now?" Other responses included, "There is no power; God is all powerful"; "The church has the power"; "God himself is the almighty power"; "I require no power in my church"; "I have the power to pray"; and power should be used "just as it is, nonexistent."

The issue of women's subordination and their seeming acquiescence to male-dominated religious tenets, illustrated by some of the previous quotes, is not new. Feminist scholars and activists have traced this problem back to the usurping of the goddess religion with a monotheistic male god. In the video *Seneca Reflections: Celebrating 150 Years of Women's Rights* (1998), Sally Roesch Wagner, director of the Matilda Joslyn Gage Foundation, says that suffragettes Elizabeth Cady Stanton, Mary Baker Eddy, and Matilda Joslyn Gage believed there was an issue greater than getting the vote, which was

> the teaching of the church, that women must be subordinate to men. They said that it was the removal of the female in the godhead and the creation of a single male god that had pushed women into a devalued position. [This was done] along with the inclusion of the teachings of St. Paul, of women's subordination, that had taken Christianity away from its original foundation. They believed that the true work that they had to do was to rid women of what they called their "religious superstition"—that is, the belief that they were indeed created by god to be inferior to men. The true religion, Gage said, is that which sets people free.

The change to a male-oriented, hierarchical, monotheistic religious structure may well be one of the original sources of power-over relationships that still exist today. This power-over relationship is especially evident between man and woman. Daly (1973) argues that

> As a power-relation, then, monotheism invariably creates a hierarchy—of one god over others, of stronger over weaker, of believer over unbeliever. In addition, the new concept of a personal relationship between man and his god, since God has chosen to create him in his own image, led to the idea of the Father God as vested in every human patriarch. [Therefore], woman could not recover from one primal overwhelming disability—she was not male. . . . If God was male and woman was not male, then whatever God was, woman was not. (pp. 69-70)

Contemporary feminist scholars supply one possible explanation why the women we interviewed were more opinionated about the role of power in family and work than they were about religion. For example, Stone (1976) suggests that "Biblical attitudes may no longer be justified to many contemporary women or men as being vital or absolute because the Lord has decreed that they were so, but centuries of having followed these religiously based precepts have provided the next argument—people have 'always' accepted them as right; therefore, they must be the natural normal way of being" (pp. 239-240). Contemporary women may be prepared to assert themselves at home and at work, but we believe that this age-old familiarity with patriarchal religion may have resulted in the few responses we received in the twenty-first century, in which power was associated repeatedly with God, the pope, priests, rabbis, pundits, pastors, ministers, and church elders. Consequently, a subordinate position was articulated by the women in responses such as "I need to pray more," and "I'm a subservient person when it comes to church."

These types of responses were not unique to the answers related to religion. They were also evident in the few responses we received in relation to questions concerning politics. It was evident, from the one question to which the women seemed to respond with some, albeit limited, enthusiasm, that several of the women were optimistic about the roles of women in politics. However, we identified three themes in the less positive responses. First, most of the women were unwilling to associate themselves with any form of political activity. Second, many of the women associated important power positions with men. Last, some of the participants believed that women are not mentally or emotionally capable or prepared to undertake political challenges. The first theme was illustrated by the fact that of the 136 women interviewed only nineteen women, or 14 percent, indicated that they were affiliated with a political organization or cause. Of these nineteen women, only a few noted that this affiliation resulted in actual voting. The second theme was evident in statements such as, "My father thinks that women don't belong in high-ranking political positions"; "Women are not as powerful as political men"; "This society is only pretending to let us see women as having power"; and "Women are still outnumbered and outspoken by male roles." As for the third theme, some of the women we interviewed suggested: "Women are still lacking the ability to achieve the highest level"; "Women are not to be trusted. They are weaker; men are stronger"; "Society never gave women a chance to become strong political leaders"; "I think women could have great power in politics if they concentrated less on becoming independent and more on family. What is their role in the family structure? They should become more oriented with nature and the natural progression of things"; and "What if the woman has a baby or PMS [premenstrual syndrome]?"

The paucity of responses to questions on politics, as well as the character of the few responses we did receive, requires some discussion. First, we suggest that a relationship between the arena of religious frameworks and political activity exists and is long-standing. According to Stone (1976), who quoted Lucy Komisar's study, *The New Feminism,* abolitionists Sarah and Angelina Grimke raised the ire of the church when they assumed political positions by speaking out against slavery. They were chastised in the following statement: "The power of a woman is her dependency flowing from the consciousness of that weakness which God has given her for her protection . . . when she assumes the place and tone of man as a public reformer, she yields the power which God has given her for her protection and her character becomes *unnatural!*" (Stone, 1976, pp. 231-232). Simone de Beauvoir argues (as cited in Stone, 1976) that it is this position by the church that led many women to shun political activism: "Man enjoys the great advantage of having a god endorse the code he writes; and since man exercises a sovereign authority over women it is especially fortunate that this authority has been vested in him by the Supreme Being. For the Jews, Mohammedans, and Christians among others, man is master by divine right, the fear of God will therefore repress any impulse towards revolt in the downtrodden female" (p. 237). Since religion has the power to describe ultimate reality and the dominant religions leave women out of their characterizations of the public sphere, then it follows that few women would risk engaging in overtly political activities.

Additional explanations are articulated by McGlen and O'Connor (1995), who say that "Five interrelated barriers exist that continue to prevent women from fully exercising their political rights: (1) negative public attitudes toward the role of women in politics, (2) the lack of appropriate careers and preparation for political activity, (3) family demands, (4) sex discrimination, and (5) the political system" (p. 93). The interview responses we quoted illustrate at least the first four barriers described by McGlen and O'Connor, and we believe that the lack of political participation by most of our respondents supports the validity of these barriers.

Although we think the women we interviewed recognized these barriers, we saw little evidence that they were willing to participate actively in creating change in their situation. Our concern with these results is that the position of women in society cannot improve without their participation. As Gloria Steinem argues in the video *Equality: A History of the Women's Movement in America* (Schlessinger, 1996),

> Most of us have learned that women's position in life is not due to biology, or Freud, or God; it's due to politics, in the deepest sense of politics. And similarly, men and women of color, their position is not due to any racial theory of intelligence, or separation of the races; it's due to a system of power. And the minute you realize that [is] the minute you realize there's hope, there's change, that there's a future that can be different.

We argue, then, that our participants' general complacency with current power relations in religious and political institutions does not bode well for women's future well-being. We address these related issues later in our recommendations.

REVISED MODEL OF RECIPROCAL EMPOWERMENT

Equality, decision making, and respect are words with which many participants in our study found some measure of power. This realization came very early in our analysis when we noticed that the women felt they had some power, but they were not necessarily describing this power using terms we associated with the four power paradigms. Although these words were used frequently throughout the interview responses, we realized that they were mentioned primarily in the context of how power *should be used* in the family. These words showed up repeatedly and across the seven cultural groups, except with Native American women who did not mention decision making (see Table 9.4).

The use of these three attributes was so prominent that we could not overlook them, and their repeated use led to a major question: How, if at all, do these words impact any or all of the four models of power we presented at the outset of our study? Taken in the context in which they appeared in the interview responses, we believe these attributes, especially the words *equality* and *respect,* are best suited to the notion of reciprocal empowerment. At the outset of our study we defined reciprocal empowerment as a discursive and behavioral style of interaction grounded in reciprocity initiated by people who feel a sense of personal authority. No form of reciprocity that we had in mind could be possible without respect for another's perspective. That is, in reciprocal empowerment we envisioned interactions com-

TABLE 9.4. New Attributes Used by Women in Response to Interview Questions

African-American Women	Asian-American Women	Caribbean-American Women	European-American Women	Latin American Women	Middle Eastern-American Women	Native American Women
Decision Making	Decision Making	Decision Making	Decision Making	Decision Making	Decision Making	—
Equality/Sharing	Equality/Sharing	Equality/Sharing	Equality	Equality/Sharing	Equality/Sharing	Equality
—	—	—	—	—	—	Tradition
Respect	Respect	Respect	Respect	—	Respect	Respect
—	—	—	—	—	Voice	—
Freedom	Freedom	—	—	Freedom	Freedom	—
—	Class/Status	—	Status	—	—	—
—	—	Color	—	—	—	—

— indicates that the word in this row was not used by this cultural group posed of respectful reciprocity. We believe that individuals who participate in such interactions must necessarily begin on equal footing in order for the reciprocal empowerment process to occur.

In addition, our original discussion of reciprocal empowerment noted that participants in the process must have enough self-confidence and respect for others to assist them without sacrificing self. Despite our realization that respect is an inherent part of this model, we neglected to consider it as an attribute; therefore, we neither included it in the graphic representation of reciprocal empowerment nor did we include it in the survey statements designed to illustrate reciprocal empowerment. We were, therefore, pleasantly surprised to find the word repeatedly used throughout the interview responses. Many of the women obviously considered respect an essential attribute of power.

Furthermore, we suggested in the book's introduction that the personal authority aspect of reciprocal empowerment provides an individual with a level of knowledge necessary to develop a heightened self-confidence that can then lead to action. This type of action can surely be evidenced in decision-making processes. It does not surprise us, then, that many women interviewed saw the ability to make decisions as a necessary component of the kind of power they prefer. At first we considered that the women's use of decision making may have been encouraged by the interview question that asked respondents who makes the major decisions in the family in the areas of child rearing, housework, and finances. A review of the results indicated, however, that decision making was touted as an attribute of power by the respondents even before they were asked this specific question. This, at least, reduced the possibility that we had encouraged the use of decision making as an attribute of power.

Table 9.4 indicates that five other words were often used by the women in our study that we could not associate with the power models: freedom, class/status, tradition, voice, and color. The women did not use these words as frequently as the three attributes just discussed. However, freedom was mentioned often by four of the groups (African-American, Asian-American, Latin American, and Middle Eastern-American women), primarily in response to the five introductory questions to the interview. Since we asked these questions to facilitate discussion about general notions of power, it appears that these women see freedom as essential to societal, cultural, and personal concepts of power. Similarly, class and status as forms of power were mentioned most frequently by Asian-American and European-American women and almost exclusively in response to the introductory questions. Research indicated that class and status resonate with the cultural and historical background of both these groups. In relevant literature, status is often mentioned as a value in many Asian cultures. For European Americans, status historically was granted to them simply due to their race or skin color. Tradition, voice, and color were each mentioned by only one group, and in all three cases these responses reflected the cultural and historical experiences of these groups. Thus, Native American women frequently mentioned tradition and customs, Caribbean-American women described color as a power attribute in U.S. society, and throughout the interview Middle Eastern-American women mentioned the importance of having a voice. The Seminole women we interviewed all worked at Big Cypress Reservation and were actively engaged in preserving their Native American culture in the face of assimilation into non-Native America. Caribbean Americans are often struck by the predominant role that race and skin color plays in U.S. society in comparison to their home cultures. Middle Eastern-American women, many of whom are Muslim, face the challenge of subverting common U.S. stereotypes about subservience and silence in Muslim women.

Since the five words just discussed surfaced only in specific groups, we chose not to consider adding them to any of the power models. However, three main reasons led us to consider adding the words *equality, respect,* and *decision making* to our model of reciprocal empowerment. First, these words were significant to nearly all the groups. Second, the women evidently saw these terms as attributes of power. Last, and most important, the very definition of these three attributes nicely complements our original conception of reciprocal empowerment. Therefore, we have refined our previous definition. Reciprocal empowerment is a discursive and behavioral style of interaction grounded in respectful reciprocity initiated by people who interact on an equal footing and have a sense of personal authority. The personal authority aspect of reciprocal empowerment provides an individual with a level of knowledge necessary to develop a heightened self-confidence that can then lead to action. This action can, in turn, facilitate movement from the private to the public sphere. Reciprocal empowerment enables people with mutual self-interests to rise above obstacles based on social and political structures and to use personal authority to discuss and act on issues openly and honestly in order to effect change. The attributes of reciprocal empowerment combine self-determination, independence, knowledge, choice, action, and decision making with competence, compassion, companionship, and consensus to enhance oneself and others, thereby creating an environment that fosters equality, mutual respect, mutual attention, mutual engagement, mutual empathy, and mutual responsiveness. We still believe reciprocal empowerment is best illustrated by the spiral, as it emphasizes both the essential quality of reciprocity as well as the fluid movement from individual to other and from private to public that we want to foster through application of this conceptual model (see Figure 9.1).

In addition, linking the three new attributes supplied by our participants to reciprocal empowerment significantly affects the results originally illustrated in Tables 9.2 and 9.3. Originally, in the interview responses reciprocal empowerment seemed virtually nonexistent, it now appears as a viable alternative concept of power for these women (see Tables 9.5 and 9.6).

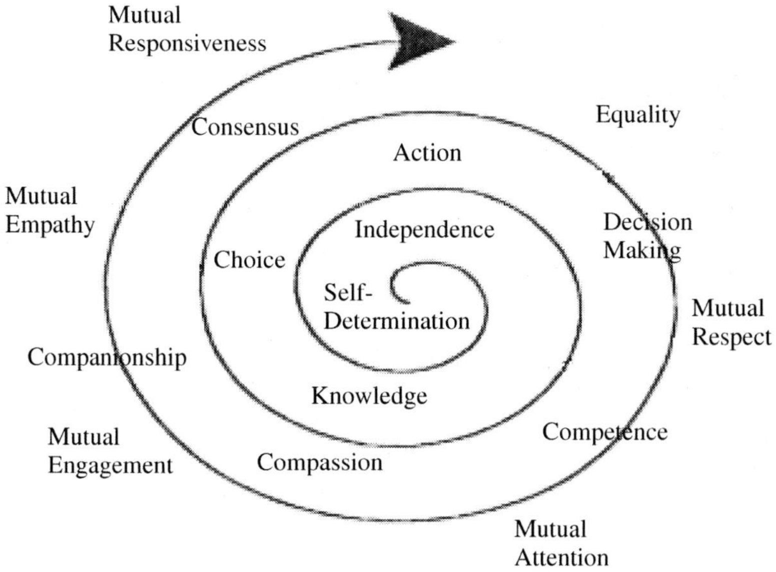

FIGURE 9.1. Graphic illustration of the revised reciprocal empowerment model

TABLE 9.5. Results from the Five Introductory Interview Questions Using the Revised Reciprocal Empowerment Model

Introductory Interview Questions	**African-American Women**	**Asian-American Women**	**Caribbean-American Women**	**European-American Women**	**Latin American Women**	**Middle Eastern-American Women**	**Native American Women**
What does the word *power* mean to you as an individual?	RE	—	RE	—	RE	—	—
What do you think the word *power* means in American society today?	—	—	RE	—	—	—	—
What do you think the word *power* means in your culture?	RE	—	RE	—	RE	—	—
As a woman, what kind of power do you think you have in U.S. society?	RE	RE	—	—	—	—	—
As a/an [insert appropriate ethnic group] woman, what do you think the word *power* means in your culture?	—	RE	RE	—	—	—	—

RE = Reciprocal empowerment

TABLE 9.6. Results from the Interview Questions Regarding How Power Is Used and How Power Should Be Used in the Areas of Work, Family, Religion, and Politics Using the Revised Reciprocal Empowerment Model

Interview Questions	African-American Women	Asian-American Women	Caribbean-American Women	European-American Women	Latin American Women	Middle Eastern-American Women	Native American Women
Work							
is	—	—	—	RE	—	—	—
should be	RE	—	RE	—	—	RE	—
Family							
is	RE	RE	—	RE	RE	RE	—
should be	RE	RE	—	RE	RE	RE	RE
Religion							
is	—	—	—	—	—	—	—
should be	—	—	—	—	RE	RE	—
Politics							
is	—	—	—	—	—	—	—
should be	—	—	—	—	—	—	—

RE = Reciprocal empowerment

RECOMMENDATIONS

Based on our findings, we would like to make some practical recommendations; we do this with the understanding that ours was a limited study. We can by no means generalize from our results that represent only a small cross section of women in one geographical region of the United States. Further studies could broaden this cross section, focus on a more in-depth examination of any or all of the groups we studied, or expand the cultural categories rather grossly constructed here. Furthermore, additional studies that examine women's notions of power in any one of the contexts we addressed (such as work, family, religion, or politics) would help flesh out the existence, usefulness, or appeal of alternative forms of power such as reciprocal empowerment.

With the need for further scholarly studies in mind, we base our recommendations here on what we have discovered thus far. The women who participated in our study did not describe reciprocal empowerment in their interview responses as we originally conceived it, but they obviously appreciated its attributes when presented with them in the survey statements. It appeared also that these women generally identified only with traditional conceptions of power, unless they were presented with another alternative. They may not have had a name for this alternative, but they recognized it and appreciated it when they saw it. In addition, when our participants did describe reciprocal empowerment, it was primarily in relation to the private sphere, or the family. Given the fact that traditional power was conceived of by men for men active in the public sphere, it follows that women might not, at first glance, associate an alternative such as reciprocal empowerment with the public sphere. This situation provides us with a two-pronged challenge: (1) How do we assist women in becoming knowledgeable about the different forms of power available? and (2) How can we assist women in recognizing that reciprocal empowerment is applicable to the public sphere? Indeed, any social or political changes beneficial to women require their active participation in a process such as reciprocal empowerment.

Although some of our findings were disheartening, especially results indicating a lack of political involvement on the part of our participants, we recognize that myriad factors influence women's behaviors. We strongly advise women to undertake the steps necessary to become viable participants in the public sphere. Thus, we would like to offer some suggestions merely as springboards.

Our first challenge, then, deals with education. We are convinced that the foundation upon which all change rests is education, and only through education can we begin to take responsibility for our own conditions. This responsibility also extends beyond ourselves to others around us. We must undertake a learning process that will help us understand how power relations are constructed. Women need to understand that power relations, as Foucault has noted, constrain certain voices by forbidding speech, by labeling some speech as madness, and by creating societal metanarratives (Gill, 1994). All of these processes have been applied, at one time or another, to the condition of women, silencing them in various areas of the public sphere as well as circumscribing their voice even in the private sphere. This has been done, for example, through religion, psychology, and politics. The writings of Saul of Tarsus, better known as the apostle Paul, still function as the foundation for much Christian teaching. He commanded the following: "A woman should learn in quietness and full submission. I do not permit a woman to teach or to have authority over a man; she must be silent" (*The Student Bible,* I Tim. 2:11-12). In the nineteenth century, Otto Weininger and Sigmund Freud were cohorts in composing pseudoscientific explanations for maintaining women's position in the private sphere. Women, frustrated by the narrow roles available to them in Victorian society, were labeled hysterical and thus prescribed "rest cures" which amounted to solitary confinement either at home or in sanitariums (Miles, 1989). In that same century, as women began the struggle to gain suffrage, they were opposed by a society that denied them the right to speak publicly. Based on the "cult of domesticity" separating work and home, no "true woman" would engage in public activity. Campbell (1989) explains, "she was to remain entirely in the private sphere of the home, eschewing any appearance of individuality, leadership, or aggressiveness. Her purity depended on her domesticity" (p. 10).

Only through understanding these historically constructed constraints can women begin to "break the bonds of power to give voice to those not in powerful roles, those who are silenced" (Gill, 1994, p. 183). We must also come to understand the interconnectedness among various social institutions and the impact they have on our positions as women. Through this educational process we may begin to recognize that the structures of these social institutions create in people subsequent feelings of power or powerlessness.

The process of educating women, we realize, is daunting since women are positioned differently as students in the classroom, as women who work at home, and as women who are employed in various positions in the paid workforce. All women must be reached. Educational curricula generally designed using the male-oriented traditional power paradigm must be revised to incorporate alternative methods of gaining and using power. Since, according to Wood (1993), "many people are unaware of the range of ways in which educational institutions devalue and disadvantage women. If lack of awareness is a problem, then a promising solution is to make people conscious of practices that inadvertently devalue and marginalize women" (p. 227). We believe the focus on traditional power does just that.

Women who work at home may be more difficult to reach; however, they cannot be ignored. As feminist researchers, we believe one of the primary values in conducting research is to take the results of such projects back into the participating communities and discuss the relevance of findings in terms of the impact they may have on women's lives. A way to do this is to conduct forums and open discussions and to make the effort to familiarize various communities with new ideas and new concepts from which they may benefit.

Women in the workplace can be reached through various networking opportunities available to them. We, as feminist researchers, have an obligation to share with these networking groups information drawn from the results of our studies. These networks allow women to "share ideas, contacts, strategies for advancement, and information. In addition to furnishing information, these networks provide women with support and a sense of fit with other professionals like them. A number of established professional women also mentor younger women in their fields, even though doing so requires heavy investments of time and energy" (Wood, 1993, p. 284). We consider this mentoring process an excellent demonstration of reciprocal empowerment.

Our second challenge rests on assisting women in applying the reciprocal empowerment process to various institutions that are a part of the public sphere. The educational process we have in mind allows women to become aware of the fact that social procedures are used to make human-made constraints appear natural. Once this educational process occurs, we believe the reciprocal empowerment many of the women seem to be practicing in their families and with their friends can then be applied more readily and frequently to their communities and to political causes and campaigns.

Bringing education regarding the formation and subversion of traditional power relations to women is an ongoing challenge not quickly met but well worth the effort. Instead of advising women to mimic stereotypically male behaviors in order to be powerful, reciprocal empowerment urges women to expand the use of tools and skills many of them already wield in the private sphere. As the resulting reciprocity and inclusiveness infiltrate the largely masculine arenas of the public sphere, women will be in a better position to positively impact their own lives as well as those of their sisters.

Bibliography

Preface

Josefowitz, N. (1980). *Paths to power: A woman's guide from first job to top executive.* Reading, MA: Addison-Wesley.

Pearson, J. C., and Cooks, L. (1995). Gender and power. In P. J. Kalbfleisch and M. J. Cody (Eds.), *Gender, power, and communication in human relationships* (pp. 331-349). Hillsdale, NJ: Lawrence Erlbaum Associates.

Chapter 1

Alcoff, L. (1988). Cultural feminism versus poststructuralism: The identity crisis in feminist theory. *Signs: Journal of Women in Culture and Society, 13* (3), 405-436.

Alcoff, L. M. (1996). *Real knowing: New versions of the coherence theory.* Ithaca, NY: Cornell University Press.

Andrews, P. (1996). *Sisters listening to sisters: Women of the world share stories of personal empowerment.* Westport, CT: Greenwood Publishing Group.

Avis, J. M. (1991). Power politics in therapy with women. In T. J. Goodrich (Ed.), *Women and power: Perspectives for family therapy* (pp. 183-200). New York: W. W. Norton.

Braxton, J. M., and Zuber, S. (1994). Silences in Harriet "Linda Brent" Jacob's *Incident in the life of a slave girl.* In E. Hedges and S. F. Fishbin (Eds.), *Listening to silences: New essays in feminist criticism* (pp. 146-155). New York: Oxford University Press.

Campbell, K. K. (1989). *Man cannot speak for her: A critical study of early feminist rhetoric,* Volume 1. New York: Praeger.

Cirlot, J. E. (1962). *A dictionary of symbols.* New York: Philosophical Library.

Clair, R. P. (1998). *Organizing silence: A world of possibilities.* Albany, NY: State University of New York Press.

Collins, P. H. (1990). *Black feminist thought: Knowledge, consciousness, and the politics of empowerment* (Perspectives on gender, Volume 2). Boston: Unwin Hyman.

Collins, P. H. (1998). *Fighting words: Black women and the search for justice.* Minneapolis, MN: University of Minnesota Press.

Connell, R. W. (1987). *Gender and power: Society, the person and sexual politics.* Stanford, CA: Stanford University Press.

Dow, B. J. (1995). Feminism, difference(s), and rhetorical studies. *Communication Studies, 46,* 106-117.

Duffy, A. (1986). Reformulating power for women. *Canadian Review of Sociology and Anthropology, 23* (1), 22-46.

Ferree, M. M., and Martin, P. Y. (Eds.) (1995). *Feminist organizations: Harvest of the new women's movement.* Philadelphia: Temple University Press.

Foss, K. A., Foss, S. K., and Griffin, C. L. (1999). *Feminist rhetorical theories.* Thousand Oaks, CA: Sage Publications.

Fox-Genovese, E. (1991). *Feminism without illusions.* Chapel Hill, NC: University of North Carolina Press.

Fraser, N. (1990-1991). Rethinking the public sphere: A contribution to the critique of actually existing democracy. *Social Text, 25/26,* 56-80.

Giddens, A. (1979). *Central problems in social theory: Action, structure and contradiction in social analysis.* Los Angeles: University of California Press.

Goodrich, T. J. (1991). Women, power, and family therapy: What's wrong with this picture? In T. J. Goodrich (Ed.), *Women and power: Perspectives for family therapy* (pp. 3-35). New York: W. W. Norton.

Habermas, J. (1989). *The structural transformation of the public sphere: An inquiry into a category of bourgeois society* (T. Burger and F. Lawrence, Trans.). Cambridge, MA: MIT Press. (Original work published 1962.)

Humm, M. (Ed.) (1992). *Modern feminisms: Political, literary, cultural.* New York: Columbia University Press.

Jaggar, A. M. (1983). *Feminist politics and human nature.* Totowa, NJ: Rowman and Allanheld Publishers.

Jaggar, A., and Rothenberg, P. S. (Eds.) (1984). *Feminist frameworks: Alternative theoretical accounts of the relations between women and men* (Second edition). New York: McGraw-Hill.

Janeway, E. (1980). *Powers of the weak.* New York: Morrow Quill paperbacks.

Josefowitz, N. (1980). *Paths to power: A woman's guide from first job to top executive.* Reading, MA: Addison-Wesley.

LaFollette, H. (1991). The truth in ethical relativism. *Journal of Social Philosophy, 22* (1), 146-154.

Landes, J. B. (1995). The public and the private sphere: A feminist reconsideration. In J. Meehan (Ed.), *Feminists read Habermas: Gendering the subject of discourse* (pp. 91-116). New York: Routledge.

Lips, H. M. (1991). *Women, men, and power.* Mountain View, CA: Mayfield.

McNay, L. (1992). *Foucault and feminism: Power, gender and self.* Boston, MA: Northeastern University Press.

Merriam-Webster's collegiate dictionary (Tenth edition). (1993). Springfield, MA: Merriam-Webster.

Miller, C. L., and Cummins, A. G. (1992). An examination of women's perspectives on power. *Psychology of Women Quarterly, 16,* 415-428.

Miller, J. B. (1977). *Toward a new psychology of women.* Boston: Beacon.

Miller, J. B. (1991). Women and power: Reflections ten years later. In T. J. Goodrich (Ed.), *Women and power: Perspectives for family therapy* (pp. 36-47). New York: W. W. Norton.

Price, B., and Markham, A. P. (1994). Fannie Lou Townsend Hamer. In K. K. Campbell (Ed.), *Women public speakers in the United States, 1925-1993: A bio-critical sourcebook* (pp. 424-435). Westport, CT: Greenwood Press.

Rampage, C. (1991). Personal authority and women's self-stories. In T. J. Goodrich (Ed.), *Women and power: Perspectives for family therapy* (pp. 109-122). New York: W. W. Norton.

Reid-Merritt, P. (1996). *Sister power: How phenomenal black women are rising to the top.* New York: John Wiley and Sons.

Schaef, A. W. (1995). *Women's reality: An emerging female system in a white male society.* New York: Harper and Row.

Starhawk. (1987). *Truth or dare: Encounters with power, authority, and mystery.* San Francisco: Harper and Row.

Steinem, G. (1983). *Outrageous acts and everyday rebellions.* New York: Signet.

Surrey, J. (1987). Relationship and empowerment. *Work in Progress, 30.* Wellesley, MA: Stone Center Working Paper Series.

Tong, R. (1989). *Feminist thought: A comprehensive introduction.* Boulder, CO: Westview Press.

Weber, M. (1969). Class, status, and party. In C. S. Heller (Ed.), *Structured social inequality: A reader in comparative social stratification* (pp. 24-34). New York: Macmillan.

Weedon, C. (1987). *Feminist practice and poststructuralist theory.* Oxford: Basil Blackwell Ltd.

Wheeler, C. E., and Chinn, P. L. (1991). *Peace and power: A handbook of feminist process* (Third edition). New York: National League for Nursing Press.

Yeatman, A. (1987). Women, domestic life, and sociology. In C. Pateman and E. Gross (Eds.), *Feminist challenges: Social and political theory* (pp. 157-172). Boston: Northeastern University Press.

Yoder, J. D. (1999). *Women and gender: Transforming psychology.* Upper Saddle River, NJ: Prentice-Hall.

Chapter 2

Berlin, I. (1974). *Slaves without masters: The free Negro in the antebellum South.* New York: Random House.

Berry, M. F., and Blassingame, J. W. (1982). *Long memory: The black experience in America.* New York: Oxford University Press.

Blassingame, J. W. (1972). *The slave community: Plantation life in the antebellum South.* New York: Oxford University Press.

Burnside, M., and Robotham, R. (1997). *Spirits of the passage: The transatlantic slave trade in the seventeenth century.* New York: Simon and Schuster.

Davis, A. Y. (1981). *Women, race, and class.* New York: Random House.

Davis, M. W. (Ed.) (1982). *Contributions of black women to America*. 2 volumes. Columbia, SC: Kenday Press.

Giddings, P. (1984). *When and where I enter: The impact of black women on race and sex in America*. New York: William Morrow.

Gilmore, E. G. (1996). *Gender and Jim Crow: Women and the politics of white supremacy in North Carolina, 1896-1920*. Chapel Hill, NC: The University of North Carolina Press.

Gutiérrez, L. (1990). Working with women of color: An empowerment perspective. *Social Work, 35* (2), 149-153.

Harding, V. (1981). *There is a river: The black struggle for freedom in America*. New York: Harcourt Brace Jovanovich.

Harley, S., and Terborg-Penn, R. (Eds.) (1978). *The Afro-American woman: Struggles and images*. Port Washington, NY: Kennikat Press.

Hemmons, W. M. (1996). *Black women in the new world order: Social justice and the African American female*. Westport, CT: Praeger.

hooks, b. (1981). *Ain't I a woman: Black women and feminism*. Boston: South End Press.

Jewell, K. S. (1993). *From mammy to Miss America and beyond: Cultural images and the shaping of U.S. social policy*. New York: Routledge.

Johnson, D. M., and Campbell, R. (1981). *Black migration in America: A social demographic history*. Durham, NC: Duke University Press.

Jones, J. (1985). *Labor of love, labor of sorrow: Black women, work, and the family from slavery to the present*. New York: Basic Books.

Joseph, G. I., and Lewis, J. (1981). *Common differences: Conflicts in black and white feminist perspectives*. New York: Anchor Books.

Lerner, G. (Ed.) (1972). *Black women in white America: A documentary history*. New York: Random House.

Levine, L. (1977). *Black culture and black consciousness: Afro-American folk thought from slavery to freedom*. New York: Oxford University Press.

Litwack, L. (1979). *Been in the storm so long: The aftermath of slavery*. New York: Alfred A. Knopf.

Lowenberg, B. J., and Bogin, R. (Eds.) (1976). *Black women in nineteenth-century American life: Their words, their thoughts, their feelings*. University Park, PA: Pennsylvania State University Press.

Myers, L. W. (1980) *Black women: Do they cope better?* Englewood Cliffs, NJ: Prentice-Hall.

Neverdon-Morton, C. (1989). *Afro-American women of the South and the advancement of the race, 1895-1925*. Knoxville, TN: The University of Tennessee Press.

Owens, L. H. (1976). *This species of property: Slave life and culture in the old South*. New York: Oxford University Press.

Ransom, R. L., and Sutch, R. (1977). *One kind of freedom: The economic consequences of emancipation*. New York: Cambridge University Press.

Reid, P. (1984). Feminism vs. minority group identity. *Sex Roles, 10,* 247-255.

Reid-Merritt, P. (1996). *Sister power: How phenomenal black women are rising to the top*. New York: John Wiley and Sons.

Rodgers-Rose, L. F. (Ed.) (1980). *The black woman*. Beverly Hills, CA: Sage.

Stack, C. (1974). *All our kin: Strategies for survival in a black community*. New York: Harper and Row.

Steady, F. C. (Ed.) (1985). *The black woman cross-culturally*. Rochester, NY: Schenkman Books, Inc.

Sterling, D. (Ed.) (1984). *We are your sisters: Black women in the nineteenth century*. New York: W. W. Norton.

Sudarkasa, N. (1996). *The strength of our mothers: African and African American women and families: Essays and speeches*. Trenton, NJ: Africa World Press.

Watkins, M., and David, J. (Eds.) (1970). *To be a black woman: Portraits in fact and fiction*. New York: William Morrow and Company, Inc.

Chapter 3

Adler, S. M. (1998). *Mothering, education, and ethnicity: The transformation of Japanese American culture*. New York: Garland.

Aguilar-San Juan, K. (Ed.) (1994). *The state of Asian America: Activism and resistance in the 1990s*. Boston: South End Press.

Beauchamp, E. R. (Ed.) (1998). *Dimensions of contemporary Japan: A collection of essays*. New York: Garland.

Chan, S. (1991). *Asian Americans: An interpretive history*. Boston: Twayne.

Chow, C. S. (1998). *Leaving deep water: The lives of Asian women at the crossroads of two cultures*. New York: Penguin.

Daniels, R. (1988). *Asian America: Chinese and Japanese in the United States since 1850*. Seattle, WA: University of Washington Press.

Diggs, N. B. (1998). *Steel butterflies: Japanese women and the American experience*. Albany, NY: State University of New York Press.

Espirtu, Y. L. (1997). *Asian American women and men: Labor, laws and love*. San Diego, CA: Sage.

Fugita, S., and O'Brien, D. J. (1991). *Japanese American ethnicity: The persistence of community*. Seattle, WA: University of Washington Press.

Fukei, B. (1976). *The Japanese American story*. Minneapolis, MN: Dillon Press.

Gehrke-White, D. (2001). S. Florida sees Asian boom, census to show. *The Miami Herald,* March 17, pp.1A, 23A.

Hall, C. (1997). *Daughters of the dragon: Women's lives in contemporary China*. London: Scarlet Press.

Hom, S. K. (1999). *Chinese women traversing diaspora: Memorias, essays, and poetry*. New York: Garland.

Hosokawa, B. (1969). *Nisei: The quiet Americans*. New York: W. Morrow.

Iwao, S. (1993). *The Japanese woman: Traditional image and changing reality*. New York: The Free Press.

Jackson, R. H., and Hudman, L. E. (1986). *World regional geography: Issues for today* (Second edition). New York: John Wiley and Sons.

Kitano, H. H. L., and Daniels, R. (1995). *Asian Americans: Emerging minorities* (Second edition). Englewood Cliffs, NJ: Prentice-Hall.

Nakano, M. (1990a). Japanese American women: Three generations. *History News, 45:2,* 10-13.

Nakano, M. (1990b). *Japanese American women: Three generations 1890-1990.* Berkeley, CA: Mina Press.

Peffer, G. A. (1999). *If they don't bring their women here: Chinese female immigration before exclusion.* Urbana, IL: University of Illinois Press.

Peterson, W. (1986). *Japanese Americans: Oppression and success.* Washington, DC: University Press of America.

Song, Y. I. (1993). Asian American women's experience in the crossfire of cultural conflict. In Y. I. Song and E. C. Kim (Eds.), *American mosaic: Selected readings on America's multicultural heritage* (pp. 186-203). Englewood Cliffs, NJ: Prentice-Hall.

Spickard, P. R. (1996). *Japanese Americans: The formation and transformations of an ethnic group.* New York: Twayne.

Takahashi, J. (1997). *Nisei/Sansei: Shifting Japanese American identities and politics.* Philadelphia, PA: Temple University Press.

Tchioka, Y. (1988). *The Issei: The world of the first generation of Japanese immigrants, 1885-1924.* New York: Free Press.

Von Hassell, M. (1993). Issei women: Silences and fields of power. *Feminist Studies, 19:3,* 549-569.

White-Parks, A. (1993). Journey to the golden mountain: Chinese immigrant women. In B. Frederick and S. H. McLeod (Eds.), *Women and the journey: The female travel experience* (pp. 101-117). Pullman, WA: Washington State University Press.

White-Parks, A. (1994). *A gathering of voices on the Asian American experience.* Fort Atkinson, WI: Highsmith Press.

Yap, Stacey G. H. (1989). *Gather your strength, sisters: The emerging role of Chinese women community workers.* New York: AMS Press.

Yung, J. (1986). *Chinese women of America: A pictorial history.* Seattle, WA: University of Washington Press.

Yung, J. (1995). *Unbound feet: A social history of Chinese women in San Francisco.* Berkeley, CA: University of California Press.

Yung, J. (1998). Giving voice to Chinese American women. *Frontiers: A Journal of Women Studies, 19:3,* 130-156.

Chapter 4

Basch, L., Schiller, N., and Blanc, C. (1994). *1994 nations unbound: Transnational projects, postcolonial predicaments, and deterritorialized nation-states.* Amsterdam: Gordon and Breach Science Publishers.

Bonnett, A. (1990). The new female West Indian immigrant: Dilemmas of coping in the host society. In R. Palmer (Ed.), *In search of a better life* (pp. 139-149). New York: Praeger.

Braithwaite, E. (1971). *The development of creole society in Jamaica, 1770-1820.* London: Oxford Press.

Bush, B. (1990). *Slave women in Caribbean society, 1650-1838.* Kingston: Heinemann Publishers.

Crahan, M. E., and Knight, F. W. (Eds.) (1979). *Africa and the Caribbean: The legacies of a link.* Baltimore, MD: Johns Hopkins University Press.

Deere, C., Antrobus, P., Bolles, L., Melendez, E., Phillips, P., Rivera, M., and Safa, H. (1990). *In the shadows of the sun: Caribbean development alternatives and U.S. policy.* Boulder, CO: Westview Press.

Elliott, A. (2001). 'A quantum leap': S. Florida's Caribbean population has almost doubled in the past 10 years, a U.S. census survey shows. *The Miami Herald,* August 7, p. 1A, p. 8A.

Ellis, P. (1986). *Women of the Caribbean.* London: Zed Books Ltd.

Henry, F. (1994). *The Caribbean diaspora in Toronto: Learning to live with racism.* Toronto: University of Toronto Press.

Ho, C. (1991). *Salt-water trinnies: Afro-Trinidadian immigrant networks and non-assimilation in Los Angeles.* New York: AMS Press.

Ho, C. (1993). The internationalization of kinship and the feminization of Caribbean migration: The case of Afro-Trinidadian immigrants in Los Angeles. *Human Organization, 52,* 1: 32-40.

Ho, C. (1999). Caribbean transnationalism as a gendered process. *Latin American Perspectives, 26:* 34-54.

Johnson, H., and Pines, J. (1982). *Reggae: Deep roots music.* London: Proteus.

Mazrui, A. (1986). *The Africans: A triple heritage.* Boston: Little, Brown and Co.

Minitz, S. W., and Price, S. (Eds.) (1985). *Caribbean contours.* Baltimore, MD: Johns Hopkins University Press.

Nettleford, R. (1978). *Caribbean cultural identity.* Los Angeles: Center for Afro-American Studies, UCLA Latin American Center Publications.

Patterson, O. (1967). *The sociology of slavery: An analysis of the origins, development and structure of negro slave society in Jamaica.* London: MacGibbon and Kee Ltd.

Thomas-Hope, E. (1992). *Explanation in Caribbean migration: Perception and the image.* London: Macmillan Caribbean.

Wiltshire, R. (1992). Implications of transnational migration for nationalism: The Caribbean example. In N. Glick, L. Schiller, L. Basch, and C. Blanc-Szanton (Eds.), *Towards a transnational perspective on migration* (pp. 175-187). New York: New York Academy of Science.

Chapter 5

Barron, M. L. (1962). *American minorities: A textbook of readings in intergroup relations*. New York: Alfred A. Knopf.

Bederman, G. (1995). *Manliness and civilization: A cultural history of gender and race in the United States, 1880-1917*. Chicago: The University of Chicago Press.

Caine, B., and Sluga, G. (2000). *Gendering European history: 1780-1920*. London: Leicester University Press.

Davie, M. R. (1962). American immigration and its European sources and patterns. In M. L. Barron (Ed.), *American minorities: A textbook of readings in intergroup relations* (pp. 229-240). New York: Alfred A. Knopf.

Handlin, O. (1957). *Race and nationality in American life*. Boston: Anchor.

Harzig, C., Mageean, D., Matovic, M., Knothe, M., and Blaschke, M. (1997). *Peasant maids—city women: From the European countryside to urban America*. Ithaca, NY: Cornell University Press.

Hawgood, J. (1940). *The tragedy of German-America: The Germans in the United States of America during the nineteenth century and after*. New York: Putnam's Sons.

Horsman, R. (1981). *Race and manifest destiny: the origins of American racial Anglo-Saxonism*. Cambridge: Harvard University Press.

Ignatiev, Noel. (1995). *How the Irish became white*. New York: Routledge.

Jacobson, M. F. (1995). *Special sorrows: The diasporic imagination of Irish, Polish, and Jewish immigrants in the United States*. Cambridge, MA: Harvard University Press.

Jacobson, M. F. (1998). *Whiteness of a different color: European immigrants and the alchemy of race*. Cambridge, MA: Harvard University Press.

Jones, M. A. (1960). *American immigration*. Chicago: University of Chicago Press.

Kessler-Harris, A. (1982). *Out to work: A history of wage-earning women in the United States*. Oxford: Oxford University Press.

Kessler-Harris, A., and Yans-McLaughlin, V. (1978). European immigrant groups. In T. Sowell (Ed.), *Essays and data on American ethnic groups* (pp. 107-137). Washington, DC: The Urban Institute.

Kiser, C. V. (1962). The diversity of American society. In M. L. Barron (Ed.), *American minorities: A textbook of readings in intergroup relations* (pp. 23-30). New York: Alfred A. Knopf.

Mayo, L. (1988). *The ambivalent image: Nineteenth-century America's perception of the Jew*. Rutherford: Fairleigh Dickinson University Press.

McCaffrey, L. J. (1976). *The Irish diaspora in America*. Bloomington, IN: Indiana University Press.

Moraga, C., and Anzaldua, G., (Eds.) (1981). *This bridge called my back: Writings by radical women of color*. Watertown, MA: Persephone Press.

Newman, L. M. (1999). *White women's rights: The racial origins of feminism in the United States*. New York: Oxford University Press.

Norton, M. B. (1999). "Either married or to bee married: Women's legal inequality in early America." In C. G. Pestana and S. V. Salinger (Eds.), *Inequality in early America* (pp. 25-45). Hanover, NH: University Press of New England.

Pestana, C. G., and Salinger, S. V. (1999). *Inequality in early America*. Hanover, NH: University Press of New England.

Rose, P. M. (1975). *The Italians in America*. New York: Arno Press.

Saxton, A. (1990). *The rise and fall of the white republic: Class politics and mass culture in nineteenth-century America*. London: Verso.

Shklar, J. (1991). *American citizenship: The quest for inclusion*. Cambridge, MA: Harvard University Press.

Shohat, E., and Stam, R. (1993). *Unthinking Eurocentrism*. New York: Routledge.

Sowell, T. (Ed.) (1978). *Essays and data on American ethnic groups*. Washington, DC: The Urban Institute.

West, G., and Blumberg, R. L. (Eds.) (1990). *Women and social protest*. New York: Oxford University Press.

Chapter 6

Aranda, E. M. (1997). *The life experiences of Puerto Rican women and the interlocking nature of race, class, and gender*. Unpublished doctoral dissertation, University of Florida, Gainesville.

Baldrich, J. J. (1998). Gender and the decomposition of the cigar-making craft in Puerto Rico, 1899-1934. In L. Delgado and F. Rodriguez (Eds.), *Puerto Rican women's history: New perspectives* (pp. 105-125). Armonk, NY: M.E. Sharpe.

Boone, M. S. (1989). *Capital Cubans: Refugee adaptation in Washington, D.C.* New York: AMS Press.

De Jesus, J. L. (Ed.) (1997). *Growing up Puerto Rican: An anthology*. New York: William Morrow and Company.

Delgado, L. C., and Rodriguez, F. V. M. (1998). *Puerto Rican women's history: New perspectives*. Armonk, NY: M.E. Sharpe.

Dominguez, J. I. (1978). *Cuba: Order and revolution*. Cambridge, MA: The Belknap Press of Harvard University Press.

Doran, T., Satterfield, J., and Stade, C. (1988). *A road well traveled: Three generations of Cuban American women*. Fort Wayne, IN: Latin American Educational Center.

Fox, G. E. (1973). Honor, shame, and women's liberation in Cuba: Views of working class emigre men. In A. Pescatello (Ed.), *Female and male in Latin America* (pp. 273-290). Pittsburgh, PA: University of Pittsburgh Press.

Gallart, M. F. (1998). Political empowerment of Puerto Rican women, 1952-1956. In L. Delgado and F. Rodriguez (Eds.), *Puerto Rican women's history: New perspectives* (pp. 227-252). Armonk, NY: M.E. Sharpe.

Garcia, C. M. (1996). *Havana USA: Cuban exiles and Cuban Americans in South Florida, 1959-1994*. Los Angeles, CA: University of California Press.

Gonzalez-Pando, M. (1998). *The Cuban Americans*. Westport, CT: Greenwood.

Jackson, R. H., and Hudman, L. E. (1986). *World regional geography: Issues for today* (Second edition). New York, NY: John Wiley and Sons.

Jimenez-Munoz, G. M. (1998). Literacy, class, and sexuality in the debate on women's suffrage in Puerto Rico during the 1920s. In L. Delgado and F. Rodriguez (Eds.), *Puerto Rican women's history: New perspectives* (pp. 143-170). Armonk, NY: M.E. Sharpe.

Kaufman Purcell, S. (1973). Modernizing women for a modern society: The Cuban case. In A. Pescatello (Ed.), *Female and male in Latin America* (pp. 257-271). Pittsburgh, PA: University of Pittsburgh Press.

Masud-Piloto, F. R. (1998). *With open arms: Cuban migration to the United States.* Totowa, NJ: Rowman and Littlefield.

Miller, F. (1991). *Latin American women and the search for social justice.* Hanover, NH: University Press of New England.

Monk, J., and Alexander, C. S. (1993). Migration, development and the gender division of labour: Puerto Rico and Margarita Island, Venezuela. In J. Momsen (Ed.), *Women and change in the Caribbean: A Pan-Caribbean perspective* (pp. 167-177). London: James Currey.

Morales, A. L. (1998). *Remedios: Stories of earth and iron from the history of Puertorriquenas.* Boston, MA: Beacon Press.

Muniz, V. (1998). *Resisting gentrification and displacement: Voices of Puerto Rican women of the Barrio.* New York: Garland.

Muniz-Mas, F. O. (1998). Gender, work, and institutional change in the early stage of industrialization: The case of the women's bureau and the home needlework industry of Puerto Rico, 1940-1952. In L. Delgado and F. Rodriguez (Eds.), *Puerto Rican women's history: New perspectives* (pp. 181-205). Armonk, NY: M.E. Sharpe.

Ortiz, A. (1998). Puerto Rican women workers in the twentieth century: A historical appraisal of the literature. In L. Delgado and F. Rodriguez (Eds.), *Puerto Rican women's history: New perspectives* (pp. 38-61). Armonk, NY: M.E. Sharpe.

Perez y Gonzalez, M. E. (2000). *Puerto Ricans in the United States.* Westport, CT: Greenwood.

Prieto, Y. (1979). *Women, work, and change: The case of Cuban women in the United States.* Unpublished doctoral dissertation, Ramapo College of New Jersey, Mahwah.

Prieto, Y. (1987). Cuban women in the U.S. labor force: Perspectives on the nature of change. *Cuban Studies, 17:* 73-91.

Ramos, J. F. (1998). Virgins, whores, and martyrs: Prostitution in the colony, 1898-1919. In L. Delgado and F. Rodriguez (Eds.), *Puerto Rican women's history: New perspectives* (pp. 83-104). Armonk, NY: M.E. Sharpe.

Randall, M. (1974). *Cuban women now: Interviews with Cuban women.* Toronto, Canada: Women's Press.

Rodriguez, F. V. M. (1998). Quien trabajara?: Domestic workers, urban slaves, and the abolition of slavery in Puerto Rico. In L. Delgado and R. Rodriguez (Eds.),

Puerto Rican women's history: New perspectives (pp. 62-82). Armonk, NY: M.E. Sharpe.

Stoner, K. L., and Perez, L. H. S. (2000). *Cuban and Cuban-American women: An annotated bibliography*. Wilmington, DE: Scholarly Resources.

U.S. Commission on Civil Rights (1976). *Puerto Ricans in the continental United States: An uncertain future*. Washington, DC: U.S. Commission on Civil Rights.

Viglucci, A. (2001). Hispanic diversity increasing in the U.S. *The Miami Herald,* May 10, p. 1A, p. 22A.

Weiler, J. D. (2000). *Codes and contradictions: Race, gender identity, and schooling*. Albany, NY: State University of New York Press.

Whalen, C. T. (1998). Labor migrants or submissive wives: Competing narratives of Puerto Rican women in the post-World War II era. In L. Delgado and F. Rodriguez (Eds.), *Puerto Rican women's history: New perspectives* (pp. 206-226). Armonk, NY: M.E. Sharpe.

Chapter 7

Abraham, S. Y., and Abraham, N. (1983). *Arabs in the new world: Studies on Arab-American communities*. Detroit, Michigan: Wayne State University Press.

Bodman, H. L., and Tohidi, N. (1998). *Women in Muslim societies: Diversity within unity*. London: Lynee Rienner.

Cainkar, L. (1994). Palestinian women in American society: The interaction of social class, culture, and politics. In E. McCarus (Ed.), *The development of Arab-American identity* (pp. 85-105). Ann Arbor, Michigan: The University of Michigan Press.

Collier, E. M. (1994). Arab-Americans: Living with pride and prejudice. In J. Kadi (Ed.), *Food for our grandmothers: Writings by Arab-American and Arab-Canadian feminists* (pp. 165-167). Boston: South End Press.

Haddad, Y. Y., and Esposito, J. L. (1998). *Islam, gender and social change*. New York: Oxford University Press.

Hamilton, M. J. (1994). The Arab woman in U.S. popular culture. In J. Kadi (Ed.), *Food for our grandmothers: Writings by Arab-American and Arab-Canadian feminists* (pp. 173-180). Boston: South End Press.

Kadi, J. (Ed.) (1994). *Food for our grandmothers: Writings by Arab-American and Arab-Canadian feminists*. Boston: South End Press.

Kahf, M. (1999). *Western representations of the Muslim woman: From Termagant to Odalisque*. Austin, TX: University of Texas Press.

Lobban, Jr., R. A. (Ed.) (1998). *Middle Eastern women and the invisible economy*. Gainesville, FL: University Press of Florida.

Majaj, L. S. (1994). Boundaries: Arab/American. In J. Kadi (Ed.), *Food for our grandmothers: Writings by Arab-American and Arab-Canadian feminists* (pp. 65-84). Boston: South End Press.

Majid, A. (1998). The politics of feminism in Islam. *Signs: Journal of Women in Culture and Society, 23:2,* 321-361.

McCarus, E. (Ed.) (1997). *The development of Arab-American identity*. Ann Arbor, Michigan: The University of Michigan Press.

Mikhail, M. (1979). *Images of Arab women: Fact and fiction*. Washington, DC: Three Continents Press.

Minces, J. (1984). *The house of obedience: Women in Arab society* (M. Pallis, Trans). London: Zed Books Ltd.

Orfalea, G. (1988). *Before the flames: A quest for the history of Arab Americans*. Austin, TX: University of Texas Press.

Said, E. W. (1978). *Orientalism*. New York: Pantheon Books.

Said, E. W. (1981). *Covering Islam: How the media and the experts determine how we see the rest of the world*. New York: Pantheon Books.

Shaheen, J. (1984). *The TV Arab*. Bowling Green, KY: Bowling Green State University Press.

Shakir, E. (1997). *Bint Arab: Arab and Arab American women in the United States*. Westport, CT: Praeger.

Shukri, S. J. A. (1996). *Arab women: Unequal partners in development*. Avebury, England: University of Bristol Press.

Smith, J. I. (1999). *Islam in America*. New York: Columbia University Press.

Terry, J. T. (1985). *Mistaken identity: Arab stereotypes in popular writing*. Washington, DC: American Arab Affairs Council.

Wadud, A. (1999). *Quran and women*. New York: Oxford University Press.

Chapter 8

Albers, P. (1989). From illusion to illumination: Anthropological studies of American Indian women. In Sandra Morgan (Ed.), *Gender and anthropology* (pp. 116-131). Washington, DC: American Anthropological Association.

Bataille, G. M. (Ed.) (1993). *Native American women*. New York: Garland.

Bataille, G. M., and Sands, K. M. (1984). *American Indian women: Telling their lives*. Lincoln, Nebraska: University of Nebraska Press.

Bataille, G. M., and Sands, K. M. (1991). *American Indian women: A guide to research*. New York: Garland.

Covington, J. W. (1993). *The Seminoles of Florida*. Gainesville, FL: University Press of Florida.

Fairbanks, C. H. (1973). *The Florida Seminole people*. Phoenix, AZ: Indian Tribal Series.

Garbarino, M. S. (1972). *Big Cypress: A changing Seminole community*. New York: Holt, Rinehart, and Winston.

Green, R. (1975). Pocahontas perplex. *Massachusetts Review, 16,* 698-714.

Green, R. (1980). Native American women. *Signs, 62,* 248-267.

Green, R. (1983). *Native American women: A contextual bibliography*. Bloomington, IN: Indiana University Press.

Kersey Jr., H. A. and Bannan, H. M. (1995). Patchwork and politics: The evolving roles of Florida Seminole women in the 20th century. In Nancy Shoemaker (Ed.), *Negotiators of change: Historical perspectives on Native American women* (pp. 193-212). New York: Routledge.

Kidwell, C. S. (1992). Indian women as cultural mediators. *Ethnohistory, 39,* 97-107.

Klein, L. F., and Ackerman, L. A. (Eds.) (1995). *Women and power in native North America.* Norman, OK: University of Oklahoma Press.

LaFromboise, T. D., Heyle, A. M., and Ozer, E. J. (1990). Changing and diverse roles of women in American Indian cultures. *Sex Roles: A Journal of Research, 22* (7-8), 455-472.

Maxwell, J. A. (Ed.) (1978). *America's fascinating Indian heritage.* Pleasantville, NY: The Reader's Digest Association.

Medicine, B. (1975). The role of women in Native American societies: A bibliography. *Indian Historian, 8,* 51-53.

Medicine, B. (1978). *The Native American woman: A perspective.* Austin, TX: National Educational Laboratory Publishers.

Sattler, R. A. (1995). Women's status among the Muskogee and Cherokee. In Laura F. Klein and Lillian A. Ackerman (Eds.), *Women and power in Native North America* (pp. 214-229). Norman, OK: University of Oklahoma Press.

Weisman, B. R. (1999). *Unconquered people: Florida's Seminole and Miccosukee Indians.* Gainesville, FL: University Press of Florida.

West, P. (1998). *The enduring Seminoles: From alligator wrestling to ecotourism.* Gainesville, FL: University Press of Florida.

Witt, S. H. (1974). Native women today. *Civil Rights Digest, 6,* 29-35.

Chapter 9

Campbell, K. K. (1989). *Man cannot speak for her: A critical study of early feminist rhetoric,* Volume 1. New York: Praeger.

Daly, M. (1973). *Beyond God the Father: Toward a philosophy of women's liberation.* Boston, MA: Beacon.

Gill, A. (1994). *Rhetoric and human understanding.* Prospect Heights, IL: Waveland Press.

McGlen, N. E., and O'Connor, K. (1995). *Women, politics, and American society.* Englewood Cliffs, NJ: Prentice-Hall.

Miles, R. (1989). *The women's history of the world.* Topsfield, MA: Salem House.

The Publisher, The Writings of Mary Baker Eddy with Reunion Productions (1998). *Seneca Reflections: Celebrating 150 Years of Women's Rights* [videocasssette]. Available from Reunion Productions.

Schlessinger, A. (Executive Producer) (1996). *Equality: A history of the women's movement in America* [videocassette]. Distributed by Library Video Company, P.O. 1110 Baya Cynwyd, PA 19004.

Stone, M. (1976). *When God was a woman.* Orlando, FL: Harcourt Brace.

The student Bible: New international version (1983). Philip Yancey and Tim Stafford (Eds.). Colorado Springs, CO: Zondervan Bible Publishers.

Wood, J. T. (1993). *Gendered lives: Communication, gender, and culture*. Belmont, CA: Wadsworth Publishing Company.

Index

Page numbers followed by the letter "f" indicate figures; those followed by the letter "t" indicate tables.